GW00457744

Dear S

CRUK
2·00
1/6

i

Dear Su Yen

A young woman from Taiwan discovers England
and discovers herself

Su Yen Hu and Roy Preece

SN❄WFLAKE BOOKS L^{TD}

Published by Snowflake Books Ltd
The Midstall, Randolphs Farm, Hassocks, West Sussex,
BN6 9EL, UK
First published 2010

Cover and text designed by Snowflake Books Ltd
Illustrations by Su Yen Hu
Printed in Taiwan by Choice Printing Group

ISBN 978-0-9565457-0-1

PREFACE
序

Su Yen wrote this book because, as she said, 'I wanted to show how poetry, like music, can be healing. My hope is that the book will encourage all who have a dream to believe that they do not have to compromise between that dream and reality. Perhaps I especially had in mind my friends whom I had to leave behind in Taiwan'.

I was involved as the person who introduced Su Yen to English poetry in the first place and substantial parts of the book consist of explanations of the poems and their contexts. We found that thinking and writing about the poems helped Su Yen to reconsider aspects of her life which she had been avoiding, and she responded by writing about events in her life as they seemed to relate to the poems. This was partly a healing process through which Su Yen was able to come to terms with painful incidents in her professional and family life. Perhaps more importantly the poems provide a way into understanding English history and culture, which had been her great ambition since childhood in Taiwan.

For a number of years it has been my pleasure and privilege to assist people from many countries who are studying in England for a range of professions. I have great respect for the courage and intelligence of these students and it has always seemed a pity that, despite their expressed wish to do so, they have so little time to absorb English culture during their short stay. As joint authors, we hope that such people may find, through Su Yen's stories in this book, not only sympathy and understanding for their often rather lonely struggle but at the same time an accessible and manageable introduction to English poetry, painting and history. We hope, and experience so far suggests, that students from other countries who thought that English language poetry was 'too difficult' may be pleasantly surprised after reading this book.

The poems were chosen in the first place to represent a range of types of poem and to cover English life from Caedmon's Anglo-Saxon hymn to Dylan Thomas's eccentric style. However, as Su Yen began to write about events in her life, the selection was also orientated towards these events, such as the death of her much loved grandfather and her sadness at being so far away from him, or her curiosity about why English people wear red poppies in November. Quite early on I became ill and was unable to leave my house, so the stories and the poems with their commentaries were mostly exchanged through a series of letters: hence the title of this book, *Dear Su Yen.*

For Su Yen the poems helped her to understand and mend her own life and to achieve a life of the mind, yet one rooted in the reality of society. Her story shows her progress from being an inarticulate stranger to, three years later, taking part in a traditional English Christmas where she felt that she belonged at last, not by abandoning her own culture but by discovering the universal truths of all cultures. Inter-leaved with these experiences are the poems and their contexts which become more significant as the story proceeds. We discovered that the poems, and their links with painting, architecture and history, could be an aid to living a life within a universal and imaginative context and to forming a more balanced view of the world.

We hope that this book may help others to do the same.

Su Yen Hu and Roy Preece, Oxford, 2010

ACKNOWLEDGMENTS
謝誌

We are most grateful to Lady Madden, Dr Lihui Wang and Lin Paris who kindly took on the task of reading through the draft manuscript and who have offered valuable advice and, above all, their encouragement. Su Yen especially wishes to express her deep thanks to her dear friend Lihui who has spared no effort in providing generous support and companionship. Thanks also to Pete Jones in New Zealand who laid a sound foundation for Su Yen's subsequent exploration of the English language, and to the Lu family and to Mr and Mrs Qiao for their kindness to a stranger there. We are grateful to Ersilia Cilenti of the Authors' Licensing & Collecting Society for her generous advice and assistance with copyright matters. Finally, thanks are due to all the kind colleagues at the University Church of St Mary the Virgin, in Oxford, for their consideration and friendship, and especially to Ann whose sincere invitations to afternoon tea and to Christmas Dinner with her family offered a special kind of experience of English culture.

We acknowledge the kind permission of the following persons and agencies to reproduce the works shown below.

The Society of Authors as the literary representative of the Estate of Laurence Binyon: '*For the Fallen*' by Laurence Binyon.

David Higham Associates and J.M.Dent & Sons Ltd, Publishers: '*Fern Hill*' by Dylan Thomas; in Dylan Thomas, *Collected Poems*, Dent.

The Trustees of the Faringdon Collection Trust: extract from *Buscot Park and the Faringdon Collection.*

'Fern Hill' by Dylan Thomas, from THE POEMS OF DYLAN THOMAS, copyright ©1945 by The Trustees for the Copyrights of Dylan Thomas. Reprinted by permission of New Directions Publishing Corp.

Poem: 'In Memory of Basil, Marquess of Dufferin and Ava',from Collected poems, by John Betjeman © The Estate of John Betjeman 1955, 1958, 1962, 1964, 1968, 1970, 1979, 1981,1982, 2001.Reproduced by permission of John Murray (Publishers).

Editions Grasset & Fasquelle for permission to include the extract from Voltaire by André Maurois; for details see page 314.

CONTENTS
目錄

THE POEMS

詩

The Rubaiyat of Omar Khayam, by Edward Fitzgerald (1809–1883)

Heraclitus, by William (Johnson) Cory (1823–1892)

The Deserted Village, by Oliver Goldsmith (1728–1774)

The Cottager's Complaint, on the Intended Bill for enclosing Sutton-Coldfield, by John Freeth (1731–1808)

Home Thoughts, From Abroad, by Robert Browning (1812–1889)

The Soldier, by Rupert Brooke (1887–1915)

Anthem for Doomed Youth, by Wilfred Owen (1893–1918)

For the Fallen, by Laurence Binyon (1869–1943)

The Iliad, Book XXII, tranlated by Alexander Pope (1688–1744)

The Chimney-Sweeper's Complaint, by Mary Alcock (1742–1798)

The Chimney Sweeper, by William Blake (1757–1827)

Elegy Written in a Country Churchyard, by Thomas Gray (1716–1771)

L'Allegro, by John Milton (1608–1674)

The Village, by George Crabbe (1754–1832)

An Essay on Man, by Alexander Pope (1688–1744)

Some poems are represented only in part.

浴火鳳凰

那一年，我拿著忘卻，世界經忘卻了，可是紛繁的
夢境開始困抹著我，我逐漸懼怕夜晚。

那天在 Sandham Memorial Chapel 欣賞 Stanley
Spencer 的畫作，無意引進 Stanley Spencer 作思中
找回了自我人生中失去的那部份，我試著尋那
描述中的夫為，那是什麼？他又如何失去自己人生
中的一部份？畫作題材是建立在第一次世界大戰
的背景時代，卻怎麼不見血腥的殺戮，呈現的卻
是軍人們生活作息，打掃東西，隨如布地連食
戰死後話，復活？為甚用了這樣一個奇怪的詞？
復活會像是吃飯睡覺一樣平凡的事情嗎？看
著 Stanley 的畫作，也許答案可以是肯定的。
士兵們身著身著，抵死猶生，走進自己的墓穴中
攀爬出土，拋開那刻著氏名著者的白色十字架
希望望还在名埠他們的戰友們握手。

Stanley Spencer 有一個多麼美的而充滿希望
的幻想

THE PHOENIX
鳳凰

All that year I tried to forget. I did forget. Now dreams are troubling me again and sometimes I am afraid to sleep.

Yesterday we went to see Stanley Spencer's paintings in the Sandham Memorial Chapel. The guidebook says he painted them to find part of himself again. What did he mean by that? How could he lose part of himself? The paintings are about the Great War, but they are not violent. They show the soldiers doing ordinary things: cleaning, washing, sleeping wherever they can by the road, and being resurrected. *Being resurrected!* What a strange thing I have written. Is it ordinary to be resurrected? In these paintings it seems to be. The soldiers in their uniforms, looking just as they did in life, are climbing out of their graves and throwing away the white crosses that marked them, and they are shaking hands with the friends who did not die. That thought is very beautiful and full of hope.

1

GROWING UP

成長

I think that my father used to care about me very much, when I was young. He tried his best to protect me from the complicated world which might have hurt me or spoiled my white paper soul. Apart from when I went to school, he didn't allow me to leave his sight, not just to cross the street to the supermarket. He even bought a house right next to my school: that was the best choice he could make for me since we could not live at the school itself. For my daily needs he was so generous. When I asked for a pencil, he bought a dozen for me; when I wanted to have a pudding, he bought a box of puddings which I could share with a whole class of pupils. Thus I lived under his protection completely, without going out at all. But I was not as happy as he expected; I desired to see the world beyond my home and my school.

'Father, I need to go to a store for some milk.' This was the best excuse I could think of to go out.

'You have fresh goat milk every day. Why do you want to get a bottle of cold milk which is not healthy for you?'

'But, father, I just sometimes want to have some milk, please.'

'The problem is, you will have to cross the street to the supermarket, which is too dangerous for a child.'

Next day when I came home from school, I found

three huge bottles of milk in the fridge. This shocked me so much because I was worried about how I could finish all of them by the 'use before' date. I tried very hard to drink them in time because there was no one else who would have the milk which my father had bought for me. Eventually, the last drops of milk were pouring through my throat. I felt so relieved, but just for a while.

Another *five* bottles of milk appeared in the fridge next day at the time my father came home from his office. I couldn't breathe for a moment, but didn't dare tell him the truth: that I really couldn't finish all of them in two days. Without any better solution, I poured one and a half bottles of the milk down the sink when they seemed nearly out of date.

'What a waste you've made! I work so hard to provide you with a good life, to offer whatever you need. Why did you throw the milk away?'

'I'm so sorry about that, father, but it's just too much for me in two days.'

'You can tell me if it's too much for you; or I can drink it if you don't want it. Why did you throw it away?'

I felt such regret and really wished that I had never done this bad thing to my father when I saw his eyes were so hurt, although his voice was fierce. I think I heartlessly threw my father's love away when the milk was poured into the waste basin.

I have never wanted to throw away any food since then, even though sometimes I'm too full.

♪

'Our lunch is coming!'

'How can you say that? You should say your father is coming home.'

During the summer and winter vacations, my sister and I always especially looked forward to welcoming our father home because he would bring us a good lunch from the staff restaurant of the prison. We liked the meals so much because their menus were as varied and professional as those in five-star hotels.

'Can you buy your lunch yourself from tomorrow? It's so embarrassing when people look at me carrying so many lunch boxes. They might think I'm bringing those lunch boxes out for sale.' My father's face was quite unhappy and serious.

How could I have forgotten to consider my father's situation? It must have looked very strange for the chief commissioner of a prison, still wearing his uniform, to carry out so many lunch boxes, especially as I and my sister liked the prison cooking so much that we always required two boxes for each of us; with one for my mother there would be at least five boxes in my father's hands everyday.

'I'm so sorry father; it's our fault to make this trouble for you. I have some ideas for you though. First, you can change out of your uniform before you leave your office for lunch. Second, you can tell those people in the restaurant that your daughters love their cooking so much and you don't have any other choice during vacations. And then you should rush home quickly, before more people see you there.'

My father didn't answer me, but turned his face to smile. Most importantly, however, he continued to bring us lunch everyday so that we could keep enjoying our favourite meals during our vacations.

Then one day the food was not so tasty and colourful as usual. Perhaps the chef had a day off, or he had a cold and couldn't smell or taste the flavours normally. However, the problem lasted for more than a week.

'*Baba*, we just wonder what the problem is in your restaurant; we don't like our lunches so much as before.'

'Don't ask for so much anymore. The chef had to leave the prison once he finished his sentence!'

What a surprise for me. Every one can bring happiness to other people from wherever they are.

♪

I thought I was a Christian, when I was a little older. When my father was at work, my mother sometimes took me to play in the park near my home. An old American there told me a Biblical story every afternoon. He also taught me how to pray to the God who is always around me and would protect me from evils and nightmares.

I felt so peaceful when I received a Christmas card from my father. There was a little Western girl kneeling down by a candle with her fingers crossed and her eyes closed. I imagined that was me talking to the God every night before I went to bed.

'You will be a real Buddhist when someone comes

to lead you to believe Buddhism.' One of my uncles was a fortune teller who sometimes told me if he 'saw' something.

'How come it will happen? I don't think I will be happy to give up beef and to become a vegetarian; and I prefer to wear the clothes of Christian nuns more than to shave all my hair off like those Buddhist nuns in temples.' I argued like this because I really imagined I belonged to a church like those I saw in movies, but just hadn't had time and a place to receive baptism yet due to the fact that there wasn't any mediaeval church in my hometown.

The Christian fantasy was hidden somewhere in my mind, but it just became a dream in the following years as I was growing up because I didn't go to that park, and never met that old American Holy Joe anymore, since my father bought another house next to my new school.

♪

'It's a waste of our love to care for children who are all traitors once they grow up and never remember the goodness of their parents. You are all the same sooner or later.' We knew that our father must have brought another bad story home because he was always so angry and his attitude to us was so violent when he had to 'process' those young prisoners in his work place. He somehow seemed to impute the origins of his emotions of sorrow and depression to me and my sister, within his own imagination, so that he gradually became so cold and harsh to us. I think he finally didn't love his children anymore by the time I was fourteen years of age.

'I saw his eyes were so firm, without any regret, although his parents were so sad and worried about his fate. He must have committed this criminal act on purpose as part of his long term plan for his future.'

I was not sure if it was just my father's personal judgement of that young prisoner or whether it was true that the young boy had chosen to pass his life in a prison when he killed three people in a few minutes, using only a nail-clipper. My father said it was so skilful that it must have been pre-meditated. That year, at the age of eighteen, the young boy had just been accepted into what was supposed to be the best university in Taiwan so his future had seemed to everyone to be very bright and hopeful. I think my father imagined himself in the place of those parents, wondering how their child could not see that they were going crazy over his situation in prison and expecting that he should have been so sad to die. And because this son did not show any regret, I believe it made my father very cynical and disillusioned about people until he came to doubt us all.

'But why did he do that if his future was so promising?' I was really curious about this story even though I was so scared about my father's attitude.

'He knows that everyone, especially his parents, had high expectations about his future, and he knows study at the best university is just the beginning of his journey to a successful life to impress other people, but it seems he could not bear this pressure. So he has committed a strange form of suicide. He understands that no one will dare spite him in the prison because he is such an intellectually gifted youth, and now he is a homicide he will be the king among prisoners. No one else sees this plan and all try to plead for his incautious mistake, but I know it because I saw his decision deeply from his eyes.'

My father's specialization and experience in criminal psychology seemed to lead him to a cynical and suspicious attitude which saw calculating and evil motives in everyone. But could it really be true that as I and my sister, no longer innocent children, were fast becoming adults he saw us as potentially wicked in the same way as his prisoners? I just couldn't see his logic so to draw inferences about me and my sister from those bad instances, when we thought we loved our parents so much. And could he really believe that boy would choose to live out his life in prison? I don't think my father was wrong and, though he was often shocked by those motives he saw in some prisoners, he needed to keep his impassivity in his office. I believe he must often have been right because he was highly respected by those prisoners due to his unusual understanding of them. However, he became distrustful of people when he saw more and more abnormal things which shocked him so much. In other words, I think he didn't know how to believe in normal people when he had fitted himself very well into another darker and more cynical world for many years.

These unreasonable attitudes, for so they seemed to us, drove our father to lose his kindness for us more and more. In particular, whereas he had previously been generous, even extravagant, with us, he was no longer happy to spend his money on us, even for our studies. I think now there may have been two reasons for the changes in my father. I have been told that the dispassionate study of emotions, as in psychiatry, requires emotional detachment; my father seemed to have brought this into his family life. Also I wonder whether my father was increasingly suffering from a mental condition known as paranoia, or persecution complex. Many years later I told him how he had seemed to change so much as we grew up. He didn't admit to being as cold and harsh as we thought, just a bit stern, and said it was all in my mind. I can understand now that my father only could express his real feeling of shock, that he couldn't show in his office, to us because we were his heart whom he might trust at least a bit more than the outside world. But although he might not have intended to scare me, he did scare me a lot because I took and thought about everything seriously; so I had quite a stressful childhood.

Would the adult world which was so complicated lead me to become one of these sorts of cold-blooded people to treat my parents cruelly when I grew up? I was so afraid and didn't know what to do to be a good person without making another tragedy for my family in future.

♩

Like most young teenagers, I was fond of reading romantic stories in my spare time.

Maybe sometimes my interest was too great because I would try to finish a whole novel, hiding under my duvet using a torch, even at midnight. Unlike most of my friends, however, my favourite romances were those set in the European Middle Ages with scenes of mediaeval life. Those were simple ideas I know, but the skilled novelists described everything so elaborately that the images seemed very real to me then and they attracted me so much. The shape of a castle, the design of a garden, the texture of a stone and the styles of clothing and of life, all those images came in to my mind with the ideas I received from movies and books about mediaeval times.

How could I have imagined that those castles could have survived from long ago, for I had grown up in the small island of Taiwan where frequent earthquakes have destroyed all our old buildings? The oldest building I had ever seen was built about a hundred years ago by the Japanese Government. With my limited knowledge about the world, I thought all those scenes of mediaeval times could be seen only in a movie or a book because they were too ancient to exist.

As well as reading romances, I enjoyed facing to a painting or a picture of a castle for an hour or so; I would pick out some nice place in the painting and pray hard about it. I prayed to the God to allow me to get in to the place of the painting for just a second, or maybe more; a minute would be better. I thought only a minute would be long enough for me to feel satisfied for my whole life. However, maybe the God was laughing at me because I still stood on the floor facing the painting alone. Jigsaw puzzles were my alternative method to try to get in to a castle. I prayed to each piece of a jigsaw puzzle as I put them all together and imagined that I could finally jump in to the picture once I finished the game; or at least, I could dream about it in bed.

Then the magic appeared in my life on the thirteenth day of June, 2005, when the scene of the High Street in Oxford first came to my eyes. I thought the God truly had received my wish and had come to lead me in to my dreaming picture for much more than a minute.

♩

I have been dreaming with Oxford for nearly three years since I discovered there is enough for me here to explore for my whole life in such a lively yet old city. I desire to know the story of each stone which I feel can show a different aspect of history. But I also have seen some poorly designed modern architecture intruding into this historic place, and I wonder how that can be; I often choose to close my eyes when I have to pass by those buildings which are unpleasant to me, and only to immerse my mind in the ancient air.

I was studying a book about John Betjeman and Oxford buildings for my first Master's dissertation when my tutor sent me a fragment of one of Betjeman's poems. For me it expresses the quiet mystery of Oxford and provided me with so much joy on feeling the poem with my own thoughts, although there were so many new words I had to discover.

Dear Su Yen

I'm so glad you like the book. John Betjeman had a deep respect and an affection for English buildings, which are often expressed in the way he writes. I send you here a small portion of a Betjeman poem because it describes just what you are doing, exploring Oxford in the book and in reality.

For many years Betjeman's poems were considered to be not very good. They often seem too easy, both to write and to read: the sort of simple rhyming lines which anyone might have produced. However, they are beginning to come back into favour, perhaps because he was an acute and honest observer of human life and its weaknesses, perhaps because we are now far enough from the times he writes about, the 1950s and 60s, to view his work more objectively. This is one of his better poems I think.

In Memory of Basil, Marquess of Dufferin and Ava, by John Betjeman (1906–1984)

...the long peal pours from the steeple
  Over this sunlit quad
In our University City
  And soaks in Headington stone.
Motionless stand the pinnacles.

Then there were people about.
  Each hour, like an Oxford archway,
Opened on long green lawns
  And distant unvisited buildings
And you my friend were explorer...

Dear Roy

I like the idea of each hour of time opening up like an archway that we can see through. It reminds me that time is not just the present. It also reminds me of how, when I was young, I longed to be in those mediaeval pictures. The whole poem is dreamlike in its unreality, the motionless pinnacles, the unvisited buildings, the unknown people about. Maybe at last I have found a dream I can walk into.

I had to look up many words in my dictionary before I could begin to understand the poem: such as peal – the sound of many bells ringing I think – and pinnacles and steeple, which are parts of buildings. I can see now that pinnacles would of course be motionless, but I think the poet must have chosen that word to emphasise the stillness; otherwise there's no point in using it, is there? But, to be honest, I have no idea whether it is good or not so good poetry. In Chinese poetry there are strict rules of structure and pattern which we use to judge how clever and beautiful the poem is. It seems to me that English poetry is nothing like that so I really don't know how to think about it.

Many of my friends in Taiwan feel the same. We are told how beautiful English language poetry is, and of course everyone has heard of Shakespeare. But it seems too difficult for us to read in English, and all the books about poetry are difficult too, so we can only read translations in Chinese.

Dear Su Yen

Your comments about the poem are very perceptive.

It seems to have stimulated your imagination, or we could say that the poem has imaginative quality, which is a criterion for all good art. Probably you would simply say that the poem 'speaks to you', which is a very good beginning.

♪

I was disappointed when I first met my flatmate in Oxford. We had been put together by chance, or rather by some administrator's decision taken, as far as I knew, with no consideration of our respective personalities. She reminded me of all the unhappy days when I lived in a student house, sharing with five other overseas students. But there was something special and very honest in her eyes which made me think that possibly she would not be as wild and noisy as my old housemates had been, although she dressed like a party animal just the way the old housemates did. I could see a strange curiosity and innocence in her eyes. But why did she dress like that? Why did she have such a crazy and awkward hair style that didn't fit her at all? I was more puzzled when she told me she had just received her Doctorate from Oxford University. Was she another Chinese who considered herself to be part of an Oxford elite just after a short language course somewhere? My heart sank deeper as my suspicion grew stronger.

The puzzle was slowly solved as we constantly chatted. That was a good sign. After a while, I was quite certain that what I saw the first day was true. Before she met me, the world to her was just the sky above her laboratory. When the Doctorate was awarded, she was lost and puzzled about her life. I have seen that so often: when those years of hard endeavour are over, life can suddenly seem to have lost its purpose. She tried different hair-styles, strange clothes and tried a night-club once as well and still found no direction. She was curious about everything: how to dress up, make up, socialize and speak with people who were not scientists. Her past life seemed to be just a paper with one word: STUDY. I smiled secretly in my heart now and then at all her inquisitive or even silly remarks. I did not say too much and just taught her patiently whatever she wanted to learn from the outside world. I told her how, at the age of nineteen, I dressed-up customers at a departmental store in Taiwan. I told her how, with little computing knowledge to start with, I managed to become the top sales-person at a national computer exhibition at age twenty-one. I told her how, at age twenty-three, I communicated with local people to discover a piece of local history, the local railway station in Kaoshiung City in Taiwan, which had been deserted for many years; and how I designed the project to convert this derelict railway station into a tourist attraction by convincing the local and central governments of its value.

We talked, or I talked, night by night and I felt like the princess in *The Thousand and One Arabian Nights.* I was also amazed that I could have a story to tell every night. For quite a long time, she always came home telling me how she wished to be like me to make everyone feel happy and attracted. We gain wisdom about the people and the world as we grow older, as I always told her. But deep in my heart, I really didn't want her to experience what I have experienced before to reach what I am now. If it were not for her, I would have forgotten what I did before completely. It was the first impression of curiosity and innocence that made the memories come back and I was willing to share them slowly. Am I back in the world now with all my memories resurrected in my brain?

貳

2

DISCOVERY

發覺

'I've been holding this book in my hand for three days and I don't want to return it to the library.'

'Why not? Is it really so interesting? Most of our text-books are boring I think. What's that book about anyway?' My colleague was curious about what sort of book could attract me so much.

'Well, I don't know what it's about really. I haven't finished reading the Introduction yet, and I'm not sure I understand even that.'

'But you've been reading it for three days. What have you read?'

'Oh dear! I have to say my English isn't good enough to read this conservation philosophy at present; that's why I haven't finished reading the Introduction. But I don't mind that much; I'm just dreaming with this book because it's more than a hundred years old. Can you imagine how many people have held this book during a century?'

When I found an old book in our library I was so excited. I couldn't help but to dream that in the past perhaps those people read it at a gloomy desk with a small oil lamp. I loved our library so much because it was like a big treasure house for me to explore history, although I was not an historian in the academic meaning.

'But how can you do your assignment if you don't

understand the language?' My colleague's question was quite right and practical because I finally received a failed mark for that assignment. It was a bit worrying, but not a big worry for me since I was sure that I would be able to ask for help somewhere for the reason that I was studying in a very English course with nearly all native English speakers.

♪

I do love to believe the God because he always gets my wish and lets it come true. In our library one day I discovered a whole room full of old books for sale, such as I could only dream about in Taiwan. I was determined to have some of those old books in my bookcase. I picked up about fifteen books straight away without having a second thought.

'Wow, this is lovely; I would like to have this one as well.'

'Are you crazy, Su Yen, did you check their contents? Are you sure you will like to read all of them?' My colleague was quite puzzled by my behaviour of buying so many books.

'I will read them one day; I like them.'

'But … Su Yen, you know, I think you won't read this one because this is not our language, it's French! Why do you choose this book?'

'Because … the cover is so pretty.'

'Oh my god, you buy books only for their covers?'

Why don't people understand it is very important for

us to love a cover or appearance before we can enjoy its contents in our lives? That includes food, books, or anything we can choose for ourselves. My tutor in the design course at High School told us that when producers spend plenty of money on their cover design and advertisement design, they are also careful about the quality of the contents because they don't want to lose their prestige.

♪

I thought those books looked very beautiful standing on my little student bookshelf. One day, I promised myself, I would have a whole roomful of fine books like those I saw in old houses in the movies. But first I had to pass my assignments somehow.

My course leader suggested that I should consult another tutor who was a semi-retired lecturer in the department and was always happy to help overseas students to survive those *very* English courses in our School of the Built Environment.

'Do you understand your situation now?' When Roy saw my two assignments with one low pass and one failed mark he asked me this question rather than talking about my work.

'I know my situation is quite dangerous, and I might not get my Master's degree.'

'Well it's good that you do know your situation. I just wondered, because you're smiling.'

I was smiling because I was happy; because I knew he was the person who would help me, when I saw his kindness and the wisdom in his eyes.

'Do you think you know what this assignment is about?' It was a serious question, put after he had read my work carefully.

'I think it's something more about policy rather than design …, maybe something harder to explain …, I'm not sure about this.'

'That's why your writing is so confused: your arguments are not clear in your mind so of course you can't write them clearly. What was your first degree in Taiwan?'

'I studied interior design at university.'

'Interior design? I'm wondering why you chose this course.' He spoke carefully, as though not to frighten me. 'I've never met an interior designer on this course before. Do you know it's a very different subject from your previous study? You see, a Master's course can't really make you into something different; it's meant to be based on what you've done before? It might not be too late to change if you want to.'

'But I don't want to change my course. I think it's very important for me to learn how policy makers and decision makers think and how that works out in reality. I want to make my designs useful for people rather than just beautiful.'

'Well, I'm happy to help you as much as you want because it looks as though you do need help; many of the people I see don't really need much help at all.'

Roy was very patient, explaining to me much of the basic knowledge which most students learn from their first degrees. He tried to speak especially slowly for me when he discovered that I had started learning English only a year ago, when I had impetuously decided to study in England.

I was sure that he too liked books. As we talked, I quickly realised that here was an opportunity to discover much more. I decided then that I would like to tell him the story of my short life. But not yet.

'Can we talk about my work later?' I said. 'I want to tell you that I have lots of old poetry books in my bookcase.' It was so important for me to share my happiness with someone who would understand it.

'That's good.' He said it with emphasis.

I was so pleased that he sounded genuinely interested; not many people took much notice when I wanted to tell them about my old books. They usually said that I would never read them, that they would be too difficult for me; why did I waste my money like that.

'Where did you get them? Do you read poetry?'

'I bought them from our lovely library where there were so many old books on sale. I now love our library more than before for this reason. I read poetry, but not in English; I think my English is not good enough to feel English poetry.'

'What books did you get from our library?' Again he sounded interested and enthusiastic, not just polite. I was sure then that he liked books very much.

'I don't know, because I don't remember those names of poets in English; there was one by someone called Browning I think; but I'm certain that one day I will enjoy reading them once I improve my English to that level.

But, you know, I bought them because they spoke to me. They told me to bring them home and look after them as treasure.'

♪

I wasn't sure that my language skills were good enough to understand English poetry, but Roy said poetry was a very good way to understand English culture. He said words in poetry mean so much more than the same words in ordinary writing, or prose. This is because poetry has rhythm, like music, and music seems to have meaning, even without words.

'I'm not sure I know what rhythm in poetry is.'

He began to speak slowly, using some words that were strange to me:

Full fathom five thy father lies.

'That sounds very beautiful. Why is it beautiful?'

'This is beautiful because it is soothing; and it is soothing because of the repeating of those soft 'f' sounds, four times. There are no hard or sharp sounds. And because of the rhythm.'

'What is the rhythm?'

'It's like the beat in music,' he explained.

I could understand that because I like to play the piano. My father had to make me learn to play, but I'm glad about that now because it gives me much pleasure.

I learned that the way a poem is constructed is called its

metre, and the rhythm is the musical effect this produces. In that one line of poetry, for example, there are eight bits, called syllables, like this:

Full-fath-om-five-thy-fath-er-lies.

When we say the words, we ever so slightly say each second syllable a little more strongly (but not too strongly) like this:

Full-Fath-om-Five-thy-Fath-er-Lies.

Just like music. I realised that this rhythm comes quite naturally; the pattern of the poetry cleverly uses the way we speak; well, the way English people speak. I've discovered it's very important to emphasise the correct syllable if you want to be understood in English.

The four pairs of syllables in the poem sort of balance each other so that the line feels complete and at rest and there is no tension left at the end. Another part of the complete pattern is how the fourth syllable, 'five,' has the same 'i' sound as the eighth, 'lies'. I learned that when two words have a similar sound we call that rhyme, which is not the same as rhythm. In fact this one line is really two short lines which rhyme, which is why the whole line seems balanced.

There was more, but first I asked him, 'What does "fathom" mean, doesn't it mean, "to think"?'

He explained it also meant a length, about one and a half metres, and generally it was only used at sea, so we know straightaway that this man has been drowned.

'And "thy"? I've never seen that word.'

Roy explained that it is just an old-fashioned word meaning 'your'. He said that, of course, when everyone spoke like that, poets naturally wrote in the same way, so even though we don't use those words these days some people still think they sound 'poetic'.

'But the words are all in the wrong order,' I argued, 'we were taught to put the subject at the beginning.'

'The order is changed to make the rhythm, and the rhyme,' he pointed out. 'In ordinary writing we might say, "Your father is drowned at sea, seven and a half metres down". But that's not beautiful is it?'

'No. Is there more?'

He started again.

Full fathom five thy father lies;
  Of his bones are corals made;
Those are pearls that were his eyes;
  Nothing of him that doth fade,
But doth suffer a sea-change
Into something rich and strange:
Sea-nymphs hourly ring his knell.
          Ding-dong!
  Hark! Now I hear them,
          Ding-dong bell!

As he said each line, he quickly wrote it down and then gave me the piece of paper.

I read the poem slowly. There were still many words

which I didn't know, but I could feel their music. 'It's sad,' I said, 'But it's beautiful too. Beautifully sad, or sadly beautiful: which? When you say, "Your father is drowned at sea," and so on, it might be sad for his son, but not really for anyone else. But somehow the poem makes it sad for everyone; but it's beautiful too, so it's sort of happy as well.'

I think Roy liked my ideas. 'You thought you couldn't understand English poetry,' he said, 'But already it speaks to you'.

'Yes! And, "Of his bones are corals made," has a rhythm, but, "Corals are made of his bones" doesn't'.

'That's right, though it's a little bit different than the one in the first line. There are many different rhythms used in poetry.'

That night, as I thought about my first English poem, I was wondering why the man had been drowned, and who was supposed to be speaking those lovely words.

♩

Dear Su Yen

I said I would send you the story of the poem about the drowned man. First of all I should say it's by William Shakespeare, perhaps the greatest English poet. He lived in the sixteenth century when Elizabeth I was Queen of England. I'm sure you have heard of him already.

The poem is from a play called *The Tempest*. A king, his son and their friends are shipwrecked on an enchanted island. The young prince is very sad because his father has been drowned. A kindly, although invisible, spirit called Ariel sings this sad but beautiful song to comfort him, which it does. His father is not gone: 'Nothing of him that doth (does) fade'; but he 'suffers' (that is, he experiences) 'a sea-change, into something rich and strange,' of corals and pearls.

However, it turns out that his father, the king, has not drowned; but he has in fact undergone a deep change, for although many years ago he did a very evil thing to the owner of the enchanted island, now the king is truly sorry, and the two men have become good friends again. Perhaps that is more beautiful and strange than being made into pearls and corals.

The stories, or plots, of Shakespeare's plays are famous, but I think his greatest genius was in his interesting and beautiful use of words.

Dear Roy

The drowned father is a lovely story expressed with poetic rhythm which interests me by its mysterious words. We may normally think that the saddest situation for people is when their close families or friends leave the world physically. However, in fact, sometimes we feel sorrow as we lose our families or friends even though they have not died. I really suffered from just such a strange feeling for about ten years before I came to England. I even thought I felt more pain than a real orphan who at least can get some support from the world and lay claim to people's kind understanding when they think their help is needed. In my case, I was supposed to be from a good family and was not 'qualified' to ask for any outside help, although I couldn't get any support from my parents to pursue my dream.

The story behind this poem brings back to me what I felt during those years. I remember my father was so considerate when I was very young; but I think I have lost my father since I was fourteen years of age because I couldn't recognize him anymore and didn't feel I still had a 'father' in the world. My grandfather told me the job in the prison took my father away from us and bound his mind into another world which normal people don't reach into. I also remember that my mother always told us to be good children to understand that my father cared about us so much, but just had a stressful job which made him so cold to us. Can this be reflected in the line of the poem, 'Sea-nymphs hourly ring his knell'? Luckily, my father now has been retired from his terrible job for several years, and is gradually becoming a kind person whom I did not see for more than twenty years.

It was such a complicated emotion for me to feel this poem when I was thinking about my own experience with my father …

Nothing of him that doth fade,
But doth suffer a sea-change
Into something rich and strange.

Dear Su Yen

Having thought a bit about what poetry is with *Ariel's Song*, here is what is said to be the earliest English poem.

I know you think England is very old, with your dreams of the Middle Ages, but it is not very old compared with China and many other places, nor is the English language. Of course there were people living here thousands of years ago, but we don't know much about what they thought because they have left no writing.

The first time writing came to this country was about 2000 years ago when the Roman Empire conquered Britain; the name England did not exist then. The people were called Britons and the Romano-British society was very cultured. You might like to see one day what their life was like by visiting the Roman Museum in Cirencester.

Then the Romans had to leave at the beginning of the fifth century AD. Over the next two centuries the country was slowly invaded and settled by people called Saxons who came from Saxony, in what is now Germany, and by Angles from the south of Denmark. That is why we are still sometimes called Anglo-Saxons. During this time there was no proper government or law as there had been in Roman times and that period is often called the Dark Ages. Culture, such as reading, writing and illustration, was kept alive in monasteries and abbeys by religious communities of monks and priests and their servants.

In a monastery in Whitby, in the north-east of the country, ruled by an Abbess (that is, a woman head-priest) called Hilda, the monks, and the servants as well, used to take turns to give a little entertainment in the evenings. A servant man called Caedmon who was not very well-educated (his job was to look after the cows) was very worried because next night he had to perform and he didn't know what to do. But that night, as he slept in the cowshed, he had a beautiful dream in which he was ordered to sing a song praising God, about the beginning of all things. When he woke up he could remember his song, and he sang it that night and it has been famous ever since. Here it is.

The Hymn of Caedmon, translated from the Anglo-Saxon by A. S. Cook (1853–1927)

> *Now must we hymn the Master of Heaven,*
> > *The might of the Maker, the deeds of the Father,*
> > *The thought of his heart. He, Lord everlasting,*
> > *Established of old the source of all wonders:*
> > *Creator all-holy, He hung the bright heaven,*
> > *A roof high, upreared, o'er the children of men;*
> > *The King of mankind then created for mortals*
> *The world in its beauty, the earth spread beneath them,*
> > *He, Lord everlasting, omnipotent God.*

Unlike *Full fathom five*, the rhythm here is powerful, like drum beats, which matches the idea of power in the poem. Try saying the second line:

The-might-of-the-mak-er-the-deeds-of-the-Fath-er.

See how the words are arranged so that the strong beats also emphasise the important words. There are four beats in a line, as in *Full fathom five*, but the arrangement of syllables makes a quite different effect: here there are two soft syllables, instead of one, between the strong ones.

I said this was the earliest known English poem, but neither you nor I would be able to read it in its original form. It has had to be translated into modern English. That is because it was written in the Anglo-Saxon language. This language gradually changed into the English we know today, but not until about the fourteenth century did it reach a form which most modern people might begin to understand, and only then with great difficulty.

But a few hundred years before that, the land of the Angles, *Angle-land*, became known as England.

Dear Roy

What a beautiful poem for the God. I enjoy reading this hymn because it seems to me that the poet didn't use many adjective words to decorate the whole poem: for example, 'the world in its beauty,' not 'beautiful world,' which perhaps is what makes the poem so strong. However, maybe it was the modern translator who wrote it in that way. That's why sometimes I desire to learn to read some old languages, such as the ancient Roman Latin, in order to understand the spirits of those old stories in depth.

I think I like the story behind the poem even more than the poem itself. Caedmon must have been a very good person whom the God also preferred to bless very much and didn't want to see him unhappy just because he didn't know how to entertain people. However, people often think the God is somehow not so caring about them when they feel they need help or protection, so sometimes people maybe choose not to believe in the God anymore. But in my own opinion, only the God knows how to judge whether we are good enough or if we really need his help. As it is said in Chinese, 'God helps people who help themselves'. I believe that the God usually comes to help me only when the mission is too difficult to me to cope with on my own. For example, I dreamt of Old Headington before I had been there in my real life; and this beautiful dream led to my decision to apply for Oxford Brookes University later on. I can't forget that day when I first came to England: I saw a familiar scene of Headington from the coach on my way to Oxford; I then realised that the God had chosen the best place for me, even a long while before I decided to come.

Dear Su Yen

You asked me to write a bit about a poem you had read in Chinese, *He wishes for the Cloths of Heaven*, because it seems to relate to your dreams. Well, I think your dreams are different to those of the poet, but the plea that these dreams might not be trampled over, whatever they are, will find sympathy in every person.

Since the poet, W. B. Yeats, calls the things he is describing the, 'cloths of heaven,' and since his description seems to suggest a beautiful sunset and twilight, we may suppose that was the source of his inspiration for this poem. He then imagines that these are finely woven and expensive coloured materials that would delight any woman and, thinking of the woman whom he loved, he wishes that he possessed such materials so that he might, as he writes, 'spread the cloths under your feet'. But he is poor and does not possess such cloths; he has only his dreams to spread before her.

If we did not know the story of Yeats' life we could see this poem, as you did when you read it in Chinese, as a very beautiful and happy poem, and think that she did tread softly and, perhaps, gratefully. Knowing the story of Yeats' life, however, it is likely that the person to whom he was expressing this devotion was Maud Gomme, a woman who did indeed often trample on his dreams even though at times she seemed to share some of them at least. Clearly the last two lines speak to you strongly because of those tutors who trampled on your dreams in Taiwan. So a great poet can treat a personal theme in a way that has a wide appeal.

In terms of poetry this poem may be called a 'lyric': that is, an expression of personal and, usually, deeply held feelings. You can compare this with the 'ode' which today is a term used for a poem which praises something: famous odes have been written to, for example, a bird called a skylark, and to a Grecian urn or vase. I suppose Caedmon's song was an ode to God, but because it is to God we call it a hymn.

He wishes for the Cloths of Heaven, by W. B. Yeats (1865–1939).

> *Had I the heavens' embroidered cloths,*
> *Enwrought with golden and silver light,*
> *The blue and the dim and the dark cloths*
> *Of night and light and the half-light,*

I would spread the cloths under your feet:
But I, being poor, have only my dreams;
I have spread my dreams under your feet;
Tread softly because you tread on my dreams.

Dear Roy

I liked to look down to the city and look up to the sky from a mountain for the whole night till dawn when the sun wakened up the world. Those stars on the sky were so peaceful and were so different from those stars busily moving on the road. I thought my mind stayed in between.

We all have our dreams from childhood to adulthood. Sometimes a dream is so tiny and sometimes it's so huge; sometimes a dream can be so strong and sometimes it's so fragile; and sometimes a dream is easily achievable and sometimes it's just unreachable. No one should judge our dreams with their own understandings of the world, but many people seem to enjoy destroying those dreams of other people. How can we expect other people to know how to cherish or embosom our dreams which are braided with our hearts? I think I don't understand the normal meaning of dream, or of the state of dreaming. Usually, when people say, 'you're dreaming,' or, 'let it stay in your dream,' they mean the thing does not truly belong to our lives or shouldn't be attained. Our dreams are broken so easily by the age of our growing mind. I don't know how many people can still remember how they were laughed at as fools because when they were very young, they ever wanted to be so great like Einstein.

It seems to me the poem shows the great desire of

sharing his treasure with someone who might be his family or his love; he cannot help himself, but only can beg of people that they might, 'Tread softly because you tread on my dreams'. Does the sun brighten the world or reveal the cloths of heaven? Should we always need someone to appreciate or share with us our dreams, and can't enjoy our joy alone? Maybe it's true that we all sometimes need to please someone to please ourselves.

3

DROWNING

沉没

'My coat sales queen, show us again how you sell a woollen coat in such hot weather.' My colleagues sometimes had fun pretending to worship my 'talented' selling ability and tried some interesting ideas to provoke me into making some business achievements on their behalf. I didn't mind doing this because I enjoyed working with them, although we were also competing with each other for sales.

'Which one do you want me to sell to the next customer?'

'Do you say *which one*? You mean you can sell whatever I tell you.' My colleague didn't believe me because customers usually had their own opinions and preferences in their minds.

'Don't worry about it, please tell me the least popular coat in your brand.'

'This funny green coat is the one which I've never sold any of this year.'

'OKay, it's the one I will sell to the next customer who comes into our shop.'

'Are you kidding? We have so many other brands in our shop; do you want to take back your word? I just worry that you'll feel embarrassed if the customer ignores you and goes to other brands.'

'How can I let that happen? I will cloak her eyes and stop her way before she sees other clothes.'

'Hello, ladies, are you looking for coats?' I stood at the entrance to accost two young ladies who were rambling into our shop.

'Not really, we just like to have a look and don't intend to find anything.'

'But now our coats are on sale; and most importantly, they're one hundred per cent woollen coats which are quite good value. I realise the spring is coming but, you know, these types of coats are never out of fashion and can be worn for more than ten years.'

'Hmm, which type of design do you have here? I am happy to have a look, but I'm not sure I will buy if you don't mind,' one of them replied.

'How about this? This one I think is quite special for you.' I picked the funny green coat right away, confidently. But she frowned and looked at her friend with some doubt. I then turned to talk to her friend: 'What do you think? The colour suits your friend because she is so white which is not so usual here. I think you are quite sensitive to fashion, according to your style. Where did you get this top from? I like the V curve of the collar which helps to show the figure of your neck very well.'

I think my innocent attitude relaxed their feelings a little and they started smiling and chatting to me. So, they didn't have any chance to look around in our shop.

'Oh, I bought this top in a normal shop; I didn't realise the collar is different till you told me. Do you like it? I can show you where the shop is.'

'Thank you very much. You should come to show me more of your clothes when you are shopping around; I enjoy looking at pretty women with smart clothes.' I returned to the customer and told her, 'You're so lucky with this friend who can be your fashion consultant.'

'Yes, that's why I'm shopping with her.'

'Now, you should ask her opinion about this coat; maybe she has some different ideas from mine. It's also good for me to learn different styles from people,' I said.

Her friend then came to stand at my side and began to convince the customer that the colour was quite suited to her skin.

'But I like brown more than this funny green; the design of the coat is fine, just the colour, I don't like the colour at all.' The customer was beginning to feel a little sympathy with the coat I had *chosen* for her.

'Funny colour? How can you use that word to describe this special green? It's special because it's not accepted by most people. It's not so popular with other people because their skin is too yellowish to match this green. If they really wanted to have it, I would discourage them because they would need heavy make-up to brighten their skin while wearing this coat. So, that's why I said it's a special coat for you because you will rarely see the same one as yours on the street. Do you still want to try the brown one which is so ordinary for you?'

'I appreciate your suggestion. But I think I still want to try the brown one because I feel better with that colour.'

'That's fine, of course you can try on just whatever you like; it's very good for me to get the chance to see how these coats look when you're trying them on.'

'Do I make too much trouble for you because you need to tidy up the shop all the time?' The customer was still worried that I might scold them if they didn't buy anything in the end. I could understand their concern because I had heard that our sales ladies were so unkind to customers who didn't buy anything after trying on for a while.

'Don't worry about me, it's my job to tidy up the shop all the time; otherwise I will be so bored if I have nothing to do here. I enjoy looking at customers trying on different clothes which are so smart. I appreciate no one will buy everything they've tried in a day. Please feel free when you're with me. It's so interesting to talk to you like friends.' Once customers felt I treated them as friends, they lost their defensive reaction and began to enjoy trying on whatever they wanted.

'Do you still like the brown coat you tried on just now? I think you can see the difference from the green one.' I still didn't give up persuading her to buy that green coat.

Her friend echoed my idea again. 'Yes, the green one is more special than the brown one, and it seems fine the way that colour matches your skin.'

'Is it easy to match with other colours?' The customer had finally entertained the idea of wearing the green coat.

'Yes, because it's an earth colour with some grey colour mixed with the green; you can match any colour you have in your cupboard. I can show you here. Don't worry; it's not good for me to hear you have lost face when your friends laugh at your funny clothes which you bought from me.' I matched the green coat with many other colours in our shop to show her the different effects; I also taught her how to make various effects for different occasions.

'Will you give me some discounts? Your prices are much higher than other places and are a bit outside my budget.'

Oh, I was so glad that she finally talked about the price because it was the last step to closing the sale.

'Yes, I can give you some discounts because I believe you will come here again when you feel comfortable with this coat. As you know, there is a saying that you get what you pay for. That's why our prices can't be any lower when the materials and quality are the main concerns of our designers.'

'Thank you for your patience; I will bring my other friends here and you should remember me every time when I see you. We like you as a friend rather than as a sales lady.'

It was always the best gift when I won friendship from my customers. I knew I also won friendships with my colleagues by making our job interesting and creating good business achievements for them.

'I can't help but worship you again because you really made it, our coat sales queen. It's often so hard to sell a woollen coat in hot weather, but you made it again.' My colleague made a bow to me after I saw the customers out from our shop with the bag containing that funny green coat.

I think that customer was quite happy with her special green coat because I didn't receive any complaint from her afterwards.

I found that job in a rather strange way. I had just finished High School in Taipei and had no idea about my future life.

'Su Yen, a manager of a department store called you just now. I think he wanted to discuss with you about when you can start working.' My mum told me to call back to the manager for my new job.

'A department store? Which one? Why do they want to offer me a place? Are you sure they mentioned my name?' I really had no idea about a job in a department store because I didn't think I had accepted a job anywhere.

'How can I know which one you visited today? They said you had been there. I think it's better to call back and check if they really want you.'

'But I didn't accept any job today.'

'He seems to think you did.'

What had I done now?

'Hi, this is Su Yen Hu. Did you call me today about a job or something?'

'Yes, I want to know if you can start working from tomorrow because one of our cashiers is away from tomorrow afternoon till next week. I hope you can learn the work from her in the morning.'

'Cashier? Are you sure you didn't call the wrong number? I don't think I applied for any job as a cashier.'

'What do you mean? You came to our shop to apply for a job, and I talked to you for about an hour this morning.

Do you mean you don't want this job?'

'Can you please give me an hour to think about it and call me later?'

I received another call just about an hour after, but really I didn't want to do that job because my subject was advertisement design, which was not exactly relevant to that situation. In fact my main concern just then was to spend quite a long time trying to think what I had done that day; finally, I felt quite embarrassed when I re- membered the morning.

I had gone to the post-office with a friend of mine when I was still in a dream-state and had not quite woken up. It meant I didn't dress up carefully and might not have done up my hair at all. Afterwards, we were rambling around the shops when, outside a store, we saw a board which showed: 'Sales Ladies Wanted' .

'Are you looking for a shop assistant?'

'Yes, do you have any experience? We need a senior sales lady to work for a designer's brand of women's clothing.'

'I've just graduated from my design course at High School, so I don't really have any work experience, but I think I can do this job because I learnt colour psychology and design concepts at school, and also I had some experience on special dresses for our costume balls.' I explained this so confidently, flourishing my hands quite professionally I thought. However, the manager looked at me strangely and didn't say a word for some moments. As he hesitated, I glanced quickly around the store and realised that all the sales ladies were very sophisticated. I suddenly felt so green and strange there.

The manager eventually said something, but still stared curiously at my scruffy hair and clothes. 'Hmm, we also have a place for a cashier. I think you might be able to deal with that job.'

'But I studied design. I did do some modules on accounting, but I don't think I can do a cashier's job because it's not my subject.'

'I will teach you about what you need to do for everyday. It's a job which doesn't require any experience to start with.'

'Oh, I have to think about it then.' I answered the manager quite aloofly.

The manager gazed at me again, and hardened his voice to *remind* me that he was kindly trying to offer me something. 'Sure. I also have to think about whether you're capable of working in this place.'

When we had left I just forgot about that shop right away because it was too complicated for me to think about accounting, or working with that funny till or that strange machine for credit cards which I had never seen before in my life; and then we visited many other places that day.

Another one hour passed; the manager called me again and asked if I wanted to work there. It was difficult for me to understand why he called me three times to persuade me to take that job. Did it mean that he couldn't find anyone for that place? If so, it must be because it was a very hard job, or perhaps the manager was a harsh person to work with.

'Su Yen, you should take this job as your first one because I think you only need to work with female colleagues and customers, which is better for you. Most importantly, it is a big company which will be useful for your records on your CV. However, to be honest, I also wonder how they will be able to teach you anything when you've never been very clever about money.' What was my father talking about? In his opinion was I too stupid for accounting?

'Yes, I accept this offer and will start working from tomorrow morning. By the way, can you remind me again where you are and what the name of your company is?'

I hoped I wouldn't make a fool of myself, even though I had no work experience. But, never mind, I would try to make it if only for the reason to prove to my father that I could be quite good in accounting.

♩

'What's she doing here? She can do nothing but make trouble!'

'What's the problem with our company? Can't they find anyone else to do this job? We don't need a child who doesn't have any experience, like her!'

'Oh, dear, she even can't make the till open.'

There was a great fiasco on the first week of my first job. I was told off the whole day long without any break. People sometimes can be so unkind and don't sympathise with any mistakes made by other people who are still learning.

'Are you all right? Do you have any problem?' Our manager came very late to rescue me, but it might not be too late because, although I was dying, I hadn't died yet.

'I have a huge problem with this job. I can't recognize the differences between credit cards, and I can't find any information on the card. When I called the bank to ask for a customer's authorized code, they asked me something about issue date, valid date, card number and card holder. I just hung up the phone-set immediately because I was so scared.'

The manager seemed not surprised at all and just showed me several cards and taught me how to read different cards using different swipe machines. However, that didn't help me much when I still needed to remember which sales lady worked for which brand and there were about thirty brands in our store. I also needed to learn telephone manners when answering the phone during the busiest times. But even these sorts of things during the day were not the most terrible for me.

The biggest nightmare always came at the end of the day when finally I had to work out the differences between those confusing accounts and the cash before closing off the till.

'Su Yen, we've been working overtime for three days; when will you start finishing your work on time? I always need to wait for you before I can shut the shop.' Our chief manager couldn't help but complain at 11 PM on the third day of my work.

'Please, don't push me so hard, I'm so new and confused. Other cashiers come to help me sometimes, but they are so fast and they don't give me enough time to see what they are doing. Can you show me slowly how to balance the account? I promise I will remember everything from tonight.'

I think I was quite patient and clever because gradually my colleagues stopped complaining about me and started asking me to help them to cope with some complicated accounting problems when the department store had a sale on during the busiest period of the year. Sometimes I went to serve customers myself to settle an account when the store was too busy. I then discovered that talking to customers was much more interesting than sitting by the till. I felt so satisfied when people decided to buy something from me. So I arranged my holidays to replace those sales ladies when they were off in the second month of my work and then I could show my name and my business achievements on the report which our manager would see every day.

It seemed that my strategy of sacrificing my holidays to work in the shop was quite successful because after a month the chief manager came to talk to me about my new position. 'Do you want to shift your place from being a cashier to become a sales lady? Your manager now wants us to train you to be a million-sales-lady.' This opportunity didn't just fall from the sky: I had several times reached the highest business achievements that they had ever seen for the different brands I stood in for.

And then my life was nearly destroyed.

♪

I thought I would never again feel anything like that I had felt at the first touch of his eye. I believed that he would be my first and my last love who would lead me to a happy-ever-after marriage. But the same tragedy has been played out many times, all over the world; only the leading roles are changing, played by different people, from the past until now, and will be played again by new people in the future. I was just another one of those heroines in the old continuing story when I had that longing for, as I thought then, the happy light of marriage. It would not be too much overstated if I say that I felt this experience almost snatched away my life. I realise now that I might simply have undergone a so-called broken-hearted re-lationship, like those suffered by many other people, but such an event may leave so much pain in our lives for so long that we can almost forget what a happy life is.

Without much choice I entered for the National United Examination for Universities with the aim of choosing a university as far as possible from my home town, in order to escape that grieving space where I had so much memory of him. But this decision was a disastrous mistake.

'Ha-ha-ha-ha; you're so lucky and you've passed your exam to a university.' A child, wearing ancient-style Chinese clothes, sat on a high chair by a big wooden table and talked to me confidently.

'How can you know it? I haven't gone to the exam yet which is taking place next week.' I was so puzzled and had no clue as to what he was talking about, but a hope arose in my mind that he might be able to tell me something which occupied my heart and hadn't seemed to move away for many months. 'If you can tell my future, can you also tell me about my boyfriend?'

The child then read to me and wrote out a poem. When he gave me the paper I saw that the poem was in the shape of a rabbit. I couldn't understand the poem right away and I felt strangely uneasy to see the rabbit made up of lines of poetry.

'Your study and your love are going together.'

I didn't quite understand what he meant, but I knew that the birth year of my boyfriend was Rabbit and the year after this year would be Rabbit as well. The problem was that I didn't think I would take the exam again if I failed to pass it this year which was the year of Tiger and a year earlier than the year of Rabbit. However, I might consider taking the exam again in the year of Rabbit if my life and my love story could turn around to be brought together brightly ever after. But, how could I believe without doubt a child who told my future like this?

'Ha-ha-ha-ha; do you want to have a bowl of noodle? I will cook for you; and those candies, take whatever you want.'

I was more puzzled and didn't understand how to reply to his apparently kindly invitation.

'Who are you?' Then I was not sure that this question was a clever one to ask when the only answer I heard was his giggle and, as his sound gradually disappeared in to my ceiling, I suddenly realized I was in a dream which had been just a bit too real for me to believe I was asleep.

I didn't tell anyone about that dream until after I entered university, because I didn't study for the exam at all, and did not really believe I could pass it unless someone in heaven blessed me a lot.

'Su Yen, please spend some time on preparing for this exam because it might affect your whole future.' My friendly colleagues took me to a library and showed me some previous exam papers. But maybe I did not want to pass it in the year of Tiger.

'Oh, no, I know nothing about the exam and can't do anything for it now. People spend one or two years preparing for it and there's only a week left. I don't know where to start. Or, maybe I will be lucky because they will test me only on what I've learnt already.'

Amazingly, a miracle came to me during those days of my exam. I was too surprised to think when I saw the first exam paper. Right through to the last paper, during the whole progress of the examination, I just kept answering those various questions with their requirements of drawing, choosing answers and painting so quickly, without wasting any time on hesitating, because almost all of those questions were so familiar and were those I had reviewed in that final week. Therefore it wasn't a surprise for me to learn later that I was qualified to get in to a university. But it was a huge shock for other people to believe it.

'YOU ARE KIDDING! If it's true that you have passed that exam then I can buy you whatever you want and take you to a five-star restaurant anytime you wish.'

'You must give the God a big chicken leg in exchange for your result. How can I believe you because I never saw you study this year?'

'Are you sure they didn't send the wrong result to you? Are you sure your name is correct on the transcript?'

'What are you doing here? This place is only for people to sign up for their universities today. I think you're a bit lost.'

I admit I had some doubt in my mind and was a bit worried that something bad would happen to take my place away because that year was Tiger, not Rabbit.

'But I saw my name on the board and it's right beside your names.' I said.

They all were suddenly so quiet while I pointed out my name and result to them. Most sadly, it seemed no one remembered their promises to buy anything I wanted, or to take me to a restaurant afterwards.

Why should they think I might have lied to them when everyone could check every examinee's name and result on the notice board outside the signing-up place? Or maybe it really was just too unbelievable for all the people who knew me. I decided to tell them how, in the week before my exam, I had dreamed of that child because I thought they might find it easier to trust in some supernatural power than to believe in my actual strength. It is strange that people think like that, but often it is so.

♫

'The character of the child you saw may be the deity of Taoism. He was the third son of an *Aga* and was apotheosized before growing up. That's why you only saw his appearance as a child.' A friend of mine told me the story of the child and showed me that I could read some books about those Taoist ideas if I wanted to learn more about them.

'I'm not a Taoist at all. I don't understand why he came to my dream and wanted to cook noodle for me? I'm more worried now if you're right about him because he told me that my study and my love are going together in the year of Rabbit. But I'm puzzled about this because I've been given a place at university this year of Tiger.'

'There might not be a problem about your religion if the God wants you to go with your dream. I reckoned originally that you might pass your exam next year, but he has already given you a rabbit in your dream; so now you have everything and don't need to wait for another year. It means your boyfriend will come to see you shortly according to the prescription of your dream.'

This explanation by my friend sounded quite logical and cheerful and it comforted me; but I did hope she was certainly right rather than just trying to give me some hope. Nevertheless, I brought a hopeful mind to the start of my new life at university and expected to see some positive change in my love.

However, it's always difficult to believe in a dream and to take directions from a dream for our lives. I made an absolutely wrong decision to start my new life in such a cultural desert as my new university town where nothing could be compared with the place I had studied in before. I regretted often that I hadn't listened to my father when he told me, 'I don't think you will like any city other than Taipei because you like crowds'. Suddenly I realised that my father was the only person who truly understood me once I saw the environment around my university. The university was claimed to be newly established for design courses, but I didn't find much modern equipment nor enough qualified lecturers there. The site was surrounded by many huge derelict fields and so far no library, or exhibition centre, or arts gallery for designers to see the latest fashion tendencies of the world had been built. In other words, the whole world was cut off by the boundary of that strange city. Perhaps it was unfair to complain too much because the university had been built for only two years and the whole city was just starting to be developed when I first arrived. But when I considered my own situation, I still did not feel I could live a free and happy life there when one disaster after another seemed to come through; as it is said, 'Misfortunes never come singly'. I left my university after a few months and painfully gave up on my love story when the situation didn't seem to be turning to a good ending. I understood now that it had been a warning when the child in my dream told me that *my study and my love were going together.* He meant that, eventually, both of them together would go away from me.

Dreams are so unreal, but sometimes they are too real to be believed in reality. I've been attracted to live in a world of interpretation of dreams since that time.

Dear Su Yen

The beginning of your last story reminded me of an evocative and rather sad poem by Robert Browning called *Two in the Campagna*. I'm sure it will be in that book of Browning's poems you bought from the library. As he says, we do not choose to love or not to love; it is not rational, and maybe we fall in love with love itself and not with a person; very few people will be good enough for that perfect dream so there is always loss because we cannot grasp the infinite. But I feel that while the poet here is sad because he did not find perfect love he knows that it was not perfect and so is not too sad; he is not like someone who believes they had found perfect love and have lost it forever.

Here are just a few verses.

Two in the Campagna, by Robert Browning (1812–1889)

How say you? Let us, O my dove,
* Let us be unashamed of soul,*
As earth lies bare to heaven above!
* How is it under our control*
To love or not to love?

I would that you were all to me,
* You that are just so much, no more.*
Nor yours nor mine, nor slave nor free!
* Where does the fault lie? What the core*
O' the wound, since wound must be?

I would I could adopt your will,
  See with your eyes, and set my heart
Beating by yours, and drink my fill
  At your soul's springs—your part my part—
In life for good or ill.

No. I yearn upward, touch you close,
  Then stand away. I kiss your cheek,
Catch your soul's warmth,—I pluck the rose
  And love it more than tongue can speak—
Then the good minute goes.

Already how am I so far
  Out of that minute? Must I go
Still like the thistle ball, no bar,
  Onward, wherever light winds blow,
Fixed by no friendly star?

Just when I seemed about to learn!
  Where is the thread now? Off again!
The old trick! Only I discern—
  Infinite passion, and the pain
Of finite hearts that yearn.

'The old trick,' the old story: as you say, repeated so many times.

Dear Roy

    I think I forgot the struggle of how to love or not to love, or perhaps I never worked out the feeling of love, so that I chose at last to return to reality; I mean, chose to return to university and made myself as busy as possible to feel life another way round.

Hence, I can't really tell if I was in the old trick when it is too difficult for me to think I was in or I didn't want to believe I was in. My ex-boyfriend said that the most beautiful feeling always comes with grief and is momentary like shooting stars that disappear on the sky quickly, but leave the brightest moment to our mind. I felt melancholy, but didn't realize that in the beginning of our meeting he had already foretold our breakaway. I was stuck in that uncertain situation with him several times and never understood why the most beautiful moment in our mind should go with sadness. However, eventually, exhaustedly, I confessed to myself that I could not control things which have to be kept between two people; therefore I decided to give up trying to appreciate this complicated romantic 'theory' of shooting stars. The only things I can certainly control are my own mind and my life which I can share with other people naturally, but which don't require intercommunicating with someone else to keep those things just for each other. I could decide to gain more work experience in companies when I was not satisfied with the air of my university; and I could leave those jobs to try some other chance to achieve my dream when I was not happy with those people who used my strength and took it for granted. Likewise, I can try my best to stay in a strange country where I have found my dreaming place to keep my cloud-castle forever.

肆
4
SONNETS
十四行詩

Dear Su Yen

You said you had heard about a special sort of poem called a sonnet, and you wondered whether *He wishes for the Cloths of Heaven* was a sonnet. Well it isn't, but it is a bit like one, as you will see.

In the nineteenth century a lady called Elizabeth Barrett lived with her parents in a gloomy house in London. She was no longer young, and often she was ill. She wrote poetry and read poetry and she particularly liked the poems of a man called Robert Browning. The two wrote to each other and exchanged poems. At last Elizabeth persuaded her parents to let Robert come to visit her. They fell in love straight away; perhaps they had already fallen in love through their letters and poems. They married and went to live in sunny Italy, near Rome; Elizabeth's health improved and, as far as we know, they lived happily ever after and continued to write poetry. It is one of the great love-stories of English life.

Elizabeth wrote a number of sonnets about her feelings for her husband: these are some of the best-loved poems in English culture. This one is about the great change in her life when she met Robert. The first part describes her 'melancholy' life. Women in well-off families at that time were not supposed to work and they were not allowed in universities, and if they did not marry they often had a restricted and boring life, although married life often was restricted and boring too; some did write books or poetry. It seemed Elizabeth's life would continue like that until her death which might be soon because of her ill health. Then, in an instant, her future changed from death to life and love. You will see that the last two lines of the poem are abrupt and not smooth like the first slow part of the sonnet: this is a poetic device to express the sudden shock as her life was transformed, though I don't like this abruptness; do you? Compare this with the last two lines of the Shakespeare sonnet which I have sent also. Do you think Elizabeth could have written more beautiful lines and still expressed the sudden transformation just as well? She describes it in terms of the common trick of English children, and of lovers, of creeping up behind someone, putting their hands over the person's eyes and saying, 'Guess who?' although I doubt that actually happened; do children do that in Taiwan?

A little explanation: Theocritus was a Greek poet from Syracuse who lived in the third century BC. He is thought of as the father of pastoral poetry: that is, poetry which idealizes the country and the lives of farmers. Perhaps his main importance is that his work was a strong influence on the Roman poet Virgil three centuries later. Virgil's bucolic (that is, country) poetry, when it was translated from Latin into English around the end of the seventeenth century, had in turn a great influence on English life, poetry, art and landscape design. Elizabeth could read ancient Greek, 'his antique tongue,' (that is, his ancient language) and in the first part of the sonnet she compares the happy rural life depicted in Theocritus' poetry with her own 'sweet sad years'.

The only other explanation you might need is the use of 'ware' for 'aware' to reduce the syllables from two to one to keep the metre.

The story is true, but there is also a play about it, called *The Barretts of Wimpole Street*, which you might find in a second-hand-book shop.

I have hurt my back working on my boat and cannot do very much at present so it is quite pleasant sitting here thinking about poetry and writing letters. But if the poetry interferes too much with all the other work you have to do you must say so.

Sonnets from the Portuguese, by Elizabeth Barrett-Browning (1806–1861)

> *I thought once how Theocritus had sung*
>   *Of the sweet years, the dear and wished-for years,*
>   *Who each one in a gracious hand appears*
> *To bear a gift for mortals, old or young:*
> *And, as I mused it in his antique tongue,*
>   *I saw, in gradual vision through my tears,*
>   *The sweet, sad years, the melancholy years,*
> *Those of my own life, who by turns had flung*
> *A shadow across me. Straightway I was 'ware,*
>   *So weeping, how a mystic Shape did move*
> *Behind me, and drew me backward by the hair;*
>   *And a voice said in mastery, while I strove,—*

'Guess now who holds thee?'—'Death,' I said. But there,
The silver answer rang,—'Not Death, but Love.'

William Shakespeare is famous for his sonnets as
well as for his plays. The Shakespearean sonnets and the
Elizabeth Barret-Browning sonnets are two of the best
known collections of sonnets in English poetry. If you
have studied the little article on prosody, or how to make
poems, (I'm sure you have) you know that all sonnets have
fourteen lines; however, the rhyming pattern may vary. In
particular, in Italian style sonnets the last two lines do not
rhyme, as you can see in Elizabeth's sonnet; in English
Elizabethan, or Shakespearean, sonnets they do. The form
of a sonnet is that the first eight lines set the background,
or build up the idea for the sonnet, and the last six lines
resolve the idea; the last two lines state the conclusion. I
feel that when the last two lines do rhyme the conclusion
is stated with greater force—like two hammer blows!

In Shakespeare's sonnet, *Shall I compare thee to a
summer's day*, he first develops the theme that in fact a
summer day does not last forever, but changes (eight
lines); in the last six lines he resolves this by saying that
as a result of his poetry, however, this person will be remembered always: the last two lines sum this up with great
force. Elizabeth uses the first eight lines and a half to state
what her life was like (she should not have used that extra
half line, but perhaps it does not matter) and the last five
and a half to show how the problem was resolved. But I
don't find the last two lines mellifluous (that is, they do not
flow sweetly) for three reasons: first, they do not rhyme,

but that is correct for an Italian sonnet; second, they are not musical or beautiful, but that was done for poetic effect, and, third, I don't like the choice of words: would a man's voice ring like silver? I think it makes him sound like a large expensive clock striking the hour: 'The silver answer rang ...' or a dinner gong maybe! Or perhaps that is what she meant. These are only my personal preferences, but I have tried to give reasons for my choices.

You will have to judge for yourself what you like and how you understand it.

You say you are puzzled by words like 'thee' and 'thou': these are the old forms of 'you' which were used when speaking to one person only and were less formal than 'you'. You do need to understand these words quite often when reading poetry. They are no longer shown in most books of English grammar, but are quite easy to use. 'Thou' is the subject of a sentence: 'Thou art more fair' means 'You are more fair'; 'thee' is the object: 'Shall I compare thee' means 'Shall I compare you'; 'thy,' as you already know, shows possession: 'thy father,' means, 'your father'; 'thine' is used before a vowel, 'thine eyes,' means, 'your eyes'; it can also stand alone: 'I give thee what is thine' means 'I give you what is yours'. In the past, poets used these words naturally as it was the everyday way of speaking, but by the nineteenth century many poets used them to create what they thought would be an old-fashioned feel to their poems. In part this was due to the Romantic style which often tried to recreate a mediaeval atmosphere. This can sometimes be irritating, especially when the subject of the poem is not mediaeval.

For example, here is just the first stanza, or verse, of the well-known *Ode to a Skylark* by Shelley who was born in 1792 and lived for just thirty years. He is many people's favourite English poet. An ode, you remember, is a poem which praises something. Here he is praising the skylark, a tiny English bird which in summer hovers so high in the clear blue sky that you cannot see him; yet his song is beautiful and so strong that he can be heard on the ground. The skylark's song is a popular symbol of the English countryside. *Lark Ascending* is a beautiful and evocative piece of music by Ralph Vaughn-Williams, a very English composer; I hope you will hear it one day.

Ode to a Skylark, by Percy Bysshe Shelley (1792–1822).

> *Hail to thee, blithe spirit!*
> *Bird thou never wert—*
> *That from heaven or near it*
> *Pourest thy full heart*
> *In profuse strains of unpremeditated art.*

That second line means, 'Bird you never were,' or perhaps, 'surely you cannot be just a bird'. I have always found that 'wert' ugly, although it is correct old English, as is 'thou'. Perhaps it was the only word he could think of to rhyme with heart and art. He means this beautiful song surely cannot come from a mere little bird, but must come from a happy spirit.

Anyway, here is a one of Shakespeare's best-loved sonnets.

Sonnet XVIII, by William Shakespeare (1564–1616)

Shall I compare thee to a summer's day?
  Thou art more lovely and more temperate:
Rough winds do shake the darling buds of May,
  And summer's lease hath all too short a date:
Sometime too hot the eye of heaven shines,
  And often is his gold complexion dimm'd:
And every fair from fair sometime declines,
  By chance, or nature's changing course untrimm'd;
But thy eternal summer shall not fade,
  Nor lose possession of that fair thou ow'st,
Nor shall death brag thou wander'st in his shade,
  When in eternal lines to time thou grow'st;
    So long as men can breathe, or eyes can see,
    So long lives this, and this gives life to thee.

Here I feel the old-fashioned, or archaic, language seems natural and beautiful.

Dear Roy

That poem by Elizabeth Browning is great fun, particularly because there is a real story behind it. First, about the common trick of children, and lovers, of creeping up behind someone, putting their hands over the person's eyes and saying, 'Guess who?': for me, I only saw this in a movie, and I think if somebody does this to me in reality, I will hit them right away rather than try to guess. But maybe it's sweet or romantic for other people, just not me.

If I compare this poem to the Shakespeare, well, I'm

trying to think about it, but so far, in my knowledge, it is still too hard to have a clear opinion on my own. But I feel Barrett's poem is modest and pure. Shakespeare's poems are more complicated in expressing feeling and more imaginative. You mentioned you don't like the abruptness in her poem. But in my feeling, my mind was as though in a picture when following her words and I felt her life was just so hopelessly ill until she met Robert. It is always believed that love is such a unique, powerful thing which can change everything suddenly, either with better or worse effect. The abruptness at the end of her poem strongly made me understand what the magic of love was in her life. Besides, I find I have a book, *The Poems of Robert Browning,* which I bought from the library that time. I'm so excited that I can read more about him. And starting from what you send me I am using keywords on the websites to build my own learning information. I'm so grateful to you for sharing your wisdom and knowledge with me. Although I'm happy that you can have more time to send me more works, it's still not good news to hear you have hurt your back.

Dear Su Yen

I liked your description of Elizabeth's sonnet as, 'modest and pure'; I might have said, 'sincere,' or, 'honest,' (not all love poetry is that), but when I think more about it I think your words are better. And you are right about Shakespeare being more complex and imaginative. I also thought fun was not the right word for such a serious subject, but perhaps it is fun at the end for I'm sure they would have laughed a lot.

It is always a pleasure for a teacher in England when a student has his or her own ideas and maybe even disagrees; perhaps it is different in Chinese culture. It is said that the great Dr Samuel Johnson, who wrote his famous dictionary in the eighteenth century and helped to standardize our English spelling for the first time, loved to be contradicted; I suppose because he loved an argument to sharpen his mind and to consider new ideas. As I said, I don't claim that what I tell you is true; these are just ideas for you to think about. Different people will like different poems for different reasons.

I thought you might like to try some more recent English poetry. I hope you will find this next poem to be a happy one for you, although for me it has a deep sense of loss too. The poet Dylan Thomas was born in 1914 into a Welsh family; he became an alcoholic, and as a result his life was a short one. He used words in an unconventional way which is very intriguing and stimulating to a reader and which creates vivid 'word-pictures'. *Fern Hill* describes the experiences of a young boy growing up and playing on a farm. To an English person this may seem to be an ideal life, though perhaps not to a Chinese person. The poem is full of the things which he remembers and which evoke that happy life: the apple boughs, or branches; the starry nights; the wagons; the daisies; the foxes barking; the owls; the horses; the farmhouse; the hayricks; the swallows; the lambs; the 'lamb-white days'.

The poet avoids clichés, or over-used phrases, by changing them. To appreciate how clever this is you need to know what the original phrase would have been. For example, in England we conventionally start a children's fairy story, which is the name we use for a magic story, with the phrase, 'Once upon a time'. He changes this to, 'And once below a time,' which means the same, but is refreshingly different. We say, 'All the day long,' for all day; he says, 'all the sun long,': the sun makes the day. We say, 'Happy as the day is long,' meaning very happy; he says, 'happy as the grass is green,' which has the same recognisable form and means the same, but is different and original: the summer day is very long, the grass is very green, the boy is very happy; but now the ideas of green grass and of happiness are merged together, or conflated, to produce a word picture of a child playing on the cool, fresh grass with, perhaps, little white and gold daisy flowers in it.

Thomas describes the house as, 'lilting,' that is as singing; can a house sing? A lilt is an apparently simple and primitive song sung by people in remote areas and especially in the Celtic areas of Britain, such as Wales; perhaps he means the idea of the house effects the same homely feelings in him as do the songs, and so the house 'sings' to him. He talks of, 'The tunes from the chimneys': smoke, not tunes, rises from chimneys: curling, formless and always changing yet always the same, like the tunes of the lilting songs.

But the poem is really two poems twisted together; within these happy memories there is a growing sense of foreboding, a warning. It concerns that thing which affects us all: 'Time'. If a dog is attached to a very long lead he may forget he is on the lead until he reaches the end of it. The poet imagines that Time holds him on a very long lead, or chain, which he does not notice when he is young until he reaches the end and, with a great sense of loss, he, 'wakes to the farm forever fled from the childless land'. He has grown up and nothing seems the same anymore. He speaks of the, 'children green and golden': as corn ripens in the fields so it turns from green to gold: and then it dies, as does childhood. This inner, sadder poem can be picked out and made to stand alone. See if you can find any more of these sad lines.

I have to admit to a strong personal preference for this poem: it is so evocative of my own childhood that I cannot read it, or even think of it, without tears coming into my eyes. One function of poetry is to arouse our sympathies. For me this poem does this more than any other I know, though perhaps it is a personal sympathy, with the poet, and not a universal one. Maybe other people will not be so moved. However, it is a wonderful poem and full of imagination and should appeal to anyone who can look back with nostalgia to a happy childhood. If you do not understand all of it just read it aloud and enjoy the music of the words.

Dylan Thomas is best known for a long poem, *Under Milkwood*, which describes a small Welsh town and many of the people who live there; it uses words in the characteristic way we have seen here. You might find it in a bookshop.

Fern Hill, by Dylan Thomas (1914–1953)

Now as I was young and easy under the apple boughs
About the lilting house and happy as the grass was green,
  The night above the dingle starry,
   Time let me hail and climb
  Golden in the heyday of his eyes,
And honoured among wagons I was prince of the apple towns
And once below a time I lordly had the trees and leaves
   Trail with daisies and barley
  Down the rivers of the windfall light.

And as I was green and carefree, famous among the barns
About the happy yard and singing as the farm was home,
  In the sun that is young once only,
   Time let me play and be
  Golden in the mercy of his means,
And green and golden I was huntsman and herdsman, the calves
Sang to my horn, the foxes on the hills barked clear and cold,
   And the Sabbath rang slowly
  In the pebbles of the holy streams.

All the sun long it was running, it was lovely, the hay
Fields high as the house, the tunes from the chimneys, it was air
  And playing, lovely and watery
   And fire green as grass.
  And nightly under the simple stars
As I rode to sleep the owls were bearing the farm away,
All the moon long I heard, blessed among stables, the nightjars
  Flying with the Ricks, and the horses
   Flashing into the dark.

And then to awake, and the farm, like a wanderer white
With the dew, come back, the cock on his shoulder: it was all
  Shining, it was Adam and maiden,
   The sky gathered again
   And the sun grew round that very day.
So it must have been after the birth of the simple light
In the first, spinning place, the spellbound horses walking warm
  Out of the whinnying green stable
   On to the fields of praise.

And honoured among foxes and pheasants by the gay house
Under the new made clouds and happy as the heart was long,
  In the sun born over and over,
   I ran my heedless ways,
  My wishes raced through the house high hay
And nothing I cared, at my sky blue trades, that time allows
In all his tuneful turning so few and such morning songs
  Before the children green and golden
   Follow him out of grace.

Nothing I cared, in the lamb white days, that time would take me
Up to the swallow thronged loft by the shadow of my hand,
  In the moon that is always rising,
   Nor that riding to sleep
  I should hear him fly with the high fields
And wake to the farm forever fled from the childless land.
Oh as I was young and easy in the mercy of his means,
  Time held me green and dying
  Though I sang in my chains like the sea.

Dear Roy

About the poem, *Fern Hill:* I was so moved by this poem when I finally found all the words from many dictionaries; it took me two days. And I found many different dictionaries while I was surfing the internet, such as the *Shakespeare Words* and some glossaries. I think my reading speed was slowed down because of those dictionaries which, although they helped me to understand old words for poems, also confused me a lot. For example, a line from the poem: 'And as I was green and carefree, famous among the barns,' the word, 'barns', does it mean children? I found the meaning from the *Shakespeare Words* dictionary which shows 'barn' means 'a child'. And another example is: 'the calves Sang to my horn …,' does the word 'horn' mean mad, or madness? The *Shakespeare Words* shows: 'horn mad: probably, harm-mad, that is, brain mad'. I'm not sure I know how to read this dictionary. Moreover, 'As I rode to sleep the owls were bearing the farm away' I'm not sure whether 'bear the farm away' means 'remove' or 'capture' the farm, or maybe both. Lastly, when I read 'lamb white days,' in my imagination I thought he meant those lovely days just like the white and soft fur of lambs (am I right?).

Overall, there was a picturesque image being formed in my brain because the childlike enjoyment is shown completely by his vivid words. However, I couldn't quite identify with the feeling of 'time' in this poem, because I grew up from a city and never touched any country life at all. Sadly, I even don't know what the feeling of feet treading on earth can be; and the only time I walked on grass once, when I stayed with my grandmother in the countryside, there was a snake in the grass. I envy people who have experience of country life during their childhood, and feel sad that I didn't have any simple joy when I was a child. So, this poem brings me a beautiful dream which is too far away from my experience of life.

Dear Su Yen

You have worked hard on this. I didn't realize you would do so much. I worry that you may be neglecting other studies; please don't feel that you must spend a lot of time on these poems; they are only for your pleasure to do as much as you want. You don't have to answer my questions, they are just meant for you to think about. Even if you don't understand all of it you seem to have experienced some of the feelings of the poem which is perhaps the most important thing.

A Shakespeare dictionary might not be helpful here as it explains how words were used in Shakespeare's time and some meanings have changed very much since then. A 'barn' could be a child I suppose, especially in Scotland, although the word 'bairn' is more usual for that meaning. In England today barns are large buildings used to store things on a farm, especially the harvest of corn, and are marvellous places for children to play in, and that is certainly what Thomas meant. Many of these barns are hundreds of years old and very beautiful, but their conservation as buildings is a current problem because they are not so useful for modern farming. I have also sent you some pictures of a famous mediaeval barn, 700 years old, at Great Coxwell near Oxford.

A horn is a sort of trumpet for communicating out of doors, used mostly by soldiers (they call it a bugle) and by hunters. In traditional fox-hunting, the dogs, called hounds, are trained to obey the sounds of the horn. I think Dylan Thomas imagines the calves, or young cows, coming to his call as the hounds do; farmers often curl their hands like a trumpet to call their animals. I think you were right about the lamb-white days.

Yes, 'bear away' is to carry away or capture; he imagines the farm flying through the night, carried by the owls, obviously not a realistic image. The idea of one's bed or bedroom or whole house flying through the night occurs elsewhere: 'My bed is a ship and I sail through the night'. Who knows what happens when we are asleep?

On your second subject of the use of other sources for interpretation: this raises problematical issues about the use and study of literature. There is an idea in literary analysis which suggests that it is not so important to understand what an author thought he or she meant at the time of writing; what matters is what the writing means to us today, to look for universal patterns, like scientific 'laws,' in writing, by stripping away the particular circumstances of authors. While that approach is certainly important, and can produce interesting insights, it may be mis-leading considered on its own because it might not stretch our minds imaginatively and sympathetically, but only present a reflection of ourselves and our own ideas. However, there is a wide body of professional commentary on literature, commentary which might be described as traditional, which you will often find in the very good introductions, written for non-specialists, to modern editions of classic novels and philosophers. I have usually found these introductions to be interesting, informative and illuminating. You will have to use your own judgement about what is useful and interesting for you. But as I said, you are not taking an examination in this; so long as you can enjoy what you read, but at the same realise there are other and perhaps deeper points of view, that is fine. Things can be enjoyed at different levels and it is a shame when people are put off enjoying literature because, like you at first, they think it is too difficult.

伍
5
STRANGE CITY
陌生城市

I chose to try a new strange city, where few people knew me, for a whole year when I quit my university in Kaoshiung because I needed to calm myself down and to find out what I wanted to do before returning to university, or having some other plans for my life. Everything of me was well hidden in a vagrant life. I made new friends there in Taichung City in Central Taiwan and sometimes stayed with them or spent time in pubs to pass my time. A good friend of mine started running a shop and told me that I could always have a place there to go to if I was tired of travelling around, but I didn't really feel happy to do that; sometimes however it was a good place for me to hide myself from the reality of life.

'This is a different world from what you have experienced before. All these people you meet here are business people or so-called artists who might not be quite the same as those people you've met in your life so far. I will try my best to protect you as your father did for you before.'

'But please don't tell anyone about my father or my life. I don't want to bear that stress when people look at me with so many questions in their minds.' This was the only worry of mine.

'You can do whatever you want till you find your way.'

I was not sure what he had done to protect me, but it seemed I was quite safe because no one dared bother me even though there were so many complicated life-styles among the people there. For example, a landlady of the shop in the opposite corner had a boyfriend, but her husband also had some girlfriends outside. The son of the landlady was not the son of her husband, but was the son of a shop owner down the end of the street. A shoe-shop upstairs was owned by a young lady who had just received her law degree from quite a famous university. People were curious about her story because her father was a rich and powerful man in this area, and her boyfriend was a rich businessman who was divorced, but had a little son and daughter. A young shop owner on the first floor was the boyfriend of a lady who ran a woman's clothes shop on the ground floor, but they didn't admit to their relationship although many people had seen their familiarity in the middle of the night when all the shops were closed. Hearsay scandals were spread around, but no one knew how much truth there might be in them.

One day I was in the basement of my friend's shop when by chance I found some pictures on the floor with some rubbish. There was one called 'Our love wedding,' which was a photograph of a naked couple. I recognized the woman as the owner of the exhibition centre next door, but I had never seen that young boy before. I thought she was un-married, although from time to time she had various many male friends in her house.

'That young guy was an artist and was going with

the woman who provided everything for his life. He committed suicide by lying down on the railway just a few months ago. No one knows the reason.' My friend told me what he knew about the story behind those pictures.

'Was it romantic? I don't understand about this situation. It's the first time I have seen a couple naked in their wedding pictures.' It seemed such a long way from my ideal. And my ideal seemed so far away that I felt confused. I also didn't understand the way they presented their love with that strange body language in those images. Perhaps I had no talent to understand art if this was art. I think now the couple thought of themselves as Dada-ists. Maybe it's true, as a design tutor told me, that Picasso once said something like, 'If you think sex is dirty, you can't be a modern artist.' I decided I was not a modern artist, but I would be a very good designer.

'Do you have a spade? I want to bury my dog that has just died. Oh, my poor dog, you don't know how good a boy he was.' An old woman from the opposite shop came in and cried so loudly.

'Sorry, I don't have anything for you to bury your poor dog.' Maybe my voice was not kind enough to comfort her: for I had no clue why she cried so sadly and called that dog as her son when she never allowed those dogs to enter her house and they only could stay in a cold empty shed just on the corner of the street.

'Open the door! Open the door of your shop.' A big man with no shoes on his feet was knocking on the door so fiercely as I was having breakfast with my friend.

'Is he your friend?' I said,' I don't understand why he doesn't wear his shoes and seems likely to break your door?'

My friend didn't say anything and just opened the door for the man who, instead of having tea with us, took out his medicine from his bag and started cooking the medicine on a stove that we used to heat water to make tea.

'Do you know what I'm cooking now? It's the medicine to control my temper because I'm a lunatic. They will take me to the madhouse again if I don't have this medicine. Are you scared? Ha-ha! I'm not joking at all. I'm a mad man.' The man then whistled and sang like a big child while drinking his medicine. I did wonder if he was really mad. Or perhaps the whole world was mad apart from him.

'Ah-ha, I found you, you're here, my love. I've just finished some paintings in my garden, and want to invite all of you to have a look.' The girlfriend of the madman found him in my friend's shop and happily described her new works. She was an art teacher at a primary school and always acted as though she were an innocent child in her world of art. Was it the reason she loved that guy so much, because they had a common world which other people couldn't reach in to?

'Sure, we're happy to see your new works. Let's go!' I answered immediately when she invited us to her garden because I think I was quite keen to leave that room by then, although I might just be changing from one daffy space to another crazy place.

But, what is a normal world? Is there anywhere we could call normal? When I heard a group of people talking up sex in a public square; saw some artists who wore torn clothes; one who kept a cigar in her mouth all day and pulled around a big dog and appeared in art exhibitions with great displays of such mysteries as animal sexual behaviours; and when everyday I saw a man playing with an ancient sword like a knight-errant on the street: I didn't know whether it was normal or not. But it would be better for me to make no comment on people's lives which were simply beyond my understanding of the world, and I didn't want to make any judgement about people because, in just the same way, I didn't want them to judge me.

♩

By the beginning of another academic year I had decided to return to the academic world which might be simpler than the outside world, even though my university was located in an urban waste-land. It was a huge decision to sign the form to return to my university when I did not have good memories of being there after my bad start a year ago.

'Take him with you when you go back to your university. I hope he will be a good friend of yours during the following years at university.' A friend of mine brought me a little turtle because she knew I love turtles very much.

'He is so tiny, like a pound coin. Maybe I should find a small, pretty fish tank for him to live in.' I was so touched, but I felt a bit worried about how to raise a tiny turtle, especially as I was even not sure how to keep myself breathing till I could finish my study in that cultural desert.

However, it was not only the physical environment of that city which bothered me so much but, surprisingly, the atmosphere of that academic place was the biggest thing which depressed me. When I returned to my university, I came to realize that certain patterns of humanity do not change, with or without education, within all sorts of cultural environments. I saw the same people as I had seen in the strange city, on the strange street. The only difference was that I recovered my true self more quickly in the civilized world.

'I hate students like you who come in from the National United Exam for Universities; just because they have good academic results they never show respect to their tutors.' I was told off by a tutor of my university because many times I didn't go to lectures.

'Do you ever think the contents of your lectures might be too easy for good students at university? I am indeed not satisfied that the university takes in students from different levels by all sorts of ways other than the United Exam. I will attend your lectures when you improve the level of lectures to be proper for undergraduates rather than for school children.' I was so upset about our poor education system and about my tuition that did not seem to be worth much.

'I have the right to fail you even if you pass your exam, because I'm the tutor and you're the student.'

What could I say when tutors threatened me like that? I

understood that every one of my tutors could easily fail me in such a top-down education system; hence I didn't have any option, except to obey them, if I was to get my first degree.

I didn't want to waste my time on sitting in the classroom only to learn such little knowledge; but I tried to deal with my tutors carefully if only to get my special freedom to arrange my life without attending lectures. I actively offered tutors information about updated computer equipment and provided them with the best service and price when they purchased products from me. I applied my knowledge of accounting which I learnt from my first job at age nineteen to help my tutors sort out cash requirements between funding bodies and the university authority. At the same time, I also tried to get opportunities to work with tutors on design projects for the government.

'You can join our group and attend some short courses and conferences sponsored by the government; and you also can practise your design for competitions on your own. There should be no problem about your student status because we can register the whole work in the name of the qualified design teams which are run by my friends.' A tutor of mine suggested I could try to practice design in real projects by entering competitions. 'It will be no problem if you don't win anything because you're learning, aren't you? However, if you win a project, you will be the richest and most famous student in the whole country, so it's worth trying.'

It sounded very attractive and I was interested to give it a try. But I didn't realize the actual complexity behind those big projects when I was thinking about the great satisfaction of presenting my designs in the real world.

At that time I was very enthusiastic about going into communities to carry out surveys of their physical and spiritual characters, and talking to people about their needs and their lives. It was no matter for me whether the days were so baking hot or uncomfortably wet. However, residents were sometimes not so friendly.

'Are you from the government? Why do you take so many pictures and draw a map here? Do you want to knock down our society? We will become homeless if you do so.' I was not surprised to hear this because I thought it was human nature for them to defend themselves from a stranger who presumptuously appeared in their society.

'I'm sorry to disturb you. I'm not from the government and I don't want to knock down your community at all. It's part of my study to make a survey of your place where I may find something interesting for me to use in a design for my project.' I hoped my friendly attitude could make them feel better.

'What do you want to find out from our place?' One of the residents was more curious, or perhaps more brave, than his companions.

'I realize your society is full of history and tradition, so I think I may want to discover more of your history so I can plan a cultural conservation project for your place. Do you think it could work?' I grasped the opportunity to find out more from local residents.

'Yes, let me show you an abandoned rail station which was built by the Japanese Government in the core of our community. No one knows we have this heritage which is still quite complete without too much damage.'

'Yes, you must see it and make something useful for this fabulous old building.'

'We also have some romantic ruins which show skilled traditional building techniques, although only a piece of wall is left now.'

People turned out to be very enthusiastic and helpful, and vied with each other to talk to me once they felt I was not a dangerous enemy in their society. In this way I gained much valuable information from them, which inspired me to make special design proposals based on their local interests and on the objectives the government had set out for preservation of culture.

'The local authority likes this project very much, and they have decided to ask for some funding from the central government to support this design.' My design tutor told me this good news after his meeting with the local authority. But I had no chance to say anything before another tutor started talking. 'So it means three of us can share ten per cent to fifteen per cent of designers' fees from this project. That's quite a lot.'

I was shocked because I knew he was talking about those three community planners whose names were presented in this design project; there was of course nothing about my work as a student. However, I was shocked not just by the way he talked about money, but by his attitude that didn't seem to recognise that it was I who had created the design for that community in the first place.

'Can you finish the whole proposal and send it to the government by the end of this week?' If they hadn't suddenly turned to me and asked me this question, I would have thought they had already forgotten I was there and listening to their conversation.

Why didn't they ask me to explain the contents of my project, or teach me how to make a proper proposal to the government? They only demanded that I should have the formal design ready in three days. Did they ever consider that I wouldn't have a second to sleep if I had to finish the whole scheme alone in such a short time?

Next day I didn't show up at university since I was so frustrated by their attitude to me. However, a colleague passed on a word of remonstration to me. 'You should learn to benefit senior colleagues and your directors without caring too much about your own contribution because you are a junior and still a student. It's mutual: because if you understand the rules they will stand you in good stead and your tutors won't chuck you out of their place.'

I must learn to be nobody happily, even though my sleep and my health were to be stripped away in my pursuit of the most decent design for those people who needed me as an advocate for their communities and their behaviour. I still enjoyed moving around every corner and lane to gather information from each part of that society as I worked with them, and I had fun learning many interesting stories from the residents, such as the stories behind street names and the characteristics of places, which had never been recorded in written form before. However, it was a shame that in the end I couldn't do much to help those people to carry out their ideas for their community, only for the reason that, as the developers and their money took over, I was not powerful enough to make the actual construction work follow strictly the designs shown in our proposals, even though they had already been accepted by the government.

Since then it has been seen everywhere, in newspapers and on the websites, how everyone talks about their discovery of this historic site and of how hard they worked to get half a million pounds funding to preserve the little wooden station and to produce a development plan and tourism project for that area. Nevertheless, my name did not appear and was never even mentioned by any of those influential authorities who gained so much from the funding and from the media attention. I felt so wordless and helpless about my successful proposal. It has tortured me continually and I am trying so hard to forget by not touching anything related to what has been going on there all these years. I wish very much that I had not been the person who made the proposal in the first place so that I could feel no more than simple envy of other people who won the project for the whole design of that area. But, apart from my personal situation, I'm so pleased that the valuable historic building is preserved and has gained enough attention to show that many people in Taiwan also care about our cultural heritage and love to look after our old buildings carefully. It has never been an easy journey for a nearly forgotten historic building, almost drowned in a fast developing city, to be discovered and preserved. I still remember so vividly the darkness and coldness when

I first came down to the station to survey it; there was not even any street light in the night. To know it was being taken care of was the only tiny piece of happiness I could have when I accidentally saw my draft of the original design in my notebook and I felt I was so brave that I could then look at it without tears streaming down my face.

'What do you want? What do you really want?' A tutor seriously asked me this question when I was awarded a design prize and helped their design group to win another half million pounds design project. Both projects were crucial links in the whole community tourism development plan. 'You're so ambitious; do you want to be on an equal footing with me.' The tutor continued his leery thought. How could I tell him that he absolutely misunderstood me? I think no one, including myself, would truly believe that anyone would be willing to work so hard for nothing to realize my original ideas for preserving our own culture and roots by achieving three feasible projects within a year. It might be said that I did everything for some purpose of my own. However, I really never thought about taking over from anyone in our group, but only simply wanted to change the whole world one day.

♫

The busiest time in my life was the time when I was supposed to be a full time student at university; or I could say it was the craziest period in my life. I tried to work out carefully what I could do and how I could make it fit overall; it might seem like quite a puzzle, but I think now that it was somehow the most well-organised life style I have ever had.

'Why are you here?' I was so puzzled by this question when a customer asked me.

'I work here. Sorry, I don't quite understand your question.'

'Well, I bought a laptop from you some days ago in a computer shop, and just now I saw you working in a laboratory on the fifth floor. I feel so confused when I see you again here, serving in the media centre.'

'Oh, I see …. It sounds like I am crazy for making money. Unfortunately, I'm still not rich and I even cannot afford a laptop like the one I sold you a few days ago. Don't ask me why and how; I'm also very confused why I have so many part time jobs. It's a long story again, so don't worry about that now.'

There were about six roles that were mine, all at the same time. I was a student in a classroom, was a salesperson in a computer shop, was an accounting assistant as well as a member of a design group, a research assistant in an environmental lab in our university, and I was a computer operator in a media centre every evening.

Considering these jobs in themselves, each of them was fine and simple, and it should have been no problem if I managed my time well. However, things were not as easy as I had imagined. My tutors became my customers when they required some IT equipment, but I was also a customer when I used my status as an assistant at the lab to deal with the money and our purchases in the computer shop, although I was the salesperson who provided the quotation to the boss of the lab. When I went to the local authority to ask for some information for a design project, those officers were uncertain whether I was an assistant from the lab or from the design group. I often needed to print out some documents, booklets or posters in the media centre; the boss allowed me to use everything anytime because I was a member of staff there, but often he didn't give me any help when I worked alone at night, because I was not really a customer for him when I made those prints for my design group or for my tutors. But, unfairly, I was still supposed to help customers when they came during the time I was in the media centre due to my status as a computer operator.

Apart from the puzzle of my various roles, it was sometimes a problem when jobs clashed; when a computer exhibition was held for a whole week at the end of my year-four study. This was not only the time for balancing accounts or finishing off some design projects in my other jobs, but it was also a busy time in the media centre because all design students needed to print out their work by the end of the academic year. Most importantly, I was also a student and had my final examinations and a final project to finish before I could graduate. My solution was to manage my time in the best possible way. First I went to the lab and the finance office in the university at 9 AM, then went to the Exhibition Centre as soon as I could till 4.30 PM, rushed to the media centre by 5 PM, and went back to the lab at 10 PM to see if there was anything that needed to be done.

I could not switch off my mobile phone even when I was sitting in my final exams because many customers would trace their orders or make further enquiries during that month after the computer exhibition started. When I had just finished my final exams, my boss at the lab arranged a series of experiments in another city for five days. I had to ask my colleagues in the computer shop to look after my customers till I came back; I also asked my colleagues in the university to help me with some of my work, such as model-making, because I had a presentation right away after the experiments. Not surprisingly, I was extremely busy checking everything was going well, but none of my customers had any complaint about me when I arrived back.

Did I have any time to sleep? I think I didn't. I remember I saw a whole set of pretty bedding stuff one evening while I was walking around after dinner. There was a great desire in my mind to have that bedding set with its matching design for a bed covering, pillow cases and a duvet cover.

'You don't need them at all because you don't ever sleep. It's just a waste of money to buy them in your case.' A friend of mine made fun of me when I didn't want to leave that shop.

It was probably a sort of psychological compensation for a person who seriously lacked sleep. I needed the whole bedding set to 'decorate' my bed because it would have been good for me to have something to look at and to miss when I passed my bed every day. On my birthday that year, when I was twenty-three, I made a wish that I could have some time to lie down on my pretty bed with a beautiful dream and, I hoped, not have to wake up forever.

♩

'Hello,' I said, 'How do you do? I assume you're quite relaxed now. What makes you feel so happy?'

'How can you know I'm happy? You even don't know who I am?'

'From your internet alias name here: a cup of tea and a cigarette.'

'You're a senior internet surfer, aren't you?'

'I'm not, although I work with computers for twenty hours a day; it's my first time to come to this site.'

'Why don't you go and sleep? Are you waiting for something or someone?'

'My mind is full of chagrin and I need to get it out of my brain. However, I realized this place might not be quite right for me when people scolded me because I refused to talk about some silly things.'

'Do you know where you are?'

'I know I'm in an on-line chatting room.'

'Do you know what the function of a chatting room is?'

'For people to say anything they can't say in their world.'

'Partly right, but I should tell you that's only your own opinion. It doesn't matter. What bothers you too much to sleep?'

'It's not easy to say. Anyway, do you know what will happen if a shellfish is thrust up by waves onto a beach?'

'To be eaten by a bird?'

'If it's lucky it will be killed by a bird very soon before any other pain comes to harass it. If not, the shellfish may be surprised and excited to have freed itself from the uncertain and dark sea to lie down on the beach and enjoy the peaceful sunshine. However, the shellfish will shortly realize that it is being baked to become someone's seafood by being exposed to the sun on the sand beach for too long. The most terrible thing is that the shellfish will suddenly miss the sea so much when it understands how lucky it was to swim with the tide rather than lie on the beach without moving till it dries out and dies under the same sun which gives life to every thing else.'

'Are you the fish or the sea?'

'Alternately both, but sometimes I'm the sand beach or the sun or the person who eats seafood happily.'

'How about now?'

'I'm the shellfish on the baking-hot beach and miss the sea very much. I was so happy to leave my father and to come to university and to get part time jobs. But when all my bosses only squeeze my strength without reasonably paying for my work, I'm dying on the dry beach without water and start missing my father so much.'

'Wait for another big wave to take you to the sea and be careful not to come to the beach again.'

'It's too late now; I will die before the next wave comes to rescue my hopeless life because I need to get my degree and can go nowhere. The sea would never know how much I miss it or need it. Anyway, thank you very much for listening to my pointless chat. I need to finish my drawings and model making by the afternoon because I'm working in the computer shop in the evening. Lots of squeezing jobs in this terrible city are all waiting for me.'

'It's my pleasure to enjoy the way you complain for life, which is quite unusual to me. I can give you my email address to welcome your complaint anytime if you want.'

'Ha-ha, you're crazy. How can you make a friend online like this?'

'I'm happy to be your friend if you don't mind.'

'I don't mind because it's fun to talk to a computer and receive responses from the screen. It's so real and not real at all.'

'So, we should have a word then.'

'What do you mean?'

'We should always enjoy talking to our computers and never break this happiness. Do you agree with me?'

'Yes, I agree.'

I cherished very much the chance to express my thoughts freely in this science-fiction way with no gender, no image and no sound for about two years, and I think both of us were afraid to destroy our shadow-land by meeting in reality. It became my habit to send emails to this address talking about my life everyday when I arrived home although I didn't always get replies on time. I also received many life stories and thoughts from the other side and even though sometimes I didn't really intend to reply to those stories, I had fun reading them.

However, I started hating my life with computers all the time in the year I was preparing for my final design project. I made an appointment with this unseen friend online at 1 AM on a Saturday, and tried to break our word.

'Why do you want to talk in the midnight? What makes you so unhappy?'

'I want to go out.'

'Why do you ask me to come online if you want to go out? You should find your friends then.'

'I don't want to see any of my friends, but I want to go out.'

'What do you mean?'

'I think you know what I mean. I want to walk around in the city and don't want to face to my screen anymore. Can you understand it?'

'You're making a dangerous decision. You shouldn't ask a stranger to go out with you in the midnight.'

'You're not a stranger for me at all.'

'That's because I'm not real, I'm not in your world, and you should always remember this rule. People hurt each other when they know each other. I don't want to hurt you and don't want to let anyone, including you, break my imaginary world.'

'Neither you nor I will hurt each other because I just want to go out.'

'If you insist to go out now, try to find a friend you believe in to go with you and then come home to sleep. You'll be fine tomorrow.'

'I only believe you who are a real friend for me.'

'…….'

'Why don't you talk to me anymore? You're so cruel to me today.'

'What sort of company do you want?'

'I only need a safe and peaceful night walking around the city. Come to pick me up by my flat, please.'

'You're challenging me. I'm leaving from home right away and will be in your place in two hours. I still want to remind you that you shouldn't tell a stranger online where you live because it's not good for you.'

I was a bit worried, but I thought it was not the biggest issue for me to worry about, this meeting with the unseen friend. How could anything go even worse than never being understood in the world?

Without many words on our first meeting, we just went to the open-air coffee shop in the park, located in the corner of the busiest place of the city designed with many colourful lights around.

'The name of this place is the City Light Gallery. It was designed by a tutor of mine at university. His designer's fee has risen three times more than usual since he won the competition for the design for this park which was on the darkest side of the city where many crimes took place. He introduced plenty of light to make his design full of magical experience at night and to brighten the darkest corner.' I naturally talked about the story of the site because all of my brain was full only of those sorts of things such as design projects and competitions.

'How about the music they're playing now? Do you like it?'

'No, I don't. The music is not well presented by a poorly skilled pianist who is making the wrong tones for the music. My piano teacher told me to play music with our hearts following the emotion of the music, so that we can present the spirit of the music. I should confess that I'm not a good pianist myself although I'm criticizing another musician.' When he started laughing at me I realized that I might be appearing to be too indignant about everything

'You're so alike the one who emails me everyday. But do you think this music is quiet enough for you to relax for a bit even though the pianist might not be playing it professionally?'

I accepted his suggestion because I knew it might be the only time I could feel calm enough to listen to the wind, to look at the sky and to breathe some fresh air without any worry about my jobs or my design for just a few hours. We then had a rambling conversation about all sorts of things around us, from a street tree to a vagrant dog, without thinking about anything stressful in our lives, till dawn light spilled from the sky.

'Can you go to a place with me if you're not tired?' I knew I had deprived him of sleep for the whole night, but I really wanted to visit a place at that moment.

'Never mind, since I decided to come the world is all yours today.'

'I will try to remember the way to that place where I haven't been for three years.'

'Should I ask the reason?'

'I went there very often before I quit university. But I just lost my memory and couldn't find the way to go there anymore after I returned to university. Maybe I'm too afraid to see that place which might remind me of the first six months of nightmares in this cultural desert.'

'Then, why do you want to find the way now? I can't help you at all if you start crying out there; I will leave you alone because I don't want to see people looking at me as though I bully you on the street.' This funny joke he made helped to ease my apprehension of getting closer to the place.

I was not afraid of anything when the familiar scene came to my eyes. When we were serenely sitting by a turtle pond under the sun, every detail of my memories about those first six months in that city went through my brain as though a roll of photographic plates was stretched out from the first to the last image

'You don't know how much I appreciate your company which helps me to overcome a nightmare hidden in a corner of my mind for about four years.' I broke the silence, but with a truly peaceful mood.

'I'm glad to hear that. I just wonder why you came here very often before. Are you a religious person?' he asked, while looking around at the Buddhist and Taoist temples.

'I know what you mean. You can think that I need a lot of blessing from many different Gods because I'm so weak. But the most important reason for me to come here so often was the turtle pond. I know my Turtle will be jealous of those turtles here if he hears that I say so, but I really love turtles that are so intelligent and wise.'

'How do you know they are wise? Do they talk to you?' he asked, laughing.

'Yes, of course. Have I told you about my Turtle in my emails? He is so rompish and always thinks he is wiser than me, so sometimes I have to pretend to listen to him if he insists to go his own way.'

'What will happen if you don't listen to him?' My friend's voice changed to a funny incredulous tone.

'He always knows how to show me his anger if I ignore him, such as to make lots of noise and to make his mess everywhere in my bedroom. Otherwise, he is very clean and quiet. I wish to visit one more place today, don't say no, please.' I wanted to have a glass of cold drink in the tea shop where I also had gone very often before I left my university in the first year.

'It seems I have no choice.' He answered gently, with a smile.

I chose the seat next to the window and faced to the entrance because I wanted to be able to see another ice cream shop next to the tea shop. I saw an image of myself wearing a pair of red bean shoes, a matching red t-shirt and black jeans, standing and talking in the ice cream shop. I looked so young, innocent and so unaware of any dangers.

'It was just about four years ago. How could I experience so much and become so grey in only four years time?' I bemoaned my lost youth quietly, with tears in my eyes, and continued talking. 'I hated this city so much and never quenched the anger in myself till now I know everything is passed over. I will start loving this city with my true heart and will use all my knowledge to make a good design for residents here in my coming final design project. Will you come to see our final design exhibition at the end of this academic year?'

'No, I won't.' This was the first time he rejected me.

'Why not? I will hope to see you in my presentation if I

make a good design because you're the person who helps me to overpass my nightmare of this city.' I was a bit hurt when I heard his answer.

'I don't want to spoil your world or make you lose face in your presentation. I'm a rogue who is not qualified to stand with you in your professional world. People will look down on you when they see you have such a cultureless friend in your life.' I saw he was quite serious, but I didn't understand his reason.

'Are you angry because I broke our word and forced you to come with me last night?' This was the only reason I could think of.

'No, I'm so happy to see you are as pretty as you presented in your emails. When I read about your life only from your emails, I thought you may be over-proud of yourself since all your stories seemed *naturally* to say that you're a princess. So, don't worry about this, I don't regret seeing you, although I was a bit annoyed when you intended to break your promise.'

'How can I force you again to come to my final presentation?'

'I will only come when you really need me, but not in your professional world.'

He indeed is a real friend of mine and always comes to help me every time I need a hand. But he didn't appear at my final presentation and he firmly insists never to show in my professional world. I then imagined that I might receive a greeting card from him in my design display area some time during the exhibition week. However, I had been waiting and disappointed day after day till the end of the exhibition when finally I withdrew everything from the exhibition centre, including my hope of his visit.

Probably he is wise to demarcate a distinct line, not to intrude into each other's worlds with any coloured opinions and decorated manners. Therefore, we both respect each other's way of living and help the other to minimize suffering in a neutral, peaceful and magical way.

陸

6

MY DREAMS

夢想

Dear Su Yen

While I was reading your story of the unseen friend I remembered that you once said you had read a Chinese translation of an English poem by Yeats, *When You are Old*, and you would like to know more about it. Here is the original version. Again, we can call it a lyric poem because the poet is expressing his deep personal feelings.

Yeats knew he could not offer wealth or social position or conventional love to the woman whom he loved, Maude Gomme, and all he could give were what he called his 'words'; that is, his poems. But these were not enough. Here he imagines that when she is an old lady dozing by the fireside she might look at his book and feel sorry that she sent his love away lonely, 'to pace [that is, to walk] upon the mountains,' and, 'hide its face,' among the starry night.

He is really saying, 'Well, you'll be sorry when I'm gone!'; but he says it much more beautifully.

He says that other men loved her because of her outward beauty, but he loved her for herself, for 'her pilgrim soul'. Soul can be a difficult concept for Chinese because it seems to be confused with the idea of ghosts. Christians believe the soul is the intangible part of us which, when our physical body dies, goes to be with God, or perhaps with the Devil, depending on how we have lived our lives. Chinese may interpret 'soul' as a dead person's spirit which they see as a scary thing, but for us it is not scary these days. We used to think there were supernatural things such as evil spirits or ghosts in the world, but most modern people don't believe in them anymore. For people who do not believe in God the idea of a soul represents all the intangible qualities of a living person and it suggests deep, serious or sympathetic qualities.

A 'pilgrim' soul means that she will always be seeking for wisdom and enlightenment, as does a Buddhist pilgrim, but not in the same way. Yeats likes this quality. Many people expect to find answers to life in art, poetry or music. However, another writer, Laurens van der Post, in his book, *Yet Being Someone Other*, seems to suggest that art does not provide answers; it only shows that we all have the same questions. It is this awareness of the sharing of the search for truth, or sympathy, which he says is the meaning of art. His book is about a Westerner in the 1930s discovering oriental culture, in this case Japanese.

When Maude Gomme became older and her beauty faded Yeats married someone else, when he was fifty-two years old, and seems to have been happy.

When You are Old, by William Butler Yeats (1865–1939)

> *When you are old and gray and full of sleep,*
> *And nodding by the fire, take down this book,*
> *And slowly read, and dream of the soft look*
> *Your eyes had once, and of their shadows deep;*

How many loved your moments of glad grace,
And loved your beauty with love false or true,
But one man loved the pilgrim soul in you,
And loved the sorrows of your changing face;

And bending down beside the glowing bars,
Murmur, a little sadly, how Love fled
And paced upon the mountains overhead
And hid his face among a crowd of stars.

Dear Roy

With this poem, *When You are Old*, I can feel that 'pilgrim soul' because we also have similar thoughts in our culture, although I usually had my doubts when guys said that they cared about pilgrim soul rather than a woman's appearance. In my opinion, the pilgrim soul is a beautiful idea in a poem; I appreciate this romantic love expressed within the magic words of Yeats. There is a belief in our culture that the most beautiful thing in our life is the one that we will never obtain. I can see now that this poem leaks deep sorrow like purple colour which shows its pity and regret.

However, it was a surprise for me when I saw your introduction for this poem, because when I read the translated Chinese version it seemed quite different. The structure and the meanings of each word of the poem were just as logical and beautiful as in the English version, but the whole meaning of the poem was completely different from that described in your introduction. It seemed the poem described the beautiful love that eternally exists between the couple from when they were young to when they were old.

The last part of the poem, for example, was presented as a romantic feeling as the love seems to flee for the time being, but in fact their love never flees but transfers to something different, so that it may be found rambling in the mountains with his face hidden but shining among stars.

Maybe both ideas are quite right and can be combined to one when people intend to find answers to life in arts, poetry and music, which don't provide answers, but may present sympathy. A tutor of my design course told us there is no accurate answer among the arts; we think affective arts bring thoughts and meanings for people to enrich their lives; or we may say arts are influential just because they make people feel, although the thoughts and meanings may include both positive and negative sides. However, we're all human beings and have various feelings which are too complicated to say; thus it is often difficult to judge how modern tendencies in the arts will lead to new fashions of life styles in many aspects over time.

Dear Su Yen

Your alternative interpretation in the Chinese version of *When You are Old* is very interesting. Some theorists of literature argue that we should react to poems and literature just as they affect us and not interpret a 'correct' meaning based on what we know about the author's life. There seems little doubt the poet was writing about his rejected love, but I can see now the poem on its own could be understood also as you suggest.

♪

'What do you wish for?'
'Please, help me to get an honours degree from my university, and then burn my degree scroll with my body for my funeral. Although I can't be awarded my degree when I'm alive, I still wish to receive it in another world.'
'You will have your degree with you when you are asleep, my dear. You deserve more: if only they knew how you always over-worked and forgot to eat and sleep for years. It's such a sorrow for us to say goodbye here instead of seeing your future.'

I wiped tears from off my face, roughly, still holding a knife in my hand, slicing cardboard in the early morning to create my model designs and imagining I had suddenly taken down an oxygen mask in a hospital and was breathing into it with difficulty. Perhaps this was only the grand finale to show that I had exerted myself to die for my dream, although there might still be no one who would come to see me for the last time and listen to my last wish, and people would only sneer at my foolish dream to become someone important. As a Chinese saying goes, '*Our death could be light as a feather or could be heavy as the mountain Tai*'. We are taught that people will be honoured for their death when they die in the right places, as soldiers are glorified when they are killed on a battlefield. Hence I deduced that students would be honoured if they died in a classroom or at a desk.

However, things often go another way round and out of our control. As I was vituperated on the podium for my final design project presentations for the year, my mind went through a death before my body was worn out.

'Do you think it's creative? I don't think so. You just use some ideas from the golden section and geometric construction for your design concepts. It's nothing but silly.' An examiner from the city council started telling me off for the site allocation of my design proposal; and continued to abuse my idea of choosing local building materials.

'Do you think it's interesting to design an international hotel using such a poor material as sheet iron? You just try to make a point which is meaningless and awful.'

'A project for an international hotel in one year? Do you think you can make it? How can you think you can make it, even I myself can't do it? It will be enough for you if you can finish a design for the lobby.' A tutor who held a Master's degree from a European university was telling me that if I thought I could do that I must believe I was better than he was.

Rather than scold me, another tutor gave me modest advice. 'I think it's better for you to choose a new site or change your topic now. You're doing something absolutely useless and illogical. Perhaps design is not the right subject for you; please go and find something else to suit you when you finish this design project.'

It was just the beginning of my life in hell following the first presentation of our final design project proposals.

I didn't understand why my supervisor didn't back me up when he saw those examiners were so harsh on me and didn't allow me any time at all to explain my ideas. However, when I had almost given up struggling with those dragons I was not sure whether I would appreciate my supervisor's encouragement to keep me carrying on with this project with my original ideas, because he had never said a word when I was pelted with abuse for all of my presentations for the whole year.

The greatest motivation to sustain me was that, when we presented my ideas to the meeting of the community planners in the government, some community group leaders showed great interest and wished to bring my design project into reality. At that time, however, I hadn't realized the huge danger that existed for me behind this opportunity.

It was not easy when we wanted to continue our culture through the introduction of new and creative design principles. The greatest challenge was to make a new structure, but still with some old buildings on site. I carefully dealt with all the details of my project and took it very seriously because I didn't want either to destroy the original character or to compromise my design principles. I studied architectural law, building legislation and planning policies for the site and for the building structure. I measured mechanical equilibrium conditions and studied different characters of materials, both for safety and for energy efficiency issues. I also communicated with local residents and analysed their thoughts for the site in order to improve whatever they wanted for their lives and so that they would be able to stay in their society.

During the time I was gathering this information for all the aspects I could think of, I spent hours and hours to develop my design concepts and the ideal embodiment of beauty for the building and for the site; my brain couldn't stop thinking and thinking, even while I held many irregularly scheduled meetings with my customers in the computer shop and the media centre. Playing music from day to night was useful for me to ensure my brain worked well, and reading books was an interesting way for me to learn about the experiences of other designers. Eventually, after all the effort, I came to the end of my work on the day I gave my final presentation to all the assembled examiners.

Before I was even ready to talk a tutor just turned away, right at the beginning, and refused to listen to my presentation. He was the person who had shouted that I couldn't make it because even he couldn't do a design for a hotel in such a short time. But many unfamiliar faces came to stand around the stage to listen to my talk, all with their cameras.

'How do you think about your design? I think you just raped the site by making those terrible boxes.'

An external examiner showed his attitude, using the stressful word 'rape'. But I was used to listening to their abusive language without any discussion about my design. A long war of words then started from this point and lasted for about an hour. The whole progress was like an angry press meeting, full of the sounds of people's questions, with constant shooting of cameras, and all the flashes dazzling my eyes. I am not sure how I eventually survived the hail of abusive bullets for an hour, till a soft sound came to my ears.

'I think Walter Disney should invite you to design for them because your style of design is so like Disney's,' a lady standing behind the examiners said.

I returned her a forced smile instead of any reply because I didn't know whether she was satirizing me or truly liked my work. However, I appreciated her comments so much because the hurricane seemed to calm down at her soft words.

Unexpectedly, a bomb-shell suddenly assaulted me and blasted the quiet air and crushed everything, including my heart. 'I know of course this design can be achieved right away from tomorrow. But what has been your own achievement in the whole process? I think you just relied on public relationships very much to get your ideas accepted in the government.' The tutor who was talking was one of the community planners and he knew the design project might well be approved by the local authority, with feasible construction plans.

I had nothing to comment on this point, and then firmly decided to withdraw myself from this complicated world. Perhaps I should have admitted that I was not good enough to do design anymore when no one cared about whether my design was helpful for people, but was only overjoyed to empoison my work by strange, lousy jealousies. I never wanted to meet anyone after that day and only stayed at home with my flatmate without doing anything for a whole year.

From that moment, I didn't care anymore about the prize in our university because I expected to win the prize in the National Design Competition in that year and to see my design become reality, which was to be a continuous plan for the wooden station to be the centre of a whole community-tourism route development. However, things turned out like the saying that disasters never come alone; at least in my life they never come alone. When my design was finally selected to be entered in the National Design Competition of Taiwan, the disastrous epidemic called SARS broke out in China so the committee decided to cancel the competition for that year, which they had never done before and have not done since. I really couldn't believe it could happen so coincidently, just at the time I was trying my best, hoping only for the day when I would see my design in that National Design Exhibition. What could I say about it? I had never dared to think I could be selected to join that National Design Competition, because I knew it was so difficult to qualify for their standard. Now I had made it, but the opportunity was uniquely snatched away by fate.

However, in the final year of my student life at university I painstakingly worked so hard for a brilliant finale before I finished my student life in Taiwan. But the way in which I won the university prize not only brought an end to my student life, but also sent my future and my hope into a bottomless and endlessly quiet sea. After I obtained my degree, nobody even mentioned further development of my design, although the idea had been accepted by the government a long time ago. The chance to fulfil this ambitious dream of turning my designs into reality seemed to be taken away from my hand straightaway, probably because so many unbelievably profitable projects were involved where other people could make money.

Everything went into a strange silence and those close colleagues became cold and harsh, but they would not allow me to resign peacefully and at the same time they tried hard to stop me from going abroad to study for a higher degree.

Dear Su Yen

Perhaps you may find sympathy in this poem by William Blake because his poetry often shows his concern for the cruel fate of truth and innocence in the world of experience, for which he found no answer either. Blake lived in the second half of the eighteenth century and on into the nineteenth. He was a skilled engraver and painter, with a very distinctive style, and a poet. He was a radical in politics, and wrote poems expressing sympathy with people or animals that were badly treated. He was also a mystic: what he wrote does not always make logical sense; he claimed to have seen angels in the trees one morning. His best-known poem, and an English favourite, is *The Tiger*.

This appears to be a poem expressing the beauty and power, and the menace, of the tiger. But it contains ideas which even English people do not understand. 'Burning bright' could be a metaphor for the golden flame colour of the tiger's coat, but what about verse four where the tiger seems to be made of iron? Perhaps Blake was referring to the developments and machines of the industrial revolution, which were also both beautiful and menacing, and which he hated.

I have told you about poets who just repeat the first verse at the ends of their poems. Sometimes this seems to be because the first few lines they thought of are the best and their inspiration falls off after that. In the best sonnets and poems the final lines are original, strong and conclusive. Blake appears to repeat his first verse at the end, but he has a subtle variation: do you see it? God 'could' make the tiger, but after the poem has considered how terrible the tiger is, Blake concludes by asking who would 'dare' make the tiger?

There is also perhaps a more general and mystical debate here about good and evil, 'Did he who made the lamb make thee?' The lamb is a symbol of innocence and peace in Western religion; did the same God make the fierce tiger and the gentle lamb? How could the God whom we believe made all good things also make evil? This has always been a major problem for Christian belief since Christians believe in only one God who made everything.

The Tiger, by William Blake (1757–1827)

> *TIGER! Tiger! burning bright*
> *In the forests of the night,*
> *What immortal hand or eye*
> *Could frame thy fearful symmetry?*

In what distant deeps or skies
Burnt the fire of thine eyes?
On what wings dare he aspire?
What the hand dare seize the fire?

And what shoulder and what art
Could twist the sinews of thy heart?
And when thy heart began to beat,
What dread hand and what dread feet?

What the hammer? What the chain?
In what furnace was thy brain?
What the anvil? What dread grasp
Dare its deadly terrors clasp?

When the stars threw down their spears,
And water'd heaven with their tears,
Did He smile His work to see?
Did He who made the lamb make thee?

Tiger! Tiger! burning bright
In the forests of the night,
What immortal hand or eye
Dare frame thy fearful symmetry?

Dear Roy

Now, about *The Tiger*, I like that, 'burning bright',
very much. This shows the feature of the tiger's coat in
a very lively way, and I think burning bright also shows
the tiger blazing like torches from his eyes. How beautiful

that perhaps Blake may have referred to the industrial revolution using the image of the tiger! This reminds me to appreciate everything by using my imagination. When I studied the history of economic development last semester, I felt so bored and not interested in the topic of the industrial revolution. But from Blake's *The Tiger*, I have more thoughts about positive and negative effects of development. Although such a boring process in reality, and while this may not be my interest at all, I still can use an artistic view to think about it in depth, and then it will be helpful to have more knowledge for combining the reality with an ideal world.

God created the lamb, He also created the tiger. Without the tiger, the lamb doesn't know the real meaning of life; then this may lead to a life of only having to eat grass, which will become too boring.

Dear Su Yen

Your comments are very perceptive and interesting. It seems wonderful that you can find sympathy and encouragement in English poems. You have a number of good ideas: I liked your original thoughts about the lamb and the tiger. In general though I was fascinated by the way you have used art, in this case poetry, to help you come to terms with the difficulties of life: in English idiom we say 'to become philosophical about life'. This is an expression of the classical Stoic philosophy which taught that we should not allow our peace of mind to be disturbed by events in our lives over which we have no control.

I'm not sure that Blake was in fact referring to the

industrial revolution, although it seems reasonable; no one really knows what he was talking about, perhaps he did not always know himself. He was not well educated in the literary sense and his verse is in some ways a bit primitive. He never wrote anything as polished as a sonnet.

I'm sorry you gained such a dull view of the industrial revolution itself; it is sometimes the way of academics to make everything seem dull. The Michigan State University Alumni Association has some words of Albert Einstein on all its documents, which say that the art of teaching is to awaken joy in creative expression and in knowledge: not an original idea perhaps, but a very good one nevertheless and worth repeating. We need more joy at the heart of learning.

The industrial revolution in England was tremendously exciting and was not produced by academics as we understand that term today, except perhaps by those philosophers such as Bacon and Mill who developed ideas of free thought and enquiry. It was a time of amazing invention, energy, enterprise, ingenuity, craftsmanship and change: imagine; no one had ever seen a steam engine or a railway before. Huge steel- and iron-works lit up the sky at night, which must have been both exciting and terrifying. Great iron bridges were built across seemingly impossible distances and were so well made that they are still in use 150 years later. It appeared as though giants were working in England. The buildings of the time were often beautiful and elegant and classical architectural details were frequently used for modern machines. There was undoubtedly great hardship at first, but eventually the changes led to our modern standard of living so that today we all live like kings with hot running water, whole orchestras to play for us at the touch of a switch, private carriages and good food rather than working long, hard, dirty hours in agriculture all day. All this at the time inspired the imagination of artists and poets and novelists, and produced deep controversy about the meanings of nature and society. So, yes, there are other ways of understanding the industrial revolution.

♪

I lived as a disabled person, relying only on the friend-ship of my flatmate. She didn't sleep if I didn't sleep; she didn't eat if I was not hungry; she went out with me if I wanted to go shopping. She always showed her special understanding of my stories when I told her that my father was the person who loved me so much when I was very young. She never laughed at my silly thoughts such as that I wanted to drink Meng Po soup and became a baby again in my mother's womb.

'I so want to dress like a princess and enjoy sunshine on the beach.' I envied the princess in the movie of *Roman Holiday* so much.

'Let's do it. You're the princess in the world.' She then urged me to go shopping.

'But we don't have any money.'

'Oh, forget about money, or anything else; believe me.' She said this so confidently, although I knew that her family was not rich and she had already quit her job some months ago. However, she never told me where the money came from and never allowed me to worry about my life, no matter that I tried all means to find out the answer.

'You are so kind and so nice to me. Why do you want to waste your time on a useless person like me?' I worried that maybe she spent so much time to show her sympathy with me only because she was too kind.

'You're not a useless person. You're the best person I've ever met in my life.' She sounded so serious and didn't seem to say it just to comfort me.

'Why? All my life is a disaster…'

She interrupted me before I could continue talking. 'I have been inspired so much by you since three years ago when you moved in to our flat. I admire you so much because you remorselessly pursue your dream which is so touching and lovely. You just haven't found your stage to perform to your strength. I'm not helping you at all, but I am trying to avoid people hurting your dream which also provides so much hope for me. In other words, I'm protecting my hope too from being broken by reality.' She then told me that she had quit her job and wanted to do something meaningful for herself and for the people since she saw I so much enjoyed working with them; therefore she had signed up for the national exam and had started to study policies in order to prepare herself to be a helpful government officer once she passed her exam. However, I think she neglected her study for the exam for the job with the national government and borrowed much money to support my hopeless life.

For a whole year she provided a most worry-free life

for me. She dressed me up as a princess, took me to coffee shops to enjoy afternoon teas and talked with me overnight when I was too excited to sleep, without any complaint about my childish behaviour; till one night I cried out in front of her.

'I'm so useless and hopeless. After my final presentation I realized that I was not good at all to do design in reality.'

'Oh, my friend, I've been waiting for this moment for a long time. I worried about you so much because you didn't show any feeling after that presentation. I know that it's the most dangerous situation when you say nothing for your pain.'

'I'm a joke for everyone. I think all of them are laughing behind me. They would say that the most favourite student of the course leader is now nothing, and say that this silly girl could win those prizes and competitions only because she manipulated people very well; and they all ridicule me because I only indulged in self-admiration without anyone's appreciation. Even my supervisor told me that I'm nothing after the presentation.'

'But you WON the design prize in the end. Do you know who voted for your design?'

'I don't know. I haven't a clue. Even my supervisor gave up his right to vote for my design. I'm the loser, the real loser in the world. I have nothing but your support. All the time I have to try hard to find reasons to keep myself breathing for the next minute. Now everyone, including my parents, thinks I'm mad. No one but you is willing to listen to me.' I couldn't help but burn all my energy out with tears.

'Oh, my poor friend, I know how terribly you are being hurt, although you may think no one understands your feeling. I have been seeing all your experience for four years and was in your presentation with you. I really wish to do something for you to stand up again.'

It was a pity when I didn't feel better with her comfort and company, and kept crying to die. She slowly and carefully said: 'Go abroad, brandishing your wings and flying to another country to have a new life. This country is too small for you to fly.'

'It's not useful if humanity is all the same, everywhere. I will need to start again for everything, including my language and my understanding of a new country and new people; it will take me about ten years to construct a new life in another country. How many ten years do I have to run the circle again and again?' My heart felt even more painful as I imagined building a complete new life in a strange place.

'You haven't tried. The world is huge and is full of surprises for us to explore; amongst all the dazzling stars in the sky, a tiny lucky star is hidden for you to discover. You will magically resurrect like the Phoenix rising from ashes once you meet your lucky star.'

I was not sure if I could metaphor my life to be a phoenix, but it seemed to me that the only hope of mine was to fly to a fire and rebuild myself from ashes. The only risk was that I might become a roast chicken in someone's dish instead of being a phoenix to fly in the sky.

Surprisingly, in spite of all the unkind criticisms, I was awarded the prize for the outstanding final design.

That was possible because all other tutors in the faculty had the right to view my work on exhibition and to vote for the prize, and they voted for me. So, I gained my degree as well, because those examiners would look stupid if they failed the person who gained top prize. I suppose I should have felt pleased that I won the prize, and that I had shown they were wrong. But I did not know about the prize till many days afterwards, and all I could feel during those days was that I had been violated by the conduct of that inquisition. Those few days of doubt and humiliation changed me for ever I think, and I fell into a deep depression. Perhaps it was the reaction to so many years hard work with little sleep; and then what should have been the pinnacle of all that work only seemed like complete loss of everything in my life. Although I wanted to keep my innocence and believe in people's goodness as usual, because I had met so many good people, I became, like my father perhaps, distrustful of human nature which I never could have imagined could act like that.

As it is said, '*Once you have been bitten by a snake, you will be so afraid of seeing a straw rope for ten years*'. I can't stop thinking about the pain when I feel something may happen again similarly.

柒
7

UNDERSTANDING
理解

Many people have told me that art and poetry are only invented for rich people who don't need to worry about their lives. But I think I find hope for all my life from art and poetry by their beauty and interest, and by the communication they provide with those artists and poets who were also trying to find answers, although they don't have any answers to life's problems straightaway. This dreaming desire is becoming natural for me since I came to England. I feel I'm so near Western art and poetry which I not only can study from modern books, but also can touch from very old books; or possibly I can observe many original paintings so closely in the places where they have been for hundreds of years.

We saw a lovely painting at a pretty English country house called Buscot House. I call the painting, 'Sleeping Beauty,' but its proper name I think is *The Legend of the Briar Rose*. It shows the legend of a princess who had a magic spell put on her so that if she ever pricked her finger she would die. But a kind fairy was able to change the spell so that the princess would sleep for a hundred years. When she did prick her finger, although for many years her parents had tried to protect her, all her family and friends and servants and dogs went to sleep too, and rose briars grew over the palace until it could not be seen anymore.

My eyes stopped glimpsing around and stayed directly on the picture of the princess sleeping on her bed; her friends are sweetly asleep in the room around her. She looks so happy and peaceful. The colours are very subdued and restful, but they are not dull. Around the picture the briars grow; so many thorns, but lovely flowers too.

I so envy that princess: if I could sleep for one night I would be happy. I bought a postcard of her sleeping and I keep it beside my bed. I hoped it would help me to sleep. It doesn't, but still it is very beautiful and I look at it every night.

Another picture shows the prince in armour who is going to break the spell and wake everyone up, as in the legend. But in the paintings that never happens and the princess stays sleeping happily, dreaming. If I was her I would not want to be woken up. I do not want to be woken up. If I am woken up I will only be used again, and not for myself. I think I will only find myself in my dreaming.

Dear Su Yen

I was really so pleased to hear you had a few hours sleep on Thursday evening. Maybe, being more relaxed you then slept better that night. I hope so. Someone wrote about the *Briar Rose* paintings (I think it's in that guide book): '...there is no narrative progression in the cycle, for Burne-Jones' primary concern was to create a hermetic [sealed] world far from the problems of the modern world and to create a mood of languor [a sort of pleasant sleepiness]. He did this through the lazy arabesques of the briars, the abandoned poses of the sleeping figures, the shallow perspective, the intense but modulated colours, and the verses inscribed beneath, which were written by William Morris. *The Briar Rose* cycle is among the greatest achievements of Victorian painting'.

♪

I watched as the River Bus struggled to turn into the current to come alongside the jetty at Tate Modern. The River Thames was in full flood and boats were being swept downstream by the rushing water. We boarded, and the Bus began its laboured journey back against the tide. We stepped off when the boat berthed at Tate Britain which in more dignified times was known as the Tate Gallery of Art. Closing time was near so we walked quickly through the galleries to see our goal.

The Sleep of Arthur in Avalon was painted by the same artist who made Sleeping Beauty, Burne-Jones. I sat down quietly to look at this huge green painting, but it did not speak to me at all. One problem was the gallery lighting, so that wherever I sat there seemed to be parts of the painting spoiled by glare. In general I thought there was both too much going on in the painting, and not enough. The details such as the little flowers in the foreground were not painted with the care shown in other Pre-Raphaelite work. However, I have since read that the artist was dying as he painted it, and struggled to finish it; perhaps we should not judge hastily without knowledge. On that point I was told that the painting belongs to a South American millionaire who in the 1960s bought it for a thousand pounds because no one in England wanted it: 'Victorian' was out of fashion just then. Now it is worth millions. It really is a lesson that we hold beautiful things in trust for the future and should not sell them or destroy them because they do not suit us at the time. At least the painting can still be seen, unlike the many fine buildings which have been destroyed.

It is said that Burne-Jones wished to express a great nostalgia for an idealised, unattainable past. He thought that the function of art was to provide an alternative to modern existence. His definition of a painting was: 'I mean, by a picture, a beautiful romantic dream of something that never was, never will be, in a light better than any light that ever shone—in a land no one can define, or remember, only desire'.

There was a little time to spare so we went back to the Pre-Raphaelite room. My attention was caught by a large colourful painting of an English lady seated in front of a light coloured sky. Her full, flowing dress was painted in an exquisitely balanced orange tone, not too bright, not too deep: the colour of the sunrise. I was sure this must be *Aurora* whom I had read about in my *Greek Myths*, the goddess of the dawn who opens the gates of the east, pours dew on the earth, and makes the flowers grow, and whose great love for the mighty hunter Orion restored his sight (I had to look that up again). But when I saw it was called *Flaming June* the picture did not seem to be so attractive to me, which is strange because it was still the same painting, but apart from the beautiful dress there was little to hold my attention on that picture. I think the ideas we associate with a picture are very important for enjoying it.

But next to it was a grey-green-blue mousy sort of picture which did speak to me as soon as I noticed it although I knew nothing about its story. A lady dressed in subdued colours was sitting in a rowing boat on a small river; on the front of the boat were three small candles, and two candles had already gone out. I knew immediately what that meant: the lady was dying. A name was painted on the boat: *The Lady of Shallot*.

Dear Su Yen

You wondered about the story of the Lady of Shallot. You will find it in a poem by Tennyson, a very influential nineteenth century English poet; he was appointed to the post of Poet Laureate, which means he was the official poet for the nation, and he held this position for forty-three years. He often used classical and especially mediaeval stories for his poems. A well known example is a very long collection of twelve narrative poems, called *Idylls of the King*, based on the legends of King Arthur. We call them narrative poems because they tell a story or narrative. Tennyson based these poems on various mediaeval manuscripts, principally one called *Le Mort d'Arthur*, which is a French title and means 'The Death of Arthur'. When you get to know the stories perhaps that painting of Arthur's death will have more tragic meaning for you.

Tennyson used an old Norman-French manuscript for *The Lady of Shallot*. He wrote the poem early in his career when he was a young man; it was among the first of his many poems about Arthur. The Lady of Shallot spends her days in a fine castle; no one sees her, but sometimes people hear her beautiful singing. She is weaving a magic tapestry and in her mirror she sees the world passing by outside. This is rather like an idea from the Greek philosopher, Plato, who suggested our knowledge of reality is no better than seeing shadows of the world on a cave wall. So maybe she does not know much about the real world, but she seems to be quite contented.

Here are just a few verses.

The Lady of Shallot, by Alfred Lord Tennyson (1809–1892)

> *Willows whiten, aspens quiver,*
> *Little breezes dusk and shiver*
> *Through the wave that runs forever*
> *By the island in the river*
>   *Flowing down to Camelot.*
> *Four gray walls, and four gray towers,*
> *Overlook a space of flowers,*
> *And the silent isle embowers*
>   *The Lady of Shallot.*
>
> *Only reapers, reaping early*
> *In among the bearded barley,*
> *Hear a song that echoes cheerly*
> *From the river winding clearly,*
>   *Down to towered Camelot:*
> *And by the moon the reaper weary,*
> *Piling sheaves in uplands airy,*
> *Listening, whispers, 'Tis the fairy*
>   *Lady of Shallot'.*

Maybe this is something like those imaginings of the middle ages you used to have when you were young in Taiwan. The word 'fairy' suggests that she is a magic person. Camelot is of course the fabled court of King Arthur.

There she weaves by night and day
A magic web with colours gay,
She has heard a whisper say,
A curse is on her if she stay
    To look down to Camelot.
She knows not what that curse may be,
And so she weaveth steadily,
And little other care hath she,
    The Lady of Shallot.

And moving through a mirror clear
That hangs before her all the year,
Shadows of the world appear.
There she sees the highway near
    Winding down to Camelot:
There the river eddy whirls,
And there the surly village-churls,
And the red cloaks of market girls,
    Pass onward from Shallot.

The curse seems far away; and then in her mirror she sees King Arthur's bravest knight, Sir Lancelot.

All in the blue unclouded weather
Thick-jewelled shone the saddle-leather,
The helmet and the helmet-feather
Burned like one burning flame together,
    As he rode down to Camelot.

As often through the purple night,
Below the starry clusters bright
Some bearded meteor, trailing light,
   Moves over still Shallot.

Without thought, maybe, of the consequences her eyes follow where this man is going: she looks down to Camelot.

She left the web, she left the loom,
She took three paces through the room,
She saw the water-lily bloom,
She saw the helmet and the plume,
   She looked down to Camelot.
Out flew the web and floated wide:
The mirror cracked from side to side;
'The curse is come upon me,' cried
   The Lady of Shallot.

Her life is broken irreparably, like the mirror. We don't know whether she fell instantly in love, or whether intense curiosity led her to ignore the curse, but the outside world has intruded into her life. The mood of the poem changes.

In the stormy east-wind straining,
The pale yellow woods were waning,
The broad stream in his banks complaining,
Heavily the low sky raining
   Over towered Camelot;
Down she came and found a boat
Beneath a willow left afloat,
And round about the prow she wrote
   The Lady of Shallot.

This is the scene you saw in the painting; it is interesting that it spoke to you although you didn't know the story. This verse is a skilful word picture of a cold, wet, late autumn day: strong cold east wind; low dark cloud; rain, the woodland trees' pale yellow autumn leaves; the river, swollen by rain, rushing against its banks. Although the poem doesn't say so, the lady must have been very cold and wet.

And down the river's wide expanse
Like some bold seër in a trance,
Seeing all his own mischance—
With a glassy countenance
    Did she look to Camelot.
And at the closing of the day
She loosed the chain, and down she lay:
The broad stream bore her far away,
    The Lady of Shallot.

Heard a carol, mournful, holy,
Chanted loudly, chanted lowly,
Till her blood was frozen slowly,
And her eyes were darkened wholly,
    Turned to towered Camelot.
For ere she reached upon the tide
The first house by the water-side,
Singing, in her song she died.
    The Lady of Shallot.

In the story there are many things which are not explained. Certainly John William-Waterhouse chose the most dramatic moment for his painting, as the lady untied the boat and allowed the river to carry her away, though not the most visually striking. I can't remember whether the painting shows the weather as stormy; can you?

Dear Roy

That idea of Plato's, that our knowledge of reality is no better than seeing shadows of the world on a cave wall, reminds me of a well known saying, 'Life is a movie,' but I don't think that's true. We are spectators when watching other people's lives and maybe think we have objective views, but we can become too confused to judge things when we're actors in our own life movies, or we may have too much self-concern to make theoretically right decisions. For the Lady of Shallot, who we think ignored the curse, may on the contrary have accepted the curse with full courage, including sacrificing her own life, to pursue her heart which no one truly sees.

My first impression of the painting was that the melancholy girl was floating with her own chosen fate to die beautifully. The colour tone of the painting is cold brown and the weather is windy which can be seen from the two candles that have died on the prow.

Luckily, she died before being hurt by reality, which is the best ending for a never broken dreaming mind for a poem, but unluckily this cannot always be applied in reality to stop people from hurting each other too much, since we cannot see the world only on a cave wall.

Dear Su Yen

I think the candles would have blown out in very little wind so perhaps that does not show the weather is stormy; the extinguished candle is a painterly device, often called *memento mori*, to remind us that death is always near, and that beauty is fragile and elusive. Sometimes a skull or an over-turned wine glass is used as the symbol.

'Who was Arthur?' you asked when you were looking at the painting, *The Sleep of Arthur*, and, 'Was he important?'

Your questions appear to be simple, but they have rather strange answers. First, we do not know if the person we think of as King Arthur ever lived at all. He is a legendary character. Second, if he ever did live he would have been quite unlike the legends which are set in a later period. But, third, the idea and story of Arthur have been very important in our culture for hundreds of years. So we have a very important person who may never have existed.

Arthur may have been a Roman-British leader who tried to prevent the Saxons from invading Britain after the Romans left in about 420 AD. We know nothing certain about him historically, but it seems he was so famous at the time that all sorts of stories have been told about him ever since over many hundreds of years. These stories were written down in Oxford in the twelfth century by a man called Geoffrey of Monmouth; in the fifteenth century another version was made by Sir Thomas Mallory. Scholars used to consider that legends were unreliable and unimportant, but recent research is leading to the idea that many strong legends, including some Greek myths, do have a basis in fact. For example, the Ancient Greeks had a story about a man called Jason who went to search for a sheep whose wool was made of gold, *The Golden Fleece*. It seems impossible, but scholars have discovered that in that part of the world, in Asia Minor, people used to put sheep skins in the streams to catch small particles of gold washed down from the mountains.

Several English kings have tried to associate themselves with the magic and idealism which surround Arthur's name in order to recreate something of the power of Arthur's famous court of the Round Table. This is rather strange because Arthur, if he existed, would have been an enemy of the Anglo-Saxons, and he was eventually defeated by them. Each period has recreated Arthur in their own image so we now think of him as a mediaeval knight living in a castle, none of which existed in his own time.

Tennyson's, long set of narrative poems, *Idylls of the King*, re-tell the mediaeval legends about Arthur and how he tried to bring justice and peace to his threatened country by gathering together a band of brave, good and committed followers, the Fellowship of the Round Table. Like other chroniclers before him, Tennyson reworked the stories to express the values of his own time, in this case the moral values of Victorian England. But all sorts of human frailties, and sometimes treacheries, mean that Arthur's vision ultimately is defeated and he is killed in a final battle with evil forces. There is a thread of this impending tragedy present throughout the Arthur legends, which is what makes them so powerful. Like any good story, and like life itself I suppose, we think why does it have always to go wrong somewhere? So the death of Arthur is the death of a dream; do you think the painting expressed that?

Legends say that Arthur is not dead but sleeping somewhere in a cave and one day he will come back to lead his people; but whether they will be the Welsh or the English people is a tricky question.

Stories about Arthur are found in many places, including Brittany which is now part of France. There is a concentration of legends around the small town of Glastonbury in England. In the twelfth century, in the grounds of Glastonbury Abbey, a tomb was discovered which was claimed to be that of Arthur and his Queen, Guinevere. You can still see the tomb in the abbey ruins. There is a prehistoric hill-fort nearby which historians think could have been used as the base of a Roman-British warrior who may have been the original Arthur; if so the hill-fort would also be the original of the fabulous court of Camelot, but not at all like the Hollywood version.

Arthur's knights sought the Holy Grail, the cup used by Jesus just before his death. Legend says the Grail was brought to Britain, to Glastonbury, by a follower of Jesus, Joseph of Arithamea, shortly after Jesus' death. Glastonbury at that time was an island and all the flat land which now surrounds it would have been under water. This land used to flood every winter until quite recently although the drainage has now been improved; but Glastonbury is still called, 'The Isle of Glastonbury,' or sometimes, 'The Isle of Avalon,' a beautiful name from the Arthur stories.

Idylls of the King: The Holy Grail, by Alfred, Lord Tennyson (1809–1892)

> *... the good saint*
> *Arimathæan Joseph, journeying brought [the Grail]*
> *To Glastonbury, where the winter thorn*
> *Blossoms at Christmas, mindful of our Lord.*
> *And there awhile it bode; and if a man*
> *Could touch or see it, he was heal'd at once,*
> *By faith, of all his ills. But then the times*
> *Grew to such evil that the holy cup*
> *Was caught away to Heaven, and dissapear'd.*
> *To whom the monk: ' From our old books I know*
> *That Joseph came of old to Glastonbury,*
> *And there the heathen Prince, Arviragus,*
> *Gave him an isle of marsh whereon to build;*
> *And there he built with wattles from the marsh*
> *A little lonely church ...*

The little church became the most powerful abbey in England until it was destroyed by King Henry VIII in the sixteenth century. You can still see the thorn tree which is said to have grown from Saint Joseph's staff, and it does flower at Christmas.

> *... But then the times*
> *Grew to such evil that the holy cup*
> *Was caught away to Heaven, and dissapear'd.*

But then, the story says, the Grail returned. It was first seen by a holy nun who was the sister of Sir Percivale, one of Arthur's purest knights. The Grail was believed to have holy powers of peace and healing. Tennyson tells how the nun had a vision of the Grail, and how this vision inspired Arthur's knights to set out on a destructive and tragic search for the Holy Grail. Here Percivale tells how his sister described her vision.

> 'For on a day she sent to speak with me.
> And when she came to speak, behold her eyes
> Beyond my knowing of them, beautiful,
> Beyond all knowing of them, wonderful,
> Beautiful in the light of holiness.
> And "O my brother Percivale," she said,
> "Sweet brother, I have seen the Holy Grail:
> For, waked at dead of night, I heard a sound
> As of a silver horn from o'er the hills
> Blown, and I thought, 'It is not Arthur's use
> To hunt by moonlight;' and the slender sound
> As from a distance beyond distance grew
> Coming upon me—O never harp nor horn,
> Nor aught we blow with breath, or touch with hand,
> Was like that music as it came; and then
> Stream'd thro' my cell a cold and silver beam,
> And down the long beam stole the Holy Grail,
> Rose-red with beatings in it, as if alive,
> Till all the white walls of my cell were dyed
> With rosy colours leaping on the wall;
> And then the music faded, and the Grail
> Past, an the beam decay'd, and from the walls
> The rosy quiverings died into the night.

So now the Holy Thing is here again
Among us brother, fast thou too and pray,
And tell thy brother knights to fast and pray,
That so perchance the vision may be seen
By thee and those, and all the world be heal'd".'

The nun had started a sort of hysteria and nearly everyone imagined they had seen the Grail; Arthur's knights, eating in his great hall, had a vision (a waking dream) of the Grail.

'And all at once, as there we sat, we heard
A cracking and a riving of the roofs,
And rending, and a blast, and overhead
Thunder, and in the thunder was a cry.
And in the blast there smote along the hall
A beam of light seven times more clear than day:
And down the long beam stole the Holy Grail
All over covered with a luminous cloud...'

All the knights swore an oath to seek (that is, they made a holy promise to look for) the Grail. But Arthur had not been there when the Grail appeared and he was very angry that all his knights were leaving him when he needed them to keep law and order and to fight the invading Saxons. He knew it would mean the end of his Fellowship of the Round Table. I wonder, did something like this happen to the real Arthur?

'Go, since your vows are sacred, being made:
Yet—for ye know the cries of all my realm
Pass thro' this hall—how often, O my knights,
Your places being vacant at my side,
This chance of noble deeds will come and go
Unchallenged, while ye follow wandering fires Lost
in the quagmire [swamp]! Many of you, yea most,
Return no more ...'

You can read about their amazing adventures in Tennyson's poems.

'Thereafter, the dark warning of our King,
That most of us would follow wandering fires,
Came like a driving gloom across my mind.
Then every evil word I had spoken once,
And every evil thought I had thought of old,
And every evil deed I ever did,
Awoke and cried, "This Quest is not for thee".'
And lifting up mine eyes, I found myself
Alone, and in a land of sand and thorns,
And I was thirsty even unto death ...'

Dear Roy

This story is very beautiful, I almost feel it's a true story (but I think it's a legend). But I may understand why people believe in the God so deeply; those words would make people want to believe.

Your explanation of Arthur reminded me of ancient Chinese legends of kings at the beginning of the oriental civilization. I have always felt that those Chinese kings who are said to have been founders of the land are part of the history and they did exist thousands of years ago. You did say legends might be true. So I have the same feeling for King Arthur. He is not at all a legendary figure to me, but lived as a real knight hundreds of years ago with his followers in a beautiful and strong castle.

I can understand why people would rather believe that Arthur is sleeping, but not dead. He has become a symbol of order and peace. For an island with so many tribes fighting among each other and with invaders coming from over the sea constantly, as Xue and I learned when we watched David Starkey's *Monarchy*, a brave and just king like Arthur is what people would love and keep forever to deliver them from all the sufferings. So I find Tennyson's poem on the Holy Grail beautiful and touching. From past to present, mankind has been looking for beauty and peace of mind for the world so we put our hopes in super-beings like the God. When the Holy Grail appeared in the land under the rule of Arthur, I can imagine a holy and sacred feeling of hearts filled with hope. How can people let this long awaited hope go?

So I find the painting is a bit strange. Why did I not find many of his knights around Arthur's bed at such an important time? Probably he has been worn out with the treacheries from his knights. If it's true that he will wake up one day to lead his people again for another prosperity, I believe the time is coming; or maybe we'll be the next lucky people to see the Grail appear in England again and will write another poem to record the magic moment.

By the way, when we watched the film *Sense and Sensibility*, Xue wanted to find the book in a second-hand book shop. I told her you have a good second-hand book shop in your village, and she saw those books in my bookcase are all good quality, so she is happy if you can find the book for her in that shop.

Dear Su Yen

That is interesting: you think the story is a legend, but because it is beautiful you want to believe it. A poet, Keats, said that beauty is truth and truth is beauty, and that is all we can or need to know; it might seem so, but perhaps that is how religion can deceive us. Arthur's knights were not present at his last sleep when he was dying from his wounds because many of them had been killed in the search for the Grail, and more died in Arthur's last great battle. On their quest the knights met dreadful things which are rather like events in a modern horror film. I wonder, do you want to believe them too? Here are three:

> *'And then behold a woman at a door*
> *Spinning; and fair the house whereby she sat,*
> *And kind the woman's eyes and innocent,*
> *And all her bearing gracious; and she rose*
> *Opening her arms to meet me, as who should say*
> *"Rest here;" but when I touch'd her, lo! she, too,*
> *Fell into dust and nothing, and the house*
> *Became no better than a broken shed,*
> *And in it a dead babe; and also this*
> *Fell into dust, and I was left alone.'*

Or, further:

'The lightnings here and there to left and right
Struck, till the dry old trunks about us, dead,
Yea, rotten with a hundred years of death,
Sprang into fire: and at the base we found
On either hand, as far as eye could see,
A great black swamp and of an evil smell,
Part black, part whiten'd with the bones of men,
Not to be crossed, save that some ancient king
Had built a way, where, link'd with many a bridge,
A thousand piers ran into the great Sea.
And Galahad fled along them bridge by bridge,
And every bridge as quickly as he crost
Sprang into fire and vanish'd, tho' I yearn'd
To follow; and thrice above him all the heavens
Open'd and blazed with thunder such as seem'd
Shoutings of all the sons of God: and first
At once I saw him far on the great Sea,
In silver-shining armour starry-clear;
And o'er his head the Holy Vessel hung
Clothed in white samite or a luminous cloud ...'

Or:

'...only the rounded moon,
Thro' the tall oriel on the rolling sea.
But always in the quiet house I heard,
Clear as a lark, high oe'r me as a lark,
A sweet voice singing in the topmost tower
To the eastward: up I climb'd a thousand steps
With pain: as in a dream I seemed to climb
For ever: at the last I reach'd a door,
A light was in the crannies, and I heard,
'Glory and joy and honour to our Lord
And to the Holy Vessel of the Grail.'
Then in my madness I essay'd [tried] the door;
It gave; and thro' a stormy glare, a heat
As from a seventimes-heated furnace, I,

Blasted and burnt, and blinded as I was,
With such a fierceness that I swoon'd away—
And yet methought I saw the Holy Grail,
All pall'd in crimson samite, and around
Great angels, awful shapes, and wings and eyes.
And but for all my madness and my sin,
And then my swooning, I had sworn I saw
That which I saw; But what I saw was veil'd
And cover'd; and this quest was not for me.'

I don't think Hollywood could improve on that.

Only 'a tithe' (one tenth) of the knights came back...

And there sat Arthur on the daïs-throne,
And those that had gone out upon the quest,
Wasted and worn, and but a tithe of them...

The remaining knights knew they had had a sort of religious madness caused by the nun and her brother Percivale.

'... my good friend Percivale,
Thy holy nun and thou have driven men mad,
Yea, made our mightiest madder than our least.
But by mine eyes and by mine ears I swear,
I will be deafer than the blue-eyed cat,
And thrice as blind as any noonday owl
To holy virgins in their ecstasies,
Henceforward'

Arthur sadly sees that the great Order of Chivalry and Justice which he built up has been destroyed.

'And spake I not too truly, O my knights?
Was I too dark a prophet when I said

To those who went upon the Holy Quest,
That most of them would follow wandering fires,
Lost in the quagmires?—lost to me and gone,
And left me gazing at a barren board,
And a lean Order—scarce return'd a tithe—
And out of those to whom the vision came
My greatest hardly will believe he saw;
Another hath beheld it afar off,
And leaving human wrongs to right themselves ...'

So this great force for goodness was destroyed not by evil, or by a just war, but by religious madness. Perhaps there is a lesson there. Arthur's Fellowship of Knights was so weakened that it was later destroyed by the evil King Mordred. But that is another story. The term 'Holy Grail' is still sometimes used as a metaphor for an ideal but unattainable objective.

Dear Roy

I read these poems aloud, trying to follow the rhythm and the punctuation as you said, rather than only reading the stories. Amazingly, it did work sometimes. I felt so happy that I've reached another level to appreciate English poetry in its original language; although I was unable to read out the beauty of the poems properly yet, it's still a great improvement and a great leap for me to feel this poetry as I practice my spoken English.

When you started to tell me about English poetry there was always confusion in my mind about the difference of rhyme and metre between ancient Chinese and English poems, but I did not want to say so then because I was afraid you might think I was being difficult. I know they are not comparable because it's about two different languages and cultures, but I think this is possibly the main obstacle along the way for Chinese speakers to enjoy their English learning. It is only now that I feel I understand the English way enough to accept and understand the differences. Before, I was trying to judge the rhythms according to Chinese rules of poetry. Ancient Chinese poems reached their highest level in the Tang dynasty. There are two typical and most popular types: four- and eight-line poems. Each line can have either five or seven words. Within a poem, all lines have to use the same number of words. So these poems have four fixed formats: five-word-four-line, seven-word-four-line, five-word-eight-line and seven-word-eight-line. These are the basic forms of ancient Chinese poems. There are also very long poems which can have hundreds of lines. And like the English long poems, the Chinese long ones can also be broken into those short forms.

For nearly all four-line and eight-line poems, one main rhyme is used with almost every line ending with the same syllable so that it sounds more like a melody. I remember that our Chinese teacher at high school told us that ancient Chinese poems were often sung but not read. The poets sometimes competed for the popularity of their poems by counting the times people sang them at a party or in a pub.

The choice of word is also strict in each line to ensure an exact symmetry of the couplet. If the first word of the first line is a verb, the first word of the second line must be a verb too and so on and so forth, and if a number, the corresponding position should be a number as well.

Apart from this, it is much preferred if the meaning of the word can be similar or opposite. So if the first word of the first line is river, the best choice of first word for the second line should be mountain. If a five-word-four-line is 'above sea arises bright moon', a good second line should be something similar to 'below hill descends dark loon'. I know it does not sound pretty but I hope it can give you some ideas about the structure of a typical Tang dynasty poem.

After the Tang Dynasty, another type of poem appeared in the Song dynasty. This new type did not follow the rules on rhyme and words so strictly, but it is more demanding and strict in it's pattern and sometimes can be more difficult to write. So we use a description such as 'Tang poems and Song songs' to include all the ancient Chinese poems. The modern Chinese is so different from ancient Chinese, probably as modern English is from Anglo-Saxon. But modern Chinese poems are seldom able to gain popularity as ancient Chinese poems have and most of the people still love to read the Tang poems and Song songs. So I have to confess that when I first studied the English poems with you I was very much surprised about the freedom English poets could have in composing their poems. I tried to find forms like those of ancient Chinese poems where almost every line ends with the same syllable so that a poem sounds more like a melody. When I used to read English poems I remembered what our Chinese teacher taught about poems and songs because I thought this would be the basic way to judge the level of poems. But when you showed me the basic rules for English poems,

I tried to feel those poems in an English way and follow your teaching. I think at first, although I enjoyed them, I only could touch the surface and wasn't able to feel them naturally like an English person, probably because my preconceptions of the forms of Chinese poems and songs were still deeply influential in my mind. But now with the wonderful rhythms of Tennyson I feel them so much more deeply. Perhaps that is because his verse is more like speaking and doesn't rhyme (I think you said it was called blank verse, like Shakespeare's) so it is further away from the Chinese forms for me and I don't confuse them. I also see now what you meant about following the punctuation: it is so easy to pause at the end of each line in a sing-song way, but when the poet shows no comma or semi-colon there, just carrying over to the next line without a break makes the poetry come alive wonderfully.

About these poems themselves, I feel they're really ghost stories and quite like so many of our ancient Chinese religious legends, but they are written in a very different style. I heard my father tell me once that English are the most superstitious people in the world because they just treat spirits or God or anything as part of their world and never need to talk about this issue, although I've often heard English people say that they don't believe in ghosts at all in their religion. So I was quite puzzled when I read these poems about the dreadful experiences of Arthur's knights while looking for the Holy Grail. The poet produced this feeling without using any of the scary or hideous words and situations that most of our ghost stories do. I feel these poems are beautiful and magical in the way they show the horrors of a spiritual world while presenting them as beautifully as other topics of poetry. I like the part:

> *'The lightenings here and there to left and right*
> *Struck, till the dry old trunks about us, dead,*
> *Yea, rotten with a hundred years of death,*
> *Sprang into fire: and at the base we found*
> *On either hand, as far as eye could see,*
> *A great black swamp and of an evil smell,*
> *Part black, part whiten'd with the bones of men,*
> *Not to be crossed, save that some ancient king*
> *Had built a way ...'*

I particularly like the last few lines which show how the souls of men conquer the evil swamp with the symbol of their sacred bones. Hence, I think maybe my father is quite right that English people, who are in the highest level of dealing with another world, never need to talk about it nor be afraid of it because it's nature and part of our world.

Dear Su Yen

Certainly the English used to be superstitious, as were all people in the world, but I think most modern people in England like to believe that they are rational and that there are scientific explanations for everything, even though we don't always know what the explanations are. For example, the 'wandering fires' of the quagmires, or swamps, were the result of spontaneous ignition of the methane gas produced by rotting vegetation: in the old days travellers might think this was the light of a house and so get lost in the swamp. But the old explanation was that the lights were carried by magic beings, called 'Wills o' the Wisp,' which you might call ghosts, who thought it was fun to deceive travellers in this way. There are people who argue that magic and mythical stories are untrue and deceptive in themselves and so it is wrong to tell 'fairy stories' to children since this is just like telling lies. On the other hand the stories can be seen to teach truths about human nature, as the Greek myths do; even many religious people no longer believe the sacred stories of Christianity, but see them rather as symbolic teachings. Perhaps that is what your father meant.

The 'board' in the poem means a table, in this case the famous Round Table of Camelot. In the Middle Ages tables were long and narrow; they still are in Oxford college dining halls. Important people sat at one end and the nearer your place was to them the more important you were thought to be. The Round Table was supposed to mean that everyone was equal since it had no top or bottom ends, but clearly some places were nearer than others to the king. In the thirteenth-century hall of the castle at Winchester there is a large round wooden table with the names of Arthur's knights, each in his place; it is very old, but no one thinks it was Arthur's.

It is interesting that three English monarchs have given the name Arthur to one of their sons, but in each case the prince has died while still young. Perhaps there can be only one King Arthur.

捌

8

ESCAPE

逃離

In those days I never imagined that one day I might leave not just my home town, but my island home of Taiwan, perhaps for ever; but it came to be the only solution I could see when I could find no other way for my life to go. I was studying design as a full-time undergraduate at university, but I also gained experience and professional knowledge of my subject by joining local architectural design projects set up by the government. In this way I learnt to deal with people and to manage my time because I also worked part-time as a research assistant in an environmental control laboratory, and as a computer operator in a media centre, and as a sales person in a computer shop. It could be said that my student life was quite rich and colourful. But then I became the biggest fool and joke in the world when all of a sudden I waived everything and chose to be nothing in a strange country.

'I would never allow you to go away from this country. I'm sure you should be back soon once I cut off your economic sources.' This was the reply from my father. He tried all sorts of methods to stop me going anywhere after that; he even persuaded my relatives, colleagues and friends to convince me to give up my decision and to start a normal job for living.

'Su Yen, you tell a big lie to us. How can we believe that your father would ignore you and leave you to raise money on your own with so much difficulty? He loves you so much, since you were a child. And, there is no point for him to do this because he is rich enough to support you to study anywhere. You should be honest and shouldn't hurt your father using this terrible lie.'

'Study abroad? What a funny idea of hers! Even her father told everyone that he doesn't agree with this silly plan. Let us wait and see what she can do without any support.'

'Su Yen, I'm telling you about the duty of children. This first thing children should do is to listen to their parents because parents are never wrong. A daughter like you who doesn't obey your parents and makes your parents worry so about you: you're not a good daughter to go so strongly against the meaning of fealty for your family.'

'It's good to have a dream; but, be practical; I don't think you can survive in another country because you don't speak English.'

'You're just so unrealistic and insensitive, and consider yourself always right! Who do you think you are? It is fated that you cannot go anywhere. Dreamer! You think you're the dreamer; we are all dreamers, but we need to wake up in the morning because we have to work hard to fill our bellies. Let your dream stay in the night; and please learn to see the truth when the sun wakes you up every morning.'

'Are you too bored, or perhaps life is too happy for you here? You can always do your Master's degree here and get a good job here. Come on, you have a quite decent life here. Why do you try to make trouble to yourself and to your families?'

Am I a trouble maker? I didn't understand who the trouble makers were in this sense. Many of them gave their self-confessed good advice on what I should do for myself, or for someone else. I did wonder if they could truly understand the reason behind my decision.

There are always untold stories well hidden in words. Words often can be useful for people to know each other; but sometimes words can make disasters when people have different understandings in mind. That's reality. What a simple yet complex word 'reality' is, involving not only the things we can touch or feel physically, but also humanity which widely includes such emotional feelings as jealousy, envy, like, dislike, love, hatred, painfulness or happiness. When people treat each other with any of these feelings they may cause judgements to become distorted. Sometimes one goes through a hell where people only focus on how easily they can control or how much they can get from other people rather than purely caring about how good, how professional or how qualified these people really are; or on *who* they are.

'What do you want? What do you really want on earth?'

Would they give me whatever I want if I answer this question? 'I want to find out who I am with my dream.' I answered in silence.

♪

'Why (or when? or what?) do you come to New Zealand?'

Oh, gosh, I was stuck in the Customs and did not understand what the question was about? I stood tensely in front of the customs officer like a log of wood which couldn't say a word. It was so hard for me to feel calm when lots of people of different races came and went in such a huge place with so many languages mixed up in the messy air.

'I… I…come to New Zealand for…studying English…'

'—for three months.' The officer kindly helped me to finish my sentence after I had taken so long trying to work out a right answer for her question.

'Yes, yes, yes.' I was so pleased and kept nodding till she showed me a card.

'Do—You—Have—This? This? Or This? In Your Bag?' It was much better that she pointed out to me those pictures of fish, cow, pig and shoes on the card instead of asking me questions, so that I could go out to the real world from the stressful airport much more quickly.

The first scenery of this strange country that came to my eyes was huge countryside and many pretty scattered houses with pitched roofs. My friend dropped me off by a lovely detached house which was surrounded by a big dreaming garden. An old white couple came to welcome me to join their family for my first visit in their world. I thought I was walking in to a film when they showed me around the house.

♪

'Hello, are you all right with your new host family?' My friend called me five days after he had left me with my host family.

'Yes, I'm fine. I just feel a bit nervous because I often don't understand their language. But I think things are getting better now.' I thought he was just kindly caring about my new life in a strange country.

'But my parents just received a call from your host family who sounded quite upset about you; they want to request your language school to find you a new host family.'

My brain became blank suddenly because I couldn't understand what they thought was wrong with me. I was also puzzled because when I arrived home a few minutes later my host parents were quite friendly, asking about my study at school without showing any sulkiness. Were they so two-faced? I went out from my room to see my home-stay-mate next door. She told me that both of us would need to move to another house because our host parents were not happy to have us anymore.

Our host father then came in to the room and started talking. 'You both are not happy here. It's just not right for you to stay here anymore; we told your school today and they agreed to find another family for you in two weeks time.'

'Is it our fault to make you so unhappy?' I asked.

'We always told you to go out to enjoy your life in this country because it's not good for you to study in your bedroom. But it seems to me that you don't take our advice and just unflaggingly spend your time on paper-study by your desk which is not good for you at all.'

'I'm sorry, but I need to pass my English exam to apply for my Master's course—'

My host father didn't allow me to finish talking and firmly restated his opinion about my life there. 'You don't know how to enjoy our culture which can't be learnt from your text books.'

My stomach suddenly felt colicky and I couldn't say anything more. I didn't know whether it was really a sort of culture difference or they just didn't like us to stay at home too long. I remembered my father always told me to come home when it's dark outside and told me to work hard rather than join parties. But it seemed everything was wrong when I spent my time studying in my room. I couldn't believe that I was kicked out from a 'lovely old white couple' after only five days when I thought I was trying to be a good girl in their house. The silly thing was that I could have been happy there, but clearly, while they wanted our money, they did not want us around their house too much.

How could we stay there for another two weeks after this nightmare had occurred? My home-stay-mate took me out with her relatives over the weekend. We rambled around with no purpose other than to avoid facing our host parents too often. We tried hard to find another place for ourselves to stay for two weeks before our school found somewhere else for us.

'Happy Birthday, Su Yen! I'm so sorry that I can't arrange a party to celebrate your first birthday in a new country.' We met on the street and my home-stay-mate greeted me on my twenty-seventh birthday with a strange mood of dreariness.

'Thank you very much, Tip. I will never forget this moment with you.' I smiled bitterly and lowered my head while wandering around. I couldn't see where my future would be; yet I only could keep going along this endless road towards somewhere that I might finally reach in to.

♪

'You two should share one room because I don't have any spare room for you; and you need to share a bathroom with all the people in this house, which means you must get up early to use the bathroom because some of them often take showers in the morning.' We were advised by the new host mother who was a single woman and had four people in her small house at once.

'Is there any bus towards the city centre that goes near your house? How long does it take from here to our school?' I asked.

'Yes, there is one. It takes you fifteen minutes to the bus stop on foot and it would be another forty-five minutes on the bus to the city centre. But you may need to check the time-table first because the bus comes only once per hour'. She explained the situation in detail and left us to decide whether we wanted to stay. We thought it would be for only two weeks. Unfortunately, the problem was not just the difficulty of sharing the bathroom or catching a bus in the morning. A handsome Swiss guy was living next to our room and studying at the same school as us. We were totally ignored in that house because our single host mother only remembered the name of that guy, re-membered to ask only him for dinner and invited only him to join her parties.

'You're so lucky that you can come home with a handsome Swiss guy.' I didn't understand what she was talking about, and didn't know what was so special. Because we were at the same school and lived in the same house, it was unavoidable that we would meet in the same bus which only came once per hour.

'Do Asian women always love Western *min*?' My New Zealand host mother asked me an odd question when I was doing my home-work in the living room.

'I don't understand this question. Can you explain it clearly for me because my English is not good? Can you also spell the word '*min*' for me?' I didn't catch what she was talking about while she was watching television beside me.

'*Min*, M-E-N. Don't you think this pop star looks so alike the Swiss guy?' She pointed to a young man on the TV screen and asked me again an odd question.

'Oh, sorry about that, I didn't understand your accent

first time. You mean the guy who lives in our house? I don't know how to tell the difference between Western people because they all look the same for me.'

I hadn't a clue about the conversation between us because, with my poor English ability, my brain was completely stuck on my homework.

♩

'Hello, Su Yen, welcome to your new home. You will stay with me from now on. Let me tell you about our house rules and show you around.' My third host mother was a widow who kept a huge house alone. I was impressed by a piano in the drawing room and a swimming pool in her garden. However, I wasn't excited at all following the previous experiences with two strange families.

She looked at me and spoke slowly. 'First, I shall tell you that the power and water are very expensive in this country, so you can't take a long shower and can't leave the light on at night for too long.'

'I can understand we always need to save energy for the earth.'

She didn't really care about what I was trying to say and kept telling me the rules. 'I counted the time already, *three* minutes for a shower is long enough for you to wash yourself from your head to toe. You should go to bed by 11 PM because it's good for your health. Don't flush the toilet when you go to the loo at night because it's just water.' I think she saw my shocked face so she quickly turned to smile at me. 'Don't worry, my dear, you'll be fine and I will give you good food which is more important for you.'

'But I need to study more and really can't go to bed by 11 PM. I have come here to study for my English exam which is so important for me.' I hoped to get her permission to use my light at night because I could never finish my study by 2 AM.

'Your parents paid a lot for you to come here. You should enjoy our culture with your peers outside rather than put yourself in a small bedroom with text books.'

'I paid for myself to come here only for the reason that I wanted to buy a peaceful place where I can concentrate on my study for a few months.' I was so fed up that everyone here seemed to think that parents would spend money on their kids for study and then expect they should just play around in another country. Maybe she was hard up for money, but I didn't see why that meant she should exploit me. But my English was not good enough so it was simply a waste of time to try to explain my situation to people there.

When we couldn't bear the stress of staying with that old widow anymore I moved out with another home-stay-mate to a Chinese family. However, it was an even worse decision because I had to sleep on the floor even though I paid for the full rent to the Chinese family because, again, they didn't have a room for me. It was a big worry because I only had one more month left to study in that country and I would have to study very hard for my coming exam.

After an urgent and frustrating house-hunting, things finally turned a little better when I received help from a Chinese businessman who had an en-suite room in his house which he agreed to let to me with only a little rental payment till I finished my study. I so appreciated his kindness and help after my difficult situations with those host families, although I think he couldn't understand why I moved five times within two months; neither I nor anyone else could understand I think.

My mind was so unbalanced when other students shared with me their lovely stories of having great times with their host families. However, I learnt something from the first experience of my study in a foreign country. For example, it can be argued whether we really can get what we think we have paid for. I was not a bad girl; all I wanted was peace to study my English. I feel that very few land-ladies understand how to provide proper conditions for serious study. If you find one she will be a jewel.

♩

'What are you looking at?' A classmate of mine at language school was curious about why I was staring up at the building while standing on the footpath outside our classroom.

'The building,' I sighed, answering her briefly.

'It's pretty, isn't it?'

I knew we would agree that the Victorian-style building was very attractive and dreaming in its lovely landscape surroundings. However, I couldn't really enjoy or appreciate the picturesque scene.

'Yes, but I'm not looking at its beauty, I'm thinking about whether I should enter the building.'

'Oh, I know what you mean; I'm also resisting going to the learning centre because I'm so fed up with all those BBC programmes which our tutor asks us to watch and to write summaries on for parts of our home work.' She voiced my worries as well as her own when she expressed her feelings about our *harsh* English tutor.

'So maybe not today. Shall we take a break and have a cup of coffee then?' I really wanted to run away from study sometimes, but I did need someone to go with me, otherwise I would feel so guilty that only I was so lazy.

'No, I think we should study hard to improve our English quickly, so that we can leave this country for ever and never come back.'

I liked her idea to study hard with the motivation of escaping from New Zealand, but I was disappointed that we still had to enter that building and study till school closed.

What could I say about my life in New Zealand when I was so terribly unhappy? I never had such a regular life as in those months in that boring country. Perhaps I shouldn't complain at all since it was my choice to study hard for my English rather than visit or travel around. But, when it was necessary for me to get up at 7 AM, to catch a bus by 8 AM, to be in the learning centre from 9 to 11am, to attend lectures from 11.15 AM to 3.45 PM, to stay in the learning centre again till school closed at 5 PM, to move to the library of Auckland University till 8 PM, to catch a bus to go home by 9 PM, and then study again to 2 AM after dinner and a short shower, I couldn't feel anything else but stress. Although our tutor sometimes pretended that he felt so sorry about my stressful life in that country, he not only kept returning my homework many times and asking me to write it again and again, but also continued to assign new work everyday.

'Su Yen, you study, study and study. You work too hard everyday for your study. Please do have some break to enjoy your stay in this country.' My tutor told me to go out when he met me again in the learning centre.

'I have lots of homework everyday. You always ask me to write again and never give me a pass for the previous work and at the same time you never stop giving me new work. How can I enjoy my life under this pressure?' I complained about my heavy work load, even though I knew it was my problem for having a too poor English ability.

'You don't need to write them if you're not happy. Those small assignments are only some practice for your study. Please don't worry about them too much.' He smilingly told me that I had a choice to ignore my homework.

'Really? Are you sure that I don't need to amend my work again and again if I don't want? But, what will happen if I don't do it?' I felt a little hope when I heard that I didn't really have to keep improving my work for my tutor.

'Of course nothing serious will happen. I mean you won't lose an arm or a leg if you ignore your homework; you just won't get a qualification at the end of this course.'

I frowned because my little hope was soon broken when I heard this terrible answer. 'Oh, no! You're so unkind to me because I feel even worse to hear what you just said. How can I take a failed result back to my home when I've spent so much money to study my English here? Maybe you hate me very much so that you never want to give me my pass.'

Nevertheless, I felt embarrassed after complaining to my tutor about my heavy homework. He seemed to be taking care not to make me too unhappy because I saw he hid my returned work beneath my note book when I was away during a break instead of handing it to me in person. On the contrary, I appreciated my tutor very much because I could see how quickly my English had improved with his professional teaching and harsh regime.

I have to confess that my English was unbelievably terrible at the beginning of my study although I was somehow placed in an 'upper-intermediate level' class, which I think was because I accidentally had a good result in the first exam on our arrival at school. I didn't know much vocabulary so drawings and body gestures were quite helpful for me to communicate with people, if they were patient enough, such as the relatives of my first home-stay-mate whom I met in the first host family. I drew many different sorts of food I wanted to have when they asked about my favourites in a restaurant, and I also drew my feelings, thoughts and ideas on paper very quickly when I couldn't express them in English. It was the first time that I realized how important drawings are for my whole life everywhere and not just for compulsory modules of a design course.

I remember I could order my own food in a restaurant in the second month of my study, whereas in the first month I only could follow my classmate's order and always said 'same' to the waiters. Most remarkably, our head of school told me, 'You're so brave because you argue with me in English which is not your first language,' when I was complaining in his office for about one hour about my unpleasant experiences with my host families.

However, not all tutors recognised my progress in learning English.

'Most of you are very good and can finish a 150 word essay in fifteen minutes. I saw some of you even just spent five minutes to write a short essay. That's so amazing.' A tutor was looking through our work and checking the length of writing time which she had asked us to write down in the top right corner when we had finished our essay. But she suddenly seemed to be stuck somewhere and was puzzled for a few seconds. She then turned to ask me about the time I spent on the essay.

'Su Yen, I think you must have made a mistake with your writing time. I think you meant to write fifteen, not fifty, didn't you?'

'No, it took me about an hour to finish this essay. But I'm very happy because it would have taken me five hours to write a 150 word essay a month ago.'

'Oh, really! That's great progress then if you said you needed five hours to write this essay a month ago. But, can I ask, how can you manage to study in this level if such a short essay would require so much time for you?'

'That's why I never join any social programmes after school. It's a pity because I don't have any time to join those activities I've already paid for with my tuition fee.'

'Oh, your tutor must be a bad man who always gives

you lots of work.'

'This school is so strict, because I heard that my home-stay-mates are so relaxed in their schools and never have so much homework after school as we have.' I softly pretended to complain about our school, but I actually felt very lucky that I had chosen the right school for the start of my English learning. The truth was that many students saw the course as a sort of holiday on which they would learn a little English, but didn't much mind whether they passed or not.

After a draconian training in my English for three months, we had a final examination which lasted for a whole week at the end. We not only had to answer essay-based questions following lectures and selected readings for the first few days, but also had a small research project to do outside the classroom. We were required to hand in the final report on the research project and to give a fifteen minute presentation afterwards, which was observed and marked by ten tutors. I can't remember how I survived that hellish week, but I remember that my brain just went blank after all those tasks had been done. When my tutor brought my final result and talked about my progress in English learning, I couldn't speak again, not because I was too moved, but because I forgot how to speak English even for a simple word like 'happy'.

'Su Yen, I think you should feel so proud of yourself because you made it. You know, when you were given zero for your first vocabulary test, and couldn't speak a word and couldn't understand me at all at the first week of your study, I was so worried about you and wasn't sure you would pass this course. You amazingly did very well, especially with your speaking; I thought you would need a year to improve to this level you're at now.' My tutor happily handed me my certificate, but I believe he thought I was not happy because I didn't say much.

'Su Yen, you're really good, although you might have expected more for your result. Do you have any plan for your future?'

'I'm not sure where to go for my Master's course, but I'm sure I will go anywhere BUT this country, although I like you, like all our tutors and like our school very much. I was so worried before you showed me my result that I might have had to extend my visa to stay here longer if I didn't pass my exam. Now I can forget about everything in this country and will never want to come back, for ever and ever.'

I thought everything in that strange country was more than enough for me, including all the strange culture, difficult host families and hellish study in a strange environment with no mediaeval buildings and no old books, only surrounded by huge countryside and an ugly city centre, in my impression. When the flight was getting closer to my home town, the images of that strange country were going further away from my immediate memory and have been locked somewhere in my brain for many years. Perhaps I shall realize how much I've learnt from my first experience in a foreign country once I unlock my memory; as a Chinese saying goes 'disillusion starts from being disillusioned'.

♪

'Can you help me to apply for any short course for about two months?' I went to see an educational agent in Taipei a week after I came back from New Zealand. I felt I couldn't carry on my English study in my own country because everyone condemned me so much for my plan to study in Europe.

'Where do you want to do it and what do you want to do?' The agent asked about my preference.

'I have no idea; anywhere. I need some break but I have no place to go. I will appreciate it if you can find the cheapest school for me to pass time in before the next academic year starts.' My words reflected my dejected mood.

'We mainly work in England, with every sort of education, so that I can tell you that London is the most popular place for people to study English, but it's the most expensive place in England.' She told me London would be the best place if I would like to have a short holiday.

'But you said it's the most expensive place, so I may prefer to go somewhere that's near there... How about this place? I don't know why *Oxford* and *Cambridge* are printed in especially big letters, but it seems Oxford is nearer to London than Cambridge according to the map. I think I would like to go there if that place is cheaper than London, but near London.'

I pointed to the place on the map. I felt I had heard the name Oxford somewhere before, but was not sure what it was about. I hoped it would not be like Kaoshiung. And then she told me it was a good choice because Oxford was a pretty town and had a quite good public transport system to go to many famous tourist places.

'When do you want to go?'

'Now, or tomorrow, if you asked when I *want* to go.'

'Tomorrow! But you need a visa; can you give me at least a couple of weeks to have everything done, please?' She was very surprised about my answer and gave me a list of the documents required for my visa preparation.

'Oh, come on. Why do we need to show them these sorts of things? I only want to go there for two months and go to the Netherlands afterwards. I will be more worried if I find I can't get out of their expensive country again; they needn't worry about my staying on illegally.'

I didn't understand why we always had to show so many proofs to obtain a visa since I never could understand why people would choose to be permanent refugees in other countries rather than returning to their decent lives in their home towns. Although I didn't want to stay in my home town, I still didn't want to be a refugee in other countries like so many people I heard about. I assumed then that I would naturally go back to my home town sooner or later once I finished my study in Europe.

When eventually I arrived at Heathrow airport in England, with my ticket and my visa in my hand, I went straight to the place which in my ignorance I had pointed to on the map. I had no idea what my life there would be like and, as I boarded the taxi and left behind the plane and the airport which were the last links with my home, I suddenly felt very alone. I could not simply turn around and catch a coach back to Taipei. England was so much further from Taiwan even than New Zealand was. I felt I was the only forgotten person without any blessing in the world, straying from one strange place to another strange place for years and years with no root. The taxi took me from the airport to Oxford where my school was; I didn't have any enthusiasm for looking around me at this new place in order to remember any route towards anywhere; my sense of direction had been lost some time ago when I took up my vagrant life.

'Is it England or only Oxford that is such a slum area? Cars park along the streets, houses are so small, and their environment is a bit dirty,' I said in my heart. Unfortunately this was my first impression of Oxford as the taxi was driven slowly down a congested road and then turned off into the maze of little streets that make up one of Oxford's old industrial and immigrant quarters. The driver dropped me off by my shabby home-stay house. 'But never mind, I don't need to like this country because I've only come here for a short break,' I said to myself while walking into the house with my Indian host mother. She was not friendly at all, although I tried to be her friend at that moment. I was shocked again and miserable with my tiny room which only had space for a small single bed, a small desk without any drawer and a little wardrobe. And, when the door of the wardrobe was open, the door of the room couldn't be opened at all. 'Lucky I didn't choose here for my intense English study,' I thought. I comforted myself again, but realized how costly this country was. I paid double in this country what I paid in New Zealand,

and I only could stay in such a slum area. But I didn't have any energy to complain since I could not do anything about it anymore.

The first day at my school was even more shocking than these initial impressions of the country. I couldn't find any building that looked like my idea of an educational place, until a passer-by answered me, 'Look, you're here. This is the school you're looking for—'

玖

9

EXPLORATION

探索

'Are you also from Taiwan? I heard you talking about your address which sounds as though it may be in Taiwan.' A tall and pretty lady asked me this as we were all waiting for the arrival exam in a meeting room.

'Yes. Is this your first day here as well? Are you with any friend?' I felt so cosy and quickly moved to sit by her when I heard this familiar accent.

'I came here alone, and you're the first person I've met here apart from my host mother. You can call me Moly if you like. Do you know anywhere in England? I think we should make a plan for every weekend to visit somewhere in this country. Who knows, we may never come back again after we finish our study here.'

We soon became friends and decided the best use of our money would be to visit many places so that we would *tread* everywhere with our own footprints. It meant we would choose to go everywhere on foot if we could. However, neither of us knew anything about England and we would need to have a guide for our visits.

'School will show us around after the exam; maybe we can see from this day-trip where to take a bus or train to where we want to visit for weekends.' I was happy that I had such good company to explore this country and couldn't wait to start learning how to use the public transport efficiently for our travel plan.

And then, quite amazingly, my disappointing first impressions of Oxford were shortly replaced by a beautiful view when I went with our school to the city centre that afternoon. I always remember that day was the 13th of June in 2005; the vista of Oxford High Street magically brought me into a dreaming paradise shining under the sun. 'I would like to see more and more and never want to wake up.' My heart voiced its desire and turned up my glum face into a real smile.

'I never knew Oxford was so beautiful. Are these buildings still in use?' I couldn't believe what I had seen there.

'Yes, they're all university colleges which are student accommodation and dining rooms.' Moly also told me we were lucky because we studied somewhere near Oxford University, even though our school had nothing that could be compared with it.

'I think each stone and gargoyle has its own story as well about the way they built those buildings. I wonder if I could apply for Oxford University after working extremely hard for ten years to improve my English and raise enough money, just to enjoy the architecture in Oxford; and then you will often see a poor old woman holding so many books in her wrinkled hands walking on High Street; that will be me.'

I made this joke rather daringly because I thought that even if the God gave me another life to study for my English, I still couldn't get into Oxford where there was nothing about design or modern architecture that was relevant to my subject and interests at that time.

♩

'Hey, Su Yen, I met a guy in our classroom. He said he is from Taiwan as well. Do you think we should make friends with him because he came here much earlier than us?' Moly excitedly told me that we may have a good guide because that Taiwanese man called Peter looked like a good person.

However, when we asked him about travelling in England, he frowned and said, 'I have no idea about this country because I only come to our school and haven't gone anywhere yet.'

'But you've been here longer than us, you must know somewhere.' Moly didn't give up although his answer sounded not so promising.

'I've only been here a few weeks longer. I'm not local. How can I know where to go and how to get to those places?' He started to look a bit embarrassed at his limited knowledge of England.

'Don't worry; I've prepared a guidebook for you. You can study this book before this weekend.' I couldn't help but laugh very much at Peter's additional assignment from Moly.

Our first step was to see the Changing of the Guard at Buckingham Palace at 9.30 in the morning. Our guide professionally showed us to go this way, that way, turn right, turn left and cross the road; after one hour of this we finally we arrived there by 9 AM.

'Wow, it's not near at all, but we made it.' I had thought Peter was so good on finding directions before I realized it only took five minutes from Victoria Station to Buckingham Palace when I went there a second time with other friends a year later. We then stood by the jam-packed gate to watch this world-famous activity. We were more like chuffs who didn't speak proper English or Taiwanese, but kept playing around with our cameras and making jokes about everything because we thought no one could understand our own language.

'We're so without culture and uneducated here. But I'm so happy that we're enjoying our life like real tourists without any worry, including speaking English. It's also my first time to use my camera to take all these so-called rubbish pictures instead of taking serious pictures for my site surveys.' I was much energized by the way we relaxed ourselves, although people might look at us sneeringly.

'But when we see our results for our English exam later, we might feel chagrined deeply at what we are doing now when we should be studying.' Moly said this laughingly without any real worry on her face.

'So, we should practice our English all the time. Peter, go to ask someone about the way to Tower Bridge. It's a very good chance for you to practice your listening and speaking.' I pushed Peter to ask for help from a passer-by because we had been lost for many hours and had already passed the Big Ben clock tower again and again all the afternoon.

'I know the way to go now. We wasted too much time on walking in a circle around Big Ben for hours.'

We thought he really had found the right way now because we both saw him nodding while the person was pointing somewhere to show him the direction. Nevertheless, strangely we still couldn't reach the famous bridge we intended to go to.

'Peter, are we still lost around Big Ben?' I couldn't believe why we still couldn't see the bridge because I thought possibly we had walked miles.

'Don't worry, just follow me, and you will see it in a minute,' he answered me, quite confidently.

'I don't believe it's so far away and takes more than one hour to get there. Can you tell me what the person told you just now?' Moly showed her doubt and was considering finding the way herself.

'Oh, he said something like turn right or left and something about corners … I forget. But I think he always pointed in that direction, so it should be somewhere towards there.' He waved vaguely with his hand, pointing at an unseen place. I had no idea whether we would ever get there with all our energy burning out.

'We should take a ferry to go back to Big Ben and go back to Victoria Station by underground because it's fun to try anything new here.' Moly and I both liked this idea, to go back by water and underground in case we might get lost again and arrive at Big Ben at midnight and see Oxford's sunrise next morning.

But overall we had experienced so many different and rich things only in a day, although we went back with blisters on our feet and worn-out shoes.

We decided to study the map more carefully in order to see another part of London where we hadn't had time to look around on the first visit. More smartly, we prepared many plasters and some water for our second journey to London. We happily visited many museums and galleries as normal tourists would do in a morning to try to gain just a superficial understanding through cursory observation.

'We must go to the British Museum this afternoon to see how much treasure English people robbed from the world.' Moly told us the well-known joke about the abundant collections from all over the world in the Museum. We then looked at the map for the way to walk there and discussed it for some time to make sure we would arrive at the Museum efficiently.

'Should we ask someone here to make sure of our direction first?' Moly said that the best ways were all on our mouths and could be more useful than a map, so she went to ask a local person about the direction.

'Do you have a map? I can show you the way on a map which is easier to explain,' the man replied to her gently.

'Map, yes, we have a map. Peter, can you show him the map.'

'Map? Oh, I thought it was in my bag, but I can't see it now; so strange.'

'We just took the direction from the map and discussed it in the café five minutes ago, and then we came out immediately. How can we lose our map?'

'So, the map you were carrying for the whole day only appeared for five minutes and now is missing again.' The three of us were confused about the missing map and hadn't a clue where we'd left it or what to do now.

'Or I can draw a simple map for you if you have a pen

and a piece of paper because it's a long way from here to the British Museum.' The man then kindly resolved our embarrassing situation, and his drawing of the map helped us to get to the Museum quickly.

The splendid building of the British Museum made a great impression on me and I suddenly forgot how to feel tired when I walked in and saw the great round library just inside the main door. 'Wow, I wish my English can be good enough to read those books one day! How can English people collect so many beautiful books and keep them in such a good condition? I envy the English so much because they have so many classical books everywhere.' I think I was inspired to study hard by seeing so many books through the windows of this grand library, even though only for a few minutes. We then became tourists again, taking pictures of the many statues and putting our heads on the headless stone lions to make funny pictures for ourselves. We didn't mind so much when people laughed at us or looked at us as though we were naughty children. Sometimes, we tried to read the explanation cards beside the exhibits, but quickly gave up and turned to play again because there were too many new words for us to guess. It was so much fun that we spent most of our time on playing everywhere in London and didn't intend to see anything in particular.

It might seem strange to say, 'We've been to London several times and trod on its land everywhere when we first came to England; but we didn't see much of London apart from Big Ben'. Nonetheless, we indeed enjoyed so much our worry-free holiday in our childish way.

Without knowing very much about each other, the three of us had met in England, probably having different reasons for leaving our home towns to look for a new start. We found each other like lost geese getting back into the migrating formation, and we flew over London just to escape the unhappiness of where we were from. This short flight of only three geese gave us such an unforgettable support to face the many coming days living in a totally strange place, and also an everlasting happiness to remember this unusual start in experiencing English culture without even knowing many English words. Sadly, I am the only goose who stayed eventually, but the desire to understand what we saw on those happy days overcame my fear of facing hard times alone without any companions. When they had gained their Master's degrees my friends would leave with the happy memories of England to take to their home towns, while I determined to stay after such a happy start which was a constant encouragement for me not to give up halfway since I chose rather to live in reality and not in memories.

♪

Bitterly, just as it seemed to be merging into reality, my dream was destroyed. I was given a low grade in the English standard for Master's level after two months of my study in England. But that was not an impossible problem because I could soon improve my level a second time, as many people did. Better still, however, my grade was just good enough to get me on to one of the excellent pre-Master's courses which universities run for overseas students, so I could leave that private language school which had seemed so awful for me. The big problem, however, was money.

All my time in England I had been hoping some magic would happen to help me, or perhaps the most impossible thing was to expect my father would change his mind and support his daughter after all, as so many Chinese fathers did. But he did not, and no magic happened for me at all; with scarcely enough money left for my ticket home I had no choice but to go back to Taiwan, compelled by his will.

Having flown home, broken-winged, with only little achievement to show for my rebellion against my Chinese family I never imagined that I would be able to choose to go to England again. Then, a thing most bitter: I received an email from my Russian friend who told me that she had just arrived in England for her dream and would like to celebrate our two dreams in Europe together. She had arrived on the exact day I had returned to my home town. I cried for hours as though I would die. This was not because I missed my friend. It was because when we had promised we would meet again in Europe we both knew it was a promise to ourselves to live our dreams. And I was not there.

When I had almost lost my dream and had just been forced to return to my country, with several serious problems, my friend's message inspired me so much that, unbelievably, I went straight to another educational agent in the hope that she could find a suitable place to fit my need properly. I had decided that, somehow, I would find a way to go back to England as soon as possible.

♩

'I don't want to study at any language school or live with any host family anymore. But I think it's too late to apply for a Master's course because the academic year at university has started and I have to take a pre-session course for two months to meet the English standard for the Master's level.' I told my agent that I knew it was not easy to deal with this situation if I wanted to go abroad right away.

'Where do you want to go and what do you want to do then?' She asked me the normal questions, as my previous agent had asked me before.

'I would like to study a subject relevant to architecture or urban design around Oxford or anywhere near Oxford.' I was probably not so clear about my subject because I did not know much about the British education system which might be completely different to that of Taiwan. 'But please,' I said, 'Don't suggest to me anything like *that* language school again.'

'It sounds as though you've been to Oxford already. Why did you change your agent?' She told me she was curious about the reason I had come to her now because it seemed I had used another agency before.

'Two reasons. First, she sent me to the most expensive school in Oxford although I told her I wanted to choose the cheapest school there because I didn't need to study intensely after New Zealand. Second, she wasn't helpful at all when I had problems with *that* school and she simply passed on my complaints to those bloody school directors. They easily smothered my complaints with their perfect native language when my English wasn't strong enough to defend myself.' I wasn't sure if she believed me, but I felt strongly that I had been wronged there.

'I would be grateful if you don't mind telling me about your experiences at your language school in Oxford because it's good for me to hear more opinions from students. Most importantly, I can tell you that you're not the first person who has come to me and said the same thing. I do wonder why students all complain about *that* school.' She smiled as she spoke. She said she didn't dare send students there anymore since she had been listening to so many unpleasant stories from them.

I didn't quite know how to start talking about my long story there, but I knew I had to tell it if I wanted to show her my true needs for my study in future. 'You know, the appearance of the school is not good enough to represent its educational function, which is disappointing to start with, but this is not the main reason for me to complain. The quality of teaching there was terribly bad and not professional at all when compared with my learning experience in New Zealand. The school directors called me to their offices for private meetings twice and asked me why they had heard from my agent about my unpleasant life there.'

'So they did care about your feelings and tried to talk to you privately.' She naturally assumed a positive attitude; maybe she thought I was just complaining too much.

'Oh, you can have your own judgement after you've heard how they answered my questions. I asked them why they called only me to their offices, but not other students who were all not happy with their school. They said, "*We only want to talk to you because we heard you posted an article online to grumble about your life here*". So I told them that they changed tutors almost every week and none of the tutors was really responsible for the progress of our study. How do you think they replied to me?' I asked my agent what would be the normal way to resolve this problem.

'I have no idea, but it doesn't sound good for students to have to change tutors all the time.' She also said it was not right if the directors couldn't give a good reason for that.

'They told me, "*Because you changed your classes so often, of course you would always meet different tutors!*" I explained that I changed classes to *follow* my tutor, because I was not happy with the new tutors; but when I changed to a different class and did feel happy for a few days, then the old tutor was moved again.'

'It's amazing to hear that.'

'They then asked me if there was anything else that annoyed me. I told them the whole school was like an open air camp jammed with refugees because they took hundreds of students every week in such a small house which was just as big as a family house. We didn't have any place to have lunch which was always insipid and twice as expensive in school as outside. Do you know what their answer was again?' I thought no one would be able to imagine what I heard from those directors.

'I really have no idea about what they would say, but it does sound so bad.' She showed her sympathy with me even though she couldn't truly imagine what the situation was there.

'They smoothly answered me with, "*You know, prices are always going up and never will be going down; and we're an educational place rather than a restaurant to provide good food to people. We are so surprised to hear you say there is no space for you to have lunch because we see students sitting on the ground everywhere around the school and they seem to be very happy to enjoy their lunch*".'

'I was dumbfounded when I heard their reply. We sat on the ground because we didn't have any proper chairs to sit by a real table for lunch. We bought food at the school because the school was too remote and there was nowhere around for us to go for lunch. Of course, some students were lucky because their host families would prepare sandwiches for them everyday. But mine never did anything like that.'

When my agent didn't say much at first, I thought perhaps she was a bit shocked by my attitude to the school, but then she told me that she wouldn't dare now to send any student to that evil place again which seemed like a modern poor-house in the movie *Oliver Twist*.

'How about your host family? Did you have a good time with them?' She tried to change the topic and maybe thought I might feel better if I stopped talking about my unhappiness at the language school.

'I and my home-stay-mates were never full and always had to pay for ourselves to get more food from supermarkets even though food was officially included in our payment for accommodation; but my host family complained that the school didn't pay enough to them. I told those directors I thought they already knew that the host family was unfriendly because, even before I arrived in England, they re-directed me from another family to this one. This made me suspicious and I soon found out why it was.' I felt even worse when talking about my experience at the home-stay house.

'What do you mean they had known this?' Now she was confused again with my story.

'Many previous students told me they moved out from that house because they didn't like that family who never provided enough food for them. But our director told me, "*I'm so surprised again to hear you say so because no one told us this before*". I didn't believe them because the school rules stated that we must have good reasons to apply for the change of our host-family. How could they say that they didn't know the family was not good when all students had moved out for the same reason? They then told me, "*Students are never honest and they always told us it was because it was too far away from the school so that they had to move to somewhere nearer*". I was so surprised and almost lost my words, and asked them how they defined the distance as being too far, because it only took two minutes to walk from that family to our school.'

'Your previous agent should have helped you to complain to the British Council because these problems were serious indeed.' She then told me what I should do if I met any unfair situation again in the future.

'Those problems *were* serious, but the craziest thing in those private meetings was their talk about *my letter* which they brought up at the beginning of these meetings. I asked them to show me *my letter* which they insisted was written by me. I said I would like to read what I was supposed to have written because I thought I must have improved my English so much to be able to write a letter of complaint so efficiently using their poor computers which always shut down automatically every fifteen minutes. And I must be very fast when I had to finish the article by standing in front of the computer with the pressure of so many people queuing behind me.' I told her my final request at the meetings was always to read my letter which I hadn't read myself before.

'Did the letter show your name on it?'

'They told me that they couldn't show me the letter because they couldn't read it since it was written in Chinese. I was so shocked and finally chose to be silent. How could they insist on saying it was written by me when they did not seem to know a single Chinese character?'

My new agent then told me that possibly I could sue them for the calumniation in that situation. But the past was past, and everything I told her was only to help her to know what I wanted for my further successful study because I really did miss Oxford, even though the beginning of my study life there had been such a huge nightmare.

I think my new agent was quite clever and considerate about fitting students' different needs. Efficiently, she found a place which had a good learning environment, resources, tutors and working staff; altogether the description sounded very good for me. The most attractive thing was that I didn't have to stay with any host family anymore, which I think she had kept in mind as one of my requests after hearing my stories. I was so touched when she called me to have a look at the information about the place she had found for me since my subject was not so usual and common at all and could only be found around Oxford.

'Wow, it's in Oxford! No one told me this information when I was in Oxford a few months ago. All the information looks so relevant to what I want indeed. I can't wait to apply for this university.' I felt a big hope beginning to appear in my life when the name Oxford Brookes University came to my eyes.

'But I'm not sure if I can help you to get in to their Master's course because the university told me they don't guarantee anything even though you could be qualified for a pre-Master's course there. The advantage for you is that you can take some undergraduate modules which you can select either for your own interests or according to your subject. In the meantime, you're allowed to use every facility of the university's. I'm sure you will be quite satisfied because they have a very good and sophisticated library which has abundant books, journals and probably all the current information about your subject which is taught by one of their core departments.' She explained every detail about the environment and the course for me and reminded me that I shouldn't expect much from language teaching there because it is a university and not a language school. I appreciated her most when she helped me to negotiate with the course leader so that I didn't need to pay any deposit in advance and could just bring my tuition fee with me because the term had started, so that I could come along even before I had raised enough to fund my study.

However, the world is so small and unimaginable. On the plane I unexpectedly met an old classmate from the same language school. When I told her about the strange letter and those private meetings with the directors she laughed so much and told me that the letter was written by her and she had signed her name without using my name at all.

That was my experience, and maybe things have improved now. However, looking back, I think I have learned to thank that school precisely for their bullying behaviour towards me in the beginning. Otherwise perhaps I could not have appreciated and enjoyed so much every single second at Oxford Brookes University and could not be so full of gratitude towards my university for providing me with such a good learning environment and an en-suite bedroom with very good service and the best equipment. I should admit that I didn't want to leave my room at all ever since the first second I moved in, and I started missing my room so badly even after only a half an hour shopping trip to a nearby supermarket. I think it can be said that 'after miserable suffering comes true happiness' in this situation, just like *Oliver Twist* who could start his good education and upbringing only after being ill treated by so many so-called benevolent benefactors.

拾
10
LEARNING
學習

'We shall meet *somewhere* in Europe, *sometime*, although we never know when and where we're going for our future.'

It was a timeless appointment I had made with my Russian friend with whom I had studied for three months in New Zealand before we departed to our countries. I came to England with our farewell words in mind.

It's so heavy to think about these two words, *somewhere* and *sometime*, which seem to suggest so many seen and unseen difficulties in our ways to pursue our dreams. The only thing we could wish was to meet in Europe soon because it would mean we both had overcome our most difficult problems to study abroad.

Then, amazingly, we met in Oxford for our Christmas in that same year. We hugged without a word outside Oxford station; maybe we were not sure what to say for a start because it was too soon to believe that we had made it to England in half a year.

'Shall we have a cup of coffee on our way home? This time it's for celebrating our reuniting in Europe, it's not for escaping from that boring learning centre.'

'Hah, you still remember our story in New Zealand. Sorry that I rejected your coffee last time; I'm paying for your cup of coffee for today.'

For the first half an hour we didn't say much to each other and just kept looking around the cosy English coffee shop. I was not sure about her feelings and didn't know what she was thinking; perhaps she felt uncertain too because we were from totally different countries, spoke different languages, and might have different problems in our lives. It was understandable that we might feel somewhat strange since our limited English was our only common language in this strange country.

'Why did you come to England?' I was curious about her decision because she had told me this country would be too expensive for her to study for her Master's degree.

'Oh, don't tell me that you don't know the reason. I received your email a month after we left New Zealand. You told me that you were doing a short language course in Oxford. Your sudden decision surprised me a lot and inspired me to make a decision for myself rather than do nothing in my home town. How could I be so timid about going for my future when my friend had already flown to England?'

'But then I didn't receive your reply till I returned to my country again two months later.'

'Oh, my dear Su Yen, as you have experienced, it's so difficult for us to come here. I had to arrange everything and to raise money for this huge decision. I was never sure that I could get a visa to come. I didn't dare email you until I had my visa and ticket in my hand.'

'Yes, it's so hard,' I sighed, 'When I finally received your email about your arrival in England, I cried as if to die for hours because it was the day I had just arrived in my home town in Taipei and I thought I would never be able to come here again. I thought it was a joke which the God made for me on purpose. How could it happen like in a movie? My friend just arrived in England on the day when I had to go back for money again.' I stopped talking in order to stop my tears coming down from my eyes.

'Did my email call you to come here again?' Perhaps she was surprised that I decidcd to come again to England when I heard she was here.

'Could be. I indeed so wished to fly to meet you here right away; it was so painful for me to read your email in *Taiwan* because I had told you that I would show you my dreaming Oxford when we met. Then I was mad to urge everyone to help me to come again as soon as possible, even though I hadn't enough money on hand yet.'

I thought it would be embarrassing to talk about my poor situation when almost all international students in this country are from rich families. I could not tell her that I had come to England with a one-way ticket and only 2000 English pounds in my purse, all my savings from Taiwan. It was far from being enough even for my pre-Master's course and I had no idea what I could do for that. Nevertheless, I saw her relieved smile as she listened to my story. I knew her smile was not about her sympathy for me, but it gave me a funny feeling that maybe she also had the same problem in her life. She didn't intend to tell me about herself till she had heard my story because she was not sure I would understand the situation. We both comprehended deeply that it could cost our lives to study abroad for our Master's degrees. I am sure, because I was thinking the same thing about her, that she was aware of my poor clothes which were all I could manage to bring with me.

'Were you scared?' She asked this question with a laughing face.

'Were you scared?' I asked back her question.

'Maybe a bit, but not too much to stop me coming here for my dream.'

'We're sitting in the same boat then. I did not dare to imagine my future when I was walking through the customs to go on board. My parents once told me off because they said I was a fool to throw all my money away to a strange country and to become a poor student without any certainty. Now I shall be able to tell my parents that there is another fool like me in the world.' I was in a funny mood, sitting with another crazy person whom I had met on the other side of the world.

'I really can't believe that we travelled to New Zealand only in the beginning of this year, travelled back to our own countries half a year ago; and travelled to England again and again till now we meet here; it's such a long way for us to go to see each other from one side of the earth to another side. I think we're the best in the world because no one could be more stupid than us who paid everything to buy an unpromising future in a foreign country.' She voiced my feeling again as she had done in New Zealand when we were struggling to study in the learning centre after lectures.

What a great and *valuable* Christmas for each of us to know that neither she nor I was the only fool in the world.

I enjoyed my pre-Master's course at first. Not only was it very helpful, but it gave me the hope that I was on my way to do my Master's in England. The university did not charge me any rent for my lovely room for the first three months; it gave me some more time to pray for some magic to come to help me.

Then disaster struck into my life again. I had been worried for some time about how I would be able to afford the pre-Master's course fees when finally the university billed me for all my back rent before the magic appeared. That took nearly all my money and I knew then for certain that I would have to go back to my home again, perhaps for ever. I selfishly wanted to sleep to my last breath in my room if it was the only way to keep my soul in the happiest moment forever. I had been unhappy in Taiwan, but I had seen no other life for me there. However, when thinking about Oxford, the most beautiful place in the world for me, I hesitated. I couldn't allow myself to spoil the Oxford air with my poor soul without any positive contribution to the most favourite place of mine. Now I had seen and touched my dream, to live and study among these beautiful buildings and books: and for a second time I must leave my dreaming life. I decided to try the most impossible thing, of getting some help from my father by pleading to him as though from hell to heaven. At last, he was *forced* by my determined mind to pay for my second term and accommodation, but not for me to eat.

This time, however, I was even more determined. My father would not give me any more money to go to England, as he firmly claimed, but as I now had a place on a Master's course in England I was able to arrange a government loan with a bank in Taipei. For a third time I travelled to England, to study for my Master's degree. The English have a saying, 'Third time lucky'. I was sure now my future life would be in England.

So eventually my Russian friend and I both entered our Master's degrees several months after we had met in Oxford, but at different universities. However, I lost contact with her before the end of the academic year; I once dreamt that she could not resolve her problems and finish her study. I'm so afraid to think maybe that's the reason for her to disappear from my world. I do hope my dream was not true; and we will meet somewhere, sometime again soon.

♪

I normally choose to shut my mind from the outside world and only enjoy immersing myself in the ancient air surrounding old books and old buildings. But sometimes my flatmate, Xue, does bring some questions to wake me up a bit to remember the world still contains many different sorts of people around us.

'Su Yen, I was quite unhappy the whole day in the lab. The European girl I was working with didn't sleep again! We had so much to do and I told her I had arranged everything. She just gave me a tiring face and two dark circles under her eyes.' Xue told me that she was annoyed by the situation with her colleague at the lab.

'Why didn't she sleep then?' I asked.

'I really didn't know what to say. She spent a whole evening cooking for us. That's absolutely fine. But she did something so peculiar to me; she stayed up with a guy from our lab who barely talked to her once or twice, so that she had no time to sleep. How could I work with her if she was expecting me to finish all the heavy work the next day as though she could only do simple things? At least this is not my way to do science.' Xue looked at me with such a childishly angry face.

'I have no idea why you're so surprised about this; I knew your male colleague would stay with her last night.' I knew my flatmate had some doubts about my judgment in this case because I had only seen her colleagues once in my life.

'Love at first sight? They barely spoke before last night's dinner. How can love come so quickly? It is beyond my imagination. If you are right, are Europeans so romantic like those in movies; they don't really need to know each other to love?' She raised her voice to a funny level.

Three weeks later she came home with a puzzled look.

'Su Yen, you are proved right again. You are always like a fortune teller to me these days. They were together since that night.'

'Are you interested in what I saw when you left for an hour to go to the swimming course that night?' I didn't want to gossip about other people's lives unless there was something meaningful for someone who wanted to learn. 'Your European girl showed her drawings to us after you left for that swimming lesson nearby. She described gloomily how she drew them in the midnight when she couldn't sleep—'

My flatmate interrupted me before I could finish the whole story. 'Do you mean those pencil drawings of naked guys? I hid those drawings for her into a book because I thought she might have misplaced them. It would be too embarrassing for the man guests to see them.'

'Why are you so shocked like a hen with one chicken? Let me finish telling you this story.' It was so amusing when I saw the open-eyed face of my flatmate. I then changed my way to describe that situation. 'That night, at the dinner, I just caught one eye contact between your colleagues; I knew instantly a romance will happen once I read the eye.'

'Which eye?' According to Xue's puzzled face I could see she hadn't entered the story yet.

'Come on, can you please have more imagination on love? How can I continue this romance if you always interrupt me like this?' I complained, trying to bring her feeling in to the story.

'OKay, I'm trying to understand what you're saying now. But can you describe things more straight and clearly? Your roundabout explanation puzzles me a lot.'

I was also puzzled then. I didn't know whether it's a difference between designers and scientists, or it was because she was too young to see things. Of course the second reason was not possible since she was about the same age as me.

'I start again. Your female colleague talked about her drawings of those naked guys with her eyes peeping to your male colleague who also returned his special solicitude when he caught a glimpse of loneliness from that girl. That guy then told that girl how to draw nicely with an artist's heart. They enjoyed exchanging their magic eyes between each other and the rest of the people like me were seen only as air in that room. Do you get it now? Is it easier for you to understand the situation?' But I think she didn't quite get it because her face didn't show any sympathy with my explanation of the story.

'Am I too Chinese? Or I am too naïve? I thought I was protecting her when I hid those drawings. Is this the so called fast-food love? I thought it could never happen outside a Hollywood movie. Just one catch of eyes, that's all? I don't understand; I really don't understand at all.'

'Oh, my dear friend, it is not a Western and Eastern thing any more. It does happen everywhere. Lust or love at first sight, can we really define it? It might be romantic for some people to pursue love anywhere anytime; but it might be strange for us when we seek to keep our innocence, our traditional culture and moral values, away from the popular and mainstream, and value living our lives to the full as happily as we can. Various reasons lead to the world changing over time. But please don't try to criticize the world and just keep your own opinions in your mind because there is no side line between right and wrong.' I had no idea how to help her to understand that the world was not simple enough to be described in *straight* and *clear* words. At least, things often are too complicated for me to explain in words. Sometimes I did wonder if it was not right to open her eyes and minds to the outside world beyond her lab and her scientific text books, although it might be better for her to see things normally.

It is not necessary that our innocence should be lost when we grow up; but our innocence often can be destroyed deeply by other people when our journeys to a real world start.

♪

After a series of stormy condemnations of my life for many days, my father helped me eventually to return the money which I had borrowed from the bank for my study in England, without any more complaint. This implausible enigma not only greatly surprised me, but puzzled me for a long time. I cudgelled my brains to discover the real answer, and sometimes talked with my friend about this unbelievable situation.

'Can you believe that my father suddenly decided to pay back my loan to the bank?'

'Because he is your father. Just believe he still loves you very much. I can't see any reason for you to think so much about this.'

'I wouldn't want to doubt his love if he was not so cruel to me for many years. For example, he didn't help me at all when I couldn't even afford a meal and owed the university my accommodation fees for the whole term in the first year of my study here. It took me so long to beseech him to sign as my guarantor for the loan from the bank for my study. And he firmly told me a hundred times that he would never pay back the money for me although he knew my life here was so difficult, because he insisted that I should be responsible for my own choice to come here.'

'Maybe he finally was affected by your perseverance for your dream, so that he changed his mind and decided to help you a bit.'

'If this is the answer, it is not my father at all. I mean this possibility is just not a reasonable way to explain my situation because I have known him since I was born.'

'Anyway, he must be proud of you very much …'

I understood why she said that, according to the natural love between parents and children. But I interrupted her talking about this natural reason which was too normal to be worth our discussing it more.

'I don't have any doubt on this point, but when things relate to his money, nothing, including a great dream or effort, can soften his mind to spend a penny on anyone else but himself, since he has never believed in the goodness of people since a long time ago. He would think once he pays a penny for a start, he would need to pay countless pounds in future till he goes into bankruptcy. Can you understand why I'm so puzzled over this thing, that he paid back my entire loan at once without any complaint?'

We considered many possibilities, such as that maybe he had just won a large amount of money from a lottery, or perhaps he finally realized that my future was sort of promising with two Master's degrees, or he was reformed because the God went into his dream at night to tell him that he should give his daughter a hand for the greatest achievement to change the world in future.

And then we finally found the most practical reason for his changed attitude.

'Maybe he is worried that you won't go back to see him forever or that you will let your bad debt slide and become one of the criminals in the wanted list soon, which would make him lose face seriously. So it was better for him to return the money for you rather than lose his credit because he was your guarantor.'

'That's the most possible reason then.' I thought my puzzle had been resolved when we couldn't think of any more reasonable answer for why my father suddenly changed his attitude and willingly paid all the money back to the bank for me.

However, life is always full of surprises outside of our imagination. I changed my mind to believe the final answer we found when I talked with my father several months after he cleared my debt.

'I had a chat with my father just now.'

'You talk to him on-line quite often these months; it seems your cold war is finished. That's so nice to hear.'

'Yes, his attitude is getting softer and gentler recently. So we remain talking and laughing as if nothing had happened before. But I just heard an interesting story from my father.'

'What's that?'

'My father walks his dog every morning and evening on the mountain near home. He has made many friends there and sometimes they chat to each other about daily life. He told me that one of his dog-walking mates was in a bad mood for a long time so that the man unexpectedly decided to retire from his work because he couldn't face the pain at all. He told my father that his daughter had been a very good student and worked so hard at university, but he had been so shocked when she told him about a credit loan of 30,000 pounds she owed the bank. However, he was shocked again when he discovered it was not just 30,000 pounds, but was more than 50,000 pounds debt and she had spent it all on a disappearing guy as though everything was sinking in the sea without any sound. The man regretted so much that he didn't agree to send his daughter abroad when she asked to study in another country several years ago, and he thought this tragedy might not have happened at all if he had agreed at the first time.'

'I think my father just acted as a listener to hear the story before he began to realize the daughter of the man was just like me, his own daughter, and had the same dream. He might feel for the man in the beginning, but was not so shocked till he saw the entire truth like seeing the iceberg from the surface to the hidden part under the sea. I think he became aware of the difference between that man's daughter and me who ever had the same dream and met the same difficulty in the beginning, but made such different decisions in the end.'

'So he might be so touched by your remorseless heart for pursuing your dream.'

'No, I don't think so. I think he suddenly felt I had treated him very well with only 15,000 pounds debt in the bank and all this money only spent on my study for two Master's degrees, compared to throwing over 50,000 pounds to a useless guy who then went off with another woman; so my little money became like nothing for him to worry about, and he just went to the bank to clear my debt at once without any hesitating.'

'Are you sure it's the real reason?'

'People often keep silence with the true answer in their mind, and only wrangle to defend their right when they can't even be utterly convinced by themselves. My father didn't complain at all after paying back my whole loan to the bank and hid this story for many months till I made a key point about the credit loan to make him argue with me. He then became in a funny mood, which I felt from his tone of voice while talking, and he was bursting to talk about this surprising story. So, I think that's the main reason for him to return the money for me. *He thought I was a good bargain!*'

I remembered my Turtle once told me in my dream that he knew how to make my father take his money from his pocket to pay towards my study. I thought it was a joke, or perhaps I dreamt about this just because I worried about my debt too much. But now I rather believe my Turtle magically arranged this surprising meeting to compel my father to repay my debt for me on time.

♩

My fervent mediaeval dream would probably have been soon extinguished if it was true that no Santa Claus really exists to distribute gifts for Christmas.

I was feeling a bit lost concerning my life when I finished the course for my first Master's, and then went straight to study for my second Master's course after only a two-week break. I had thought I consistently had a dream and hadn't given it up even with so many uncertainties in my life. Then, by the end of my first Master's course, I wasn't sure anymore about what indeed I stood out for and pursued since my future seemed to be all at sea. Whereas it might be my fine interest to study the course for my second Master's I didn't know how I could make up my mind to enjoy another hard-working year with a brand-new subject with not only abstruse English culture but also a huge amount of strange vocabulary which I had never learnt in my life. If it was not for the winter vacation between two semesters, I possibly would have failed some of my modules when I was so weary and felt somewhat hopeless.

Perhaps this second Master's course naturally brought me so much closer to the God through the many field trips to visit historic buildings, including churches and cathedrals, almost every week to learn the work of restoration and conservation. At nearly the end of the first semester, the God handed over to a Santa Claus the task to choose Christmas gifts for me to have a happy English Christmas and to pass through the haze of my life quickly before I could fail to get my degree.

All surprises were hidden in festive wrapping paper, and were unveiled to me as I unpacked one after one my Christmas gifts which were attentively chosen for me by my Santa Claus. A fragment of an elaborate Western painting on the cover of a book was suddenly revealed to my eyes when my fingers carefully pulled away the beautiful paper.

CIVILISATION: the word was written in plain capitals above the painting of the *School of Athens* by Raphael; it greeted me and straightaway called all my memories in to my mind. I never could have imagined that I would be so close to the Western arts and could immerse my life in the ancient air in the way that I have been experiencing in England; even the mediaeval images from movies and books had been gradually hiding away in my inner heart while I was ageing. Now my sleeping soul was suddenly reviving again like a flower budding in the fresh air of spring. What a huge circle I had been running for a dozen years and had finally reached the original point again, but in such a different place which is full of the cultural treasure I've been looking for from my childhood.

Dear Roy

Thanks for everything. I had a happy Christmas and New Year with those poems and pictures. You mentioned your worry for my studies. However, I did so much for those other things for several reasons. Firstly, it's just so rare and valuable that I can learn English culture with an English gentleman who is always so kind and patient. Secondly, I thought maybe I can have a holiday from Christmas to New Year, so I want to learn something more interesting that I couldn't do during the busy semester. Thirdly, I learnt not only about those works, but also the way of thinking, the concept of study and the attitude of learning (or maybe more).

It is said, 'There is no royal road to learning'; and Chinese people believe that 'All things have hard beginnings'. In my thought, it is a good start for me to think about my learning style through studying my interests; and of course it takes time (is it a good excuse?).

Speaking of my other studies, I found some websites with glossaries for architecture, landscape and mediaeval art and architecture (they even have illustrations of words and provide pronunciations for learners). Besides, I've borrowed some books from the library for pre-reading of my modules. So, please do not worry about me, I will always remember what I should do first. Thank you for your concern about me and for correcting my English all the time.

Dear Su Yen

I do find your comments interesting: for example, 'There is no royal road to learning'. Does this mean even a king must be humble if he wants to learn. Actually I think a teacher must be humble too. Do you have a saying about that? A teacher should *share* knowledge, not *give* knowledge; there is a subtle difference.

Your comment once that, 'The most beautiful thing in our life is the one we will never obtain,' reminded me of this little poem by Blake.

Eternity, by William Blake (1757–1827)

He who bends to himself a joy
Does the wingèd life destroy:
But he who kisses the joy as it flies
Lives in eternity's sunrise.

Dear Roy

Since the beginning of this semester I have suffered from group work for a long time and felt stressed even when the assignments were completed. Everything was especially out of control when I didn't have my computer for a month; all data are in the computer, so I had to spend too much time arranging my work again. But my soul is reviving now and I have started the essay on repair at Hampton Court again, although that assignment is still very difficult for me. I think my reviving speed is too slow, but I hope I've learnt how to deal with problems more efficiently.

During break I noticed that little poem, *He who bends to himself a joy*, in your email and smiled. When I read this little poem at the first time, I didn't feel it's so strong. But now it reminds me about my attitude of life. The difference between 'cherish' and 'bend' joy makes for different levels of enjoyment for life. This maybe also can be reflected in my friendships between peers.

Dear Su Yen

I like your idea of your soul 'reviving'; I think of a plant which has been drooping from lack of water and now is beginning to grow upright and strong again.

William Blake is said to have seen things with great intensity, with an intense sense of their being. We can feel this sometimes when a stone or rock or tree may seem to have intense significance and meaning, though what that significance is we cannot explain. He believed there was a spiritual reality behind the physical reality which we see, and that the spiritual reality was in fact more real than the physical. His drawings of things express this spiritual reality rather than the physical and so, unlike some artists who may draw spiritual things in a vague mystical sort of way, his work is noted for its precision, detail and exceptional exaggerated strength.

Here is part of another poem by Blake:

Auguries of Innocence, by William Blake (1757–1827)

> *To see a World in a Grain of Sand,*
> *And a Heaven in a Wild Flower,*
> *Hold Infinity in the palm of your hand,*
> *And Eternity in an hour.*

I don't quite know what people mean by 'spiritual' these days, except that I think it is something in our own minds and expresses the wonder and connectedness of things. But here are some thoughts. In most cultures there is a very early stage of religion known as 'animism'; it is when people believed that every rock, stream or tree has its own spirit which might speak to you. For those people the whole world was full of magic. These ideas continued long into Christian times. It certainly made a walk in the country very exciting. This is shown in the Greek myths, although by that time people had human-like gods as well.

Coming to more abstract and human ideas, the Ancient Greek philosophers such as Plato and Socrates believed every person, possibly every thing, had a soul. When we are born a soul comes from some 'perfect place' where it lived happily, but then it forgets. When we see beauty or love we recognize it because it reminds our soul of that perfect place. Things in this world are imperfect, but we strive to recreate that perfection which we left behind. This is part of Plato's Theory of Ideal Forms; it had a practical application in Greek architecture where stonemasons *distorted* forms so that they would *appear* perfect, though it is possible the stonemasons had the idea before the philosophers thought of it. In Asia the minimalist Buddhist Zen gardens of Japan and China use very basic informal compositions of rocks and gravel. At one level these are very boring, but it is possible to experience intense symbolic significance when looking at them; this is vividly described in a book called *Yet Being Someone Other* by Laurens Van der Post.

I know you understand something of this because you said you preferred old books, 'Because they speak to me'. I liked that.

♪

Probably I should have been awakened already by my first visit to the British Museum three years ago, but I was not sufficiently aware or receptive at that time. The British Museum collects and displays many world treasures and grandly shows us the world's civilisation. I have admired the English ever since my visit. I think English people have mostly been tolerant and have respected various cultures from all over the world for hundreds of years. They have protected all the cultural properties very well, as invaluable treasure like their own, not only for themselves but also for the preservation of the progress of civilisation. They have done even more than any other of the countries from which those cultural characters originated. I'm sure if those cultural properties had not been moved to England *in certain perhaps unusual ways*, we wouldn't have a chance to see so much even though we could possibly travel around the whole earth. I didn't dare say so at that moment to others because I was not sure people would agree with me or might not see me as a traitor, but I voiced in my mind, 'they have done very well for the world as far as the conservation of *civilisation* is concerned'.

This was the beginning of my changing my view of England. I had started thinking seriously about changing my choice of study for my Master's degree in England in order to know more about the history and culture of this country. My childhood romantic dream of castles and princesses, and my grown-up thirst for a true understanding and knowledge of Western art and civilisation collided and sprung out bright sparkles of fire of hope on that Christmas day. The beautiful feeling in my mind led me to be brave again and strengthened my courage to explore more in this dreaming environment I'm living in. However, this exploration has never been an easy one and I started so patiently by looking up the difficult and strange words in the dictionary one by one to understand the sentences little by little while learning to study Clark's *Civilisation*. Without a dreaming mind, there could have been no pleasure in doing this word jigsaw puzzle. In that first year I could only feel the book; only later, and after much study, could I begin to understand its essence.

拾壹

11

BUILDINGS
建築

'I'm not full and I want more and more to fulfil my soul.' My heart brought out its desire and helped me to overcome all trouble such as language barriers and cultural differences which I met during study. It was quite cruel that difficulties in reality sometimes destroyed my confidence so much and depressed me a great deal. I thus at times almost wanted to give up taking any trouble to go on for my dream. For example, it's not easy to forget my first three-day field trip with our class in another part of England.

From the morning, as I departed with several colleagues in their car, the normal greeting and chatting started to challenge my listening and speaking during the whole time travelling on the motorway. The situation became more painful as we intensively visited many places within three days. However, the most difficult part was not that I couldn't catch enough information from lectures and explanations on site, it was in every break time, such as in the formal dinner, or in a pub at night when everyone seemed to relax after a long day trip. Although it was so exciting for me to learn English culture by placing myself in this group of English people, I never could fully enjoy gathering with them in the same room, including sharing a dormitory in a youth hostel. Everything was just so foreign for me that I had to concentrate very carefully all the time on what they were talking about until, at last, I was back in my own bedroom after what seemed like the year-long trip.

The strongest motivation for me to keep going was my feeling for the mediaeval air which allowed me to enjoy my own world as if I were entering many movie scenes with not only my imagined stories for the buildings, but also all the interesting technical knowledge of preservation and repair work illustrated by professionals on the sites during our visit. Therefore I was not completely unhappy or stuck too much on the trouble of language and cultural background. Nevertheless, the killing process of learning was still gradually consuming my courage to pursue my dream in this country, till Santa Claus came on time to relight my flame of exploring the Western mythical world.

I now quite like to believe that Christmas doesn't just have its religious meaning of the coming of the Good Shepherd, but contains some special meanings for people like me to revive ourselves when Santa Claus comes. Another surprise came to me after Christmas when a friend introduced me to work in the shop at the University Church of St Mary the Virgin in Oxford. I thought I was getting closer to the God and I have been receiving more blessings while working there.

♪

By the year of my second Master's course I enjoyed so much mixing with our class everywhere, including having lunch in English pubs, and now chatting normally with them during our trips. If it could be imagined that my decision to go to New Zealand to start my life in a foreign country was like the phoenix flying to the fire, my life in England could be the metaphor of that phoenix rising again from ashes.

'Su Yen, you're so happy in the pictures. I never saw you smile like this when you were in Taiwan. I can see that you're truly happy in England.' A colleague of mine from university in Taiwan was so surprised about my change when she was looking at my pictures from England.

'Those pictures are a record of my study in England. Did you see I was making a clay wall in a traditional way? It was so stirring for me to touch the materials and to make a wall with my hands. I learnt to make lime-cement mortar, make a brick wall, a straw and clay wall, and a thatch roof; and you know, I also learnt to make my own baked brick, iron nail and hook on our trips.' I talked excitingly to my friend about my colourful study life in England.

'Wow, it sounds so different from our life here. I can't imagine that your life could be so great in England because I thought language would be a huge barrier for our staying in another country.' What she was concerned about was quite right, and it was the main difficulty that put off most people from going abroad.

'Oh, come on, you can enjoy it a lot once you get used to the idea, the way a chicken talks to a duck.' I answered her easily because I didn't want to let her know my language problem could still be a balk to bother me.

'You're so optimistic. But I still can't imagine how you

can manage it when you don't understand the language.'

'That's easy. I often reply to them with a smile when I don't understand them. Of course sometimes it's quite embarrassing when people just turn away and never talk to me anymore. I had a hard experience when I was working in a community meeting in the year of my pre-Master's course; I had to ask people in the meeting many times to spell words for me, and then an old gentleman once answered me that, "*this word also has another spelling, i-d-i-o-t*;" everyone was laughing but me. Apart from this, academic people are normally quite friendly to explain everything especially slowly for me to enjoy their activities. I think life in England is interesting because it's always full of flavours for me to feel: sour, sweet or bitter, but never *toxic*, so that I enjoy all different tastes which help me to grow up, but wouldn't make me die.'

'Oh, dear, I would cry many times if I were you there. But I'm so glad that you've found a right place for you to enjoy your life.' She told me that she felt my life in England was so free and happy, as when a fish meets pure water.

I love England because England has Oxford; I love Oxford because Oxford has splendid historic buildings and books. Most importantly, I have been touched so much by all the ways English people use to protect and preserve their own culture. They would try everything to rebuild a historic house by recruiting experts and skilled craftsmen from various fields to join the rebuilding work no matter how much time and money that work might cost. I was impressed that most repair work is done by hand when it's not possible to do it using machines, such as when re-creating specific period architectural details or ornament.

My Master's course in England was quite different to my experience of university in my own country; here it was full of surprises and I was always expecting interesting learning experiences from the course. Our course leader arranged many field trips to many different places so that we could visit various historic buildings as well as practise different traditional building skills for repairing old buildings. I think I was indeed fully educated by listening to our lectures, doing assignments and joining field trips in this true English course.

I never knew before how much passion English people have spent for those marvellous old buildings which are naturally present in our everyday living environment here until I joined the historic conservation group for my study. For example, a short conversation during a visit awakened my interest in their fervour for preserving their culture.

'How could the stained glass survive the wars?' What a smart question that was, raised by someone on one of our site visits who was asking the guide about the mediaeval stained window glass in the building. I was astonished because I never had thought about this in my life. These windows have glass of many colours arranged to make beautiful patterns and pictures.

'They removed the stained glass piece by piece and put the pieces together with the furniture in a safe house far away from the war to avoid it being damaged.'

The answer amazed me so much because I thought people would all have been fleeing to save their lives, but

I never could have imagined that people would *have time* to remove their windows and furniture painstakingly in a war. I once foolishly believed that those ancient buildings stood normally everywhere because there are not so many earthquakes in England and because no one intends to demolish those buildings in this country. Gradually, I have come to admire English people more and more profoundly since I have been learning more and more from them.

On the other hand, I sometimes don't understand the way English people destroy their own historic character which has survived so impressively for hundreds of years. One day our tutor arranged for us to visit a historic building which had been successfully, or so everyone said, converted to a new use: she told us we would see Oxford Castle. I so looked forward to that. This was why I enjoyed that course so much. I knew parts of the castle were very old. I had often walked past the great green castle mound, or *motte*, which was put up quickly by the Normans soon after they had conquered Saxon England in the eleventh century, more than nine hundred years ago. And I had seen the old tower, all that remains of the twelfth century church. I had read too of how Queen Matilda, besieged in the castle in 1142, had been lowered from the battlements one snowy winter night, dressed in a white cloak for camouflage, and escaped across the frozen marshes. Most of the so-called castle, however, is really a prison building started at the end of the eighteenth century and is only two hundred years old. Only two hundred! My sense of time and history has been so altered by living in England. I was impressed by how they had restored the exterior using traditional materials and details, and the modern extensions seemed to fit in quite well. I couldn't wait to see inside and experience the spirit of the building, shut off from the modern world outside.

I was to be so disappointed. The whole spirit of the building was gone, replaced with a modern interior which can be seen everywhere, all over the world, without any specific character. The colours, types and materials of the furniture had nothing to do with the historic building at all, but only showed its new function as a hotel. I felt the design was arbitrary and rootless, lacking any association with the building's history. When someone asked why the modern cross beam in the bedroom was painted with two different colours the answer was, 'There were two people who had different opinions about the colours at that time and they weren't sure which one was the best. So they finally decided *to have both colours painted* on the beam'. I was sure that I would have been failed on my design course if I said that to our examiners at university in Taiwan, because the *interior design* seemed to me to lack any design idea or meaning. Perhaps William Morris would agree with me if he were alive to see the design which is so opposite to his idea of beauty and function; and is against his belief influenced by G. E. Street's idea of 'total' building: that each part of a building is important and full of meaning which should be comprehended by the architect. I could well imagine that all the modern equipment and furniture had been chosen from the market to put in to the building without any historic concern for interior design to match the spirit of the building.

I would think that it should be possible to keep some positive feeling for an old building while still being concerned about regeneration and enhancement of the building; I believe that it should be a most stimulating task to challenge designers' talents in such a project to achieve a better balance between preservation and renewal. I have seen other designs which are clearly modern yet have some of the enduring humane character of the traditional and vernacular.

I might be ridiculed for my limited experience in this country if I was given a chance to speak up about my opinions publicly. Maybe the argument between old and new has always been a controversial topic of philosophical debate on the definition of aesthetic objectives, which dizzies me sometimes. My mood is constantly going up and down with this argument between old and new since I have been so crazily in love with this mysterious and radiant English culture. However, I realized that not all English people understand why people like me so desire to come to England. They may not be aware of a fundamental fact in the English culture. When we say Oxford is so beautiful, we really mean that we see this beauty as the most precious fruit born by efforts from generations of the English people to sustain their culture and preserve their history alive till the modern day. We are living and breathing freely in Oxford like people who were living in the ancient buildings hundreds of years ago. Every brick, every stone and every pebble are so vividly telling us their old and interesting stories. We feel and experience Oxford with all our senses open and do not need to do a jigsaw puzzle to imagine and picture an Oxford by examining the records in museums or offices.

I will be so proud of my culture if we have so many historic buildings to show the world one day, because it also tells where our root is for ourselves.

♪

After a long process of checking in, walking through in a long queue and passing a security test that we might experience at an airport, at last we were in the London Eye, an enormous fairground-like 'big wheel,' hoping to see the whole of London from the sky. But, unfortunately, there was only one space remaining in the large enclosed cabin so, after all our efforts, we stood in the corner facing the ugliest view of London.

'Everyone is so smart to move so quickly to occupy the corner facing the view of the Houses of Parliament.' I couldn't help but complain a bit because I was disappointed that I could only stand near the door and face the modern London scene.

'Because they want to see the most attractive part of London that shows the truest character of England.' My friend said this naturally although she hadn't majored in anything about urban design or architecture.

Where would a modern architect choose to stand, I wondered? 'I feel so strange,' I said, 'about the way English people build modern architecture like those sorts of unpleasant tower blocks which destroy their own character, even though it's so clear that people fancy their traditional architecture so much, as now when they occupy the best view and don't intend to move at all.' I looked anxiously at the corner and hoped that someone could move a bit for me to see the view there. However, I didn't want to waste any second on watching people's heads which were not so good value for my expensive ticket, so I resigned myself to try to *enjoy* my view in the opposite corner. Here I could easily sympathise with Prince Charles's feelings, expressed in his book *A Vision of Britain* in 1989, when he described the view just beyond Westminster Bridge and said that although he tried very hard to appreciate that sort of architecture, he just couldn't.

'How do you feel about the environment around St Paul's Cathedral?' I asked my friend.

'What can I say about that view? When I was in the USA, I saw they had built tall buildings that followed a harmonious skyline to compose a whole scene which looks quite exciting. But here, these tall buildings don't seem to be designed to relate to each other or to fit the scene of London, and the skyline is too irregular and cacophonous. Each building seems to be trying to say, '*Look at me! I'm different,*' rather than being part of a family.'

I thought this was very perceptive of her since she was not a designer; but then, designers had permitted and made those destructive buildings. And it was not just the buildings but the views they destroyed which mattered, famous views of London. My tutor had once advised me to go to a lecture in London to be given by a very special designer who was trying to preserve those views. He showed examples such as the view of Horse Guards from St. James's Park, or of Hampstead Heath where the illusion of being in the countryside is destroyed by the intrusion of tall buildings. I'm sad to say he concluded that the struggle was almost lost for London already.

'The Cathedral is not as distinct in this environment as it was ten years ago when I was here,' my friend said. 'Luckily, the Cathedral building has been preserved very well and hasn't been knocked down yet.' She described her idea and told me that it was better than nothing when we still could see something pretty in this corner.

'Do you know, I chose the Cathedral as my first case study for my dissertation? I felt I liked it very much even before I saw it in reality.' I started talking about my special affection for the Cathedral.

'What do you mean, *even before you saw it in reality*? I think you mean that you'd read a lot about it before you visited it in person don't you?' I think she knew me quite well. I'm not the sort of person who can study much just with words without seeing or touching things in reality, particularly with English culture and historic buildings which I found difficult to imagine at first.

'When I told my supervisor I wanted to do research on lighting design in historic churches, and told him I would like to choose St Paul's in London for my case study, I think he felt uncomfortable about that because he is an architectural historian and not a designer; but he accepted my argument when I told him that my first degree was interior design, and I hoped to apply all my knowledge to this problem of keeping the character of these beautiful buildings. But he disagreed with my choice of St Paul's and advised me to study only Oxford churches, for hundreds of good reasons.' I told her what a struggle it was for me to make my supervisor consent to my idea.

'I expect he finally gave way to you because you're so stubborn!'

'No, I don't think that was the main reason because eventually he was laughing so much and told me he was happy then,' I argued.

'Why? Are you sure he was not weary of your noisiness in his office for more than one hour?' She mocked me with a funny smile.

'He didn't agree with any of my *reasons* at all for the first half hour, and I really ran short of means to convince him. So I changed my attitude and chose to tell him the truth.'

'I told him, "*I decided to do my case study in St Paul's because I once dreamt of a cathedral which was so beautiful. I saw a great dome, but I was not sure whether I was inside or outside the building. There were earth-coloured mural paintings and some words on the ceiling of the dome. A priest wearing a black gown stood by the altar and was looking up at somewhere towards sky or ceiling. I followed the line of his sight, and to my surprise saw snowflakes flying elegantly down in beautiful sunshine coming through windows. I was so attracted to this magical scene, but was so confused in my dream whether it was an indoor or outdoor scene, or whether it combined both; you know what dreams are like*"'

She interrupted me. 'How could you really know it was St Paul's Cathedral when your dream was so abstract?'

'I described my dream to a friend who then immediately answered me, "ST PAUL'S CATHEDRAL, in London". So I went to St Paul's to see if it's really the one in my dream. And then I saw the paintings on the ceiling in the dome and all the priests were wearing black gowns there. I told my supervisor, "*I think the God has chosen St Paul's for me to do the research; and most importantly I discovered there was a new award-winning lighting design in St Paul's which was so interesting for me to see how they designed for a historic building using the most advanced technique*". My supervisor then decided to agree with the God's choice.'

'Su Yen, I wonder if all designers are like you who never think and show ideas in a normal way. I have never seen anyone so remarkable and extraordinary like you in my life before. The most important thing is you finally could do research on the building you liked. I think you must be very happy doing your thesis which is such a nightmare for many students.' She envied me that I could work with my own interests. However, I shortly realized that sometimes it may be better to keep beautiful things in a dream without seeing too much in reality and I stopped talking when our turn came to go to another corner to enjoy the best view of the Houses of Parliament.

Of course the reality of doing research in St Paul's was nothing like it was in my dream, but it was quite interesting and enjoyable to evaluate its new lighting design working with my own knowledge of interior design.

I had always thought churches and cathedrals were

built in the gothic style which I love so much. So it was difficult at first to think of this splendid neo-classical building as an English cathedral at all. It was built in the Renaissance style, in the second part of the seventeenth century, to replace the old gothic cathedral which was destroyed in the Great Fire of London; so although the style is classical, the plan is gothic, which is a bit odd, but I don't think many people notice. The elaborate paintings on the dome interior and the shining golden mosaics on the ceilings were added by the Victorians in characteristically luxuriant style because Queen Victoria thought the cathedral was a bit dull inside. I was told it's the most impressive building of its type in Europe, except for St Peter's in Rome. It was a wonder to see it so well preserved in such a modern international city. I was also told that in the war all the old buildings around it were bombed and destroyed by fire, but St Paul's was saved by brave people who stayed on the roof all through the air-raids and extinguished all the fire-bombs which fell on the cathedral.

My first impression of being inside St Paul's was that it is very light. Its windows are large and filled with clear or very pale-coloured glass, not like other cathedrals I had seen. I was told that this is because its designer, Sir Christopher Wren, who was a mathematician and astronomer, intended to allow in the pure light of reason whereas the mediaeval cathedrals were intended to create a coloured world of mystery. St Paul's was a building for the new Age of Reason when scientists were no longer ordered to believe the old ideas of the church, though they did still believe in the God and saw their scientific investigations as understanding what the God had made. The marvel of St Paul's though is the huge space beneath Wren's dome, much larger than any central space that a gothic church could possibly have beneath its central tower. This space is flooded with light from the circle of windows in the dome, and I realised that this was where, so strangely in my dream, I had seen the snow falling.

I was interested to see how individual architectural details, such as the beautifully proportioned Renaissance pillars and arches, were skilfully highlighted by hidden lighting. The dome and its paintings were lit by a circle of lights high up which were invisible until we climbed to the gallery. Maybe Queen Victoria would have been pleased. Beyond the dome the gold mosaics in the choir gleamed in the lights.

That was my first impression and it was favourable. But as I looked around, and thought about what I saw, it was less pleasing. Above the pillars supporting the dome were black triple light fittings like traffic lights, or stage lights, which of course is what they were, used for illuminating performances under the dome. There was a religious service taking place under the dome just then, like an island of calm in a sea of tourists who meanwhile wandered around apparently oblivious of any religious purpose. Concentric circles of chairs formed a bastion between the tourists and the service. At the centre was a priest dressed in a green robe, equally oblivious it seemed of the tourists. Some participants, and other priests dressed in black, as in my dream, were sitting on the chairs.

To step inside that magic circle would be to enter a different world. The traffic lights were switched on to illuminate this other world, so that when, as tourists, we looked upwards to view the dome our eyes were met by intrusive glare. Those lights were disturbing too because they somehow symbolised the conflicting purposes of the cathedral, and maybe my conflicting feelings about where I belonged.

Now, when I looked at the interior more critically, as a whole picture, I saw how the various light sources from every angle confused the main lights and shadows of the architecture itself which should be the principal concepts for presenting the depth of a building interior. I don't understand why, when the simple basic idea of main light and shadow is always naturally presented in painting and sculpture, it seems to be so difficult for architects to keep this primary principle in their designs when lighting historic buildings. I remembered what I had read in Ruskin's *Seven Lamps of Architecture*, and when I reached home I looked it up again.

The power of architecture may be said to depend on the quantity of it's shadow; and it seems to me, that the reality of its works, and the use and influence they have in the daily life of men, require of it that it should express a kind of human sympathy, by a measure of darkness as great as there is in human life: and that as the great poem and great fiction generally affect us most by the majesty of their masses of shade, and cannot take hold of us if they affect a continuance of lyric sprightliness, but must often be serious, and sometimes melancholy, else they do not express the truth of this wild world of ours; so there must be in this magnificently human art of architecture, some equivalent expression for the trouble and wrath of life, for its sorrow and mystery, and this it can only give by depth or diffusion of gloom, by the frown upon its front, and the shadow of its recess.

Of course Wren wanted natural daylight to flow through his windows, and not the light of glass saints, but that doesn't mean he had no place for shadows and there are many shadowed recesses in his building as old prints show. I concluded that the lighting design project in St Paul's must have been awarded the prize mostly because of the advanced lighting techniques and controls used rather than for its presenting the spirit or beauty of the historic building.

We waited until the service had ended before approaching a black robed priest to see what he could tell us about the religious and ceremonial aspects of the lighting. He in turn asked the priest who was wearing the green robe. I had read much about how lights had been very important in the religious ceremonies of the Christian church for hundreds of years so I was a bit amazed when he told me that the priests had not asked for any particular requirements of that sort; they just said they wanted plenty of light and left the details to the architect. I didn't understand how this could happen if designers had ever considered the users of the building and designed for people as they always say they do in their design principles. More surprisingly, there were more than twice as many light fittings installed in the cathedral after the new scheme although the design concepts were all claimed to be about the representation of the *historic mood*. I was quite puzzled how they could claim to do this because there was not so much artificial light when the cathedral was built. I think they thought they did this by using lots of electric imitation candles. However, my questions were never answered because no one in that design group replied to my queries about the lighting design.

I had been inspired by the dream which I believed to be God-given to start my research with St Paul's. Probably it is because St Paul's is a witness to the history of London from being a centre of British culture to a modern multi-cultural metropolis and symbolizes the spirit of Londoners and their cultural roots. That dome used to dominate the skyline of London and I have seen the famous picture of St Paul's in war-time, surrounded by burning buildings yet standing triumphantly above the flames. However, even in a so well-preserved monumental historic building, I can still perceive a hard battle between keeping the original character and accommodating modern needs and ideas. Perhaps the God also wanted me to appreciate those difficulties and tested my perseverance to be qualified as a warrior in this battle. Afterwards, however, the God left me alone and never intervened when I was writing my thesis and was desperate because of having such scarce information. The despair I went through indeed made me more aware of my situation if I choose to remain passionate to my dreams and true to my heart, but I shall prepare myself with more studies and more detailed knowledge for my future journey since I have determined not to give up this God-given start.

♩

The day of my viva I felt perhaps a little of what I had seen in Robert Bolt's historical play, *A Man for All Seasons*, as Thomas More must have experienced sitting in front of a grand jury, fighting to the last drop of his blood not to be convicted. However, when one of More's previous servants appears before the court and uses a twisted account of their conversation to prove the crime of treason, the accused man collapses and knows he is doomed although there are rounds of applause from the audience for his penetrating final remarks. I did not quite understand the archaic English in that play completely when I watched it, but I found sympathy with the poor nobleman after my *viva voce* exam. He was regarded as one of the most intelligent men of the time in England in the time of Henry VIII, but still even he could not escape the fate of beheading because of an apparent misunderstanding about the words used in a conversation with his disloyal servant.

I realized how difficult it is to keep a middle position. More attempted to stand astride the widening space separating his king and the Pope, to be loyal to both, but fell between. It is so easy to take sides; so difficult to take an independent position. On each side are supporters; in the middle you are on your own. On my way home after my trial to determine the fate of my future research interests or of my dream to change the world, I amused myself by thinking that I should be in a play called *The Girl of Countless Winters*. Of course there would be a huge difference in my play, although it would have a similar setting, since I as the heroine am just a student who has learned the language for three, not thirty, years. I felt so much better at the thought. If all the outcomes are the same in different countries from the past to now, to parody myself might be a way to escape the bitterness of not being accepted because of a simple, unsophisticated, but different idea. Luckily my head is on my neck, not like the poor man whose head was chopped off soon after his final conflict.

'Do you think it's possible to create mediaeval light using the most advanced lighting techniques?' The examiner came directly to the first question on my dissertation, without much greeting.

'Perhaps it is possible because designers may think they can create all sorts of effects using the most updated lighting equipment.' This answer was not about my own opinion, but was learnt from those lighting design concepts which had been used in some of my case studies.

'I think it's impossible because there was no artificial light in the mediaeval time.' he argued.

'I think I agree with you, but one of my case studies showed that this ideal of replicating pre-industrial light was achieved and was awarded the lighting design prize for historic buildings. This finding interested me so much that I wanted to do more research on the ideas of mediaeval light, because I was not sure how they could both represent the historic mood and create a special lighting environment for specific needs at the same time by introducing double light fittings in the cathedral.'

'Did you talk to the architects and surveyors of this project?'

'Not really because I think they may not like me at all so that they didn't want to reply to my email or answer my enquiry about installing double light sources to represent historic mood as they have described in their design concepts.'

He laughed rather than talk about this possibility and then carried on to the next question. 'How will you deal with cables which may cause damage on the fabric?'

'As I learnt from the case study, they used a radio frequency control system to reduce wiring in the building and to overcome the problem of piercing the wall. Another case study shows how a floor was reconstructed and cables and pipes buried underneath.'

'That's a way to do it.' For the first time he showed his agreement with my answer. I then held on to this opportunity to talk more about my finding. 'The most interesting thing is that the other two converted churches didn't have any problem of damaging the fabric by installing new light fittings because in both cases all light fittings were removed from their walls.'

'That's another issue because of the new function of

the converted churches.' He seemed not satisfied with this idea.

'But these churches were converted to libraries which are often considered to require more light than other buildings, aren't they?'

He again jumped to the next question without any response to my reply; this was stressful because I didn't know how I was doing. 'How do you apply the national policies for this subject? I know people all talk about Planning Policy Guidance 15 which is about historic conservation. But I want to know how you think you can apply this policy to a lighting design project?'

This question scared me a bit and I think I was shaking in front of him while trying to answer this question because I was not sure I had studied enough about this policy; there are hundreds of phrases in a hundred pages in that policy guidance. 'PPG 15 doesn't say much on lighting design for historic buildings, but at the end of the policy it says that alterations and new service installation work can be done in listed historic buildings, but the whole project should avoid damaging the fabric. I think it means we can put cables or wiring on the surface of the wall and try to make them not so intrusive, and we can also easily remove them once we don't need them in future. This method doesn't cause too much damage to the fabric and is flexible for the changing attitudes of historic conservation.' I remembered the wires over the aisle arcades in Oxford's Christchurch Cathedral, how they lay in the curvature of the arch and were painted the colour of the stone.

He then smiled slightly which made me feel better

on hearing the next question. 'Which philosophy do you apply to the design of lighting for historic buildings?'

'Ruskin. I read a book of his which discusses light and shadow in a whole chapter. The philosophy is to remind architects that positive shadows are as important as the light to present a building in depth, which also reminds me of the ideas from arts, paintings and sculptures. It often happens that when people intend to emphasise some interesting details, they forget to maintain the principal effects of light and shadow and carelessly destroy the spirit of the building. As Ruskin says, the use of shadow for a building is more complicated and important than for a painting.'

He laughed again, but still didn't reply to my answer and carried on to the next question. 'What sorts of light fittings do you prefer for historic buildings?' May be this was a trap for me.

'I think I prefer the style which is as traditional as possible.'

'But Ruskin says that the building should be honest and I don't think he would like the idea of imitating old style because it's not honest.' He laughed as he thought he had pointed out the apparent contradiction with my previous answer about Ruskin's philosophy.

'There are some modern light fittings and sources used both for historic buildings and new buildings. I think it's not fake when we only choose a style to match the style of buildings, but don't intend to pretend that it is truly old. But in any case Ruskin was concerned with truth of materials and structure, not with style. He was quite happy for sixteenth century style buildings to be built in nineteenth century industrial England.'

'What will you do if you are a conservationist working for the city council and have to consider a lighting design project?' He always used another question to skip from one issue to another; this meant my brain was continually on a war footing.

'I will check if they really need so much light first, and then check if those proposed light fittings will destroy the spirit of the historic building.' I replied quickly, but he interrupted me.

'What will you do to check whether they need so much light or not?'

'I will use a light metre to measure the luminance *in situ* to see how much they really need to improve and how to improve without causing too much damage to both spirit and fabric. Therefore, the installation work and techniques will be the final concern only when they really unavoidably have to fix new light fittings in the building.'

'You didn't go through the details on the difference between different light fittings; I can't see how you can deal with a lighting design project without practical knowledge of different light sources.'

'I wanted to include that topic in my work, but it wasn't easy because while doing research on my six case studies I discovered this other issue of how to represent *historic mood* using the most advanced lighting techniques. Especially, when I saw those two libraries, I started thinking about the question of whether we actually need so much light. Do you think we have all been stuck for a long time on the issue of the damage done by installation work and we need to return to consider whether so much light is needed in the first place?'

'But it's not possible to avoid facing the problem of damage during installation. You didn't write about this in detail to show a way to resolve this problem.' He so insisted on his point even though I thought I had already answered the question with radio frequency control and glass-fibre optics in my dissertation.

'If we think about whether we really need so much light first, we may have no problem with the damage issue. For example, they can easily have light where they need it by using table lamps or portable lights for their working places rather than fixing light fittings onto the fabric. Hence I think the discussion of the difference between light sources and techniques should be another dissertation topic which cannot possibly be included in these 20,000 words or finished in three months. And you know, I already cut the idea of mediaeval light and window studies from 10,000 words to 3,000 words which was so painful for me and it's a pity because I found it's so interesting for people to think about the historical ideas when they all talk about *historic mood* so much for their design projects.'

'I'm interested in the reason you changed your topic from shopping centres in historic towns to lighting in churches. That's a big jump between these two topics.'

'Because it's about my first degree. I studied interior design at university in Taiwan; and I worked in an environmental control lab for three years. It was part of our job to do those experiments on lighting interiors because we needed to consider how to improve lighting for practical needs and we hoped to find how best to use natural light for the purpose of energy saving.'

'Oh, that's interesting. I heard you studied spatial planning before you came to this course. But now I assume that you have the knowledge and skills on lighting techniques already.'

'Yes, it seems so. I wanted to apply all that knowledge into this work at the beginning of the research. However, I learnt from my case studies that we should study history as the first step rather than continue to argue between the preservation of the historic buildings and installation of new light fittings which has been a debate for more than a hundred years. Most importantly, I believe strongly that we seriously need to consider whether we do indeed need so much light when processing new lighting design proposals.'

I think he didn't know how to argue with me anymore. The most dangerous question came at the end.

'You have so many research questions in the first part of your dissertation, but I don't think you answered those questions.'

'I'm so surprised when you say that, because I did this research by looking back to those questions again and again, otherwise I would be lost somewhere if I didn't keep checking my research questions. Can you provide any examples of unanswered questions for me, please?'

It was indeed surprising for me to hear this point, and difficult to answer him since I couldn't tell him the truth:

that I wrote those questions at the end of my research. In other words, how could this be so if I wrote those questions based on my answers?

On reflection it seems to me that they only opened their eyes to go through those 20,000 black words and coloured figures on white paper without opening their minds to enjoy some ideas which might be so different from their own opinions already in their minds. On the other hand, I appreciated so much that he gave me this opportunity to talk about my work for more than the suggested time limit for the viva, rather than treat me as a stupid foreigner with no sense and knowledge of English culture to deal with this very English study. But at least, unlike that poor nobleman, and unlike my experience in Taiwan, I was given a chance to defend myself. I think that is the English way now.

拾貳

12

DEATH

死亡

'Why are they all crying by my bed? What happened here? It's so painful because they scratch my face so carelessly.' My grandfather tremblingly curled in the corner of the ward, looking at himself on the bed.

'Oh, gosh, am I dreaming?' I asked myself and tried hard to open my eyes to work out the situation of my curled up grandfather in the corner beside my recumbent grandfather on the bed.

'*Baba*, this is Su Yen, I'm sorry to bother you, but can you tell me if my grandfather is all right now?' I rang my father straight away when I jumped up from my bed in the morning.

'I will call you back when we finish reciting *sutra* for the funeral of your grandfather. But, how can you know he died this early morning?' My father did not want to be interrupted during the service of final honours for my grandfather, but I knew he was surprised about my call because I was in England, which was a long way from my hometown.

'I dreamt he told me that he was so scared about the sound of crying around him just now—' I wanted to say more but my father didn't let me finish my description.

'We're so busy now preparing for the funeral and I will

tell you the whole story later. Bye.'

A deep sorrow was rising from my stomach to my heart. I breathed so slowly, but forgot how to cry. I knew I couldn't go back to see his last face because I was going to the Netherlands to study for a week soon. Time passed too slowly from that moment. A second for me was like an hour long while I was waiting for my father's call.

I think it is true when it is said, 'Don't cry around the dead person because the sound of crying will frighten them'. My grandfather was so horror-stricken and couldn't go asleep peacefully when his children cried out so sadly. What could I do for him when I was a long way from him?

'Su Yen, are you all right? We just arranged the time of burial for your grandfather.' It had been a long wait for me to receive a call from my family.

'*Baba*, I want to tell you to stop people crying beside my grandfather because he is so scared by the grieving voices.' I thought it was so important to inform them about this situation.

'How can you know that? I really don't understand why your grandfather called for help from you who was so far away and he must have to cross many seas to find you.'

I was not sure the puzzlement of my father was logical at all, but I didn't mind because I only wanted to ask them to move my grandfather gently to avoid making too much pain on his poor body. '*Baba*, I don't know if you believe me or not, I think it's quite true that people still have feelings of pain when they have just died. Can you tell those nurses to work cautiously even though they think my grandfather has died? That's the only thing I want to ask for him, please.'

The dream of the death of my grandfather again persuaded me to believe that spirits never vanish even though our physical bodies are faded for the time being. Most importantly, I consider this idea cannot be changed across the boundaries of different countries and cultures while I am still receiving those sorts of mysterious messages in my dreams, even though it is the case that I have been visiting so many English churches and my mind has been immersed in English culture entirely for some time.

Dear Su Yen

You are so worried about your grandfather that I send you this poem about how peaceful death can be. I hope it will be some comfort for you. I too think that bodies may feel pain a little while after we think they are dead, which is a disturbing thought. Here is another of the Greek myths which you like so much.

The Ancient Greeks and the Romans had mostly the same gods and goddesses, but used different names for them, which seems confusing at first. Proserpine is the name the Romans used for the Greek Goddess of Spring and Flowers. The Greek name was Persephone (pronounced Per-sef-onee) which I think is the more beautiful name. She was the daughter of Ceres (in Greek called Demeter), the Goddess of the Harvest (from which we get the word 'cereal') and Jupiter the leader of the Gods (in Greek, Zeus). One day Proserpine was picking flowers when she was carried away by Pluto, the God of Hades or the underworld, who forced her to marry him. Jupiter was very angry and made Pluto agree to allow Proserpine to return to the upper world for several months of the year: when she comes back our spring arrives; when she goes back to the underworld then winter begins.

The Garden of Proserpine, by Algernon Charles Swinburne (1837–1909)

> *She waits for each and other,*
>   *She waits for all men born;*
> *Forgets the earth her mother,*
>   *The life of fruits and corn;*
> *And spring and seed and swallow*
> *Take wing for her and follow*
> *Where summer song rings hollow*
>   *And flowers are put to scorn.*

Hades is the place where, so the Ancient Greeks believed, all people went when they died, whether they had been good or bad. The Greeks did not separate heaven and hell as Christians do. The dead person would:

> *Nor wake with wings in heaven,*
>   *Nor weep with pains in hell.*

The poet Swinburne imagines that Persephone made a beautiful garden in Hades where people, when they die,

fall into a peaceful dreamy sleep and are thankful that all
the troubles and disappointments of life are over:

From too much love of living,
  From hope and fear set free,
We thank with brief thanksgiving
  Whatever gods may be

Swinburne was a Victorian poet. He was known for his
ability to express a sense of mystery and unreality in his
poems and some people thought this was because he took
laudanum, that is a mixture of opium and alcohol, which
was commonly used as a drug in those days. He employed
unusual metres and rhymes; for example, the last four
lines of each verse have a hypnotic soothing quality, as
though someone is stroking your head.

I am tired of tears and laughter,
  And men that laugh and weep;
Of what may come hereafter
  For men that sow to reap:
I am weary of days and hours,
  Blown buds of barren flowers,
Desires and dreams and powers
  And everything but sleep.

You can feel the effect of lines five to seven all rhyming:
they seem to lead your voice naturally to fall away, as
though going to sleep. The poem is quite long and I think
very beautiful in a mysterious way. You can find it in most
anthologies of poems.

Dear Roy

I think I gained many ideas from those poems you chose for me; I can see they are not only beautiful works but also records of English life, although I'm not sure I have understood all of them in depth.

And thank you for that *Proserpine*, I like it so much and want to know more myths and legends. Am I dreaming? I have a great birthday. My grandfather will be happy when he knows my life here and maybe he will forgive me for not attending his burial. Sadly, he was not a good friend to me because he only cared about his first grandson (due to our traditional culture), but I used to see him and listen regularly to his complaint about his life. My aunt said that when he was dying he talked about me quite often. However, nobody informed me about my grandfather's death till I dreamt it. I dreamed he told me he was very hurt and scared, and then he closed his eyes with much pain. After that, I felt very sad so I called my father and checked that this news was happening during the time I was dreaming. Perhaps it's a sort of sixth-sense or because I love him so much. Anyway, I hope he can see my life here and my beautiful future.

♩

I couldn't quite remember what had happened that day and only had some memory that I had been bound with a heavy rope and my eyes covered with a piece of cloth by some people whom I had known somewhere in my life. There had been an indistinct discussion about how they would cope with me without any evidence being left for the police. I didn't remember what had gone on afterwards.

I stumbled home with my tiring body at night. It seemed a big party was hosted in my parents' house. I hadn't a clue whether it was a special day for my family or perhaps some important people had come to visit my father officially. However, when I was getting closer to my home, I saw the crowd around and some policemen were talking seriously to my father by a coffin. There was a picture of the dead person on the top of the coffin. I couldn't react in time because my thoughts were so tangled; the name and the picture of the dead person was me.

Was it my coffin? Why did they arrange a dummy funeral for me? Was it because they needed to arrange a trick to catch those people who had bound me? So many questions came to my mind at once. I went to my mother and wanted to ask her about this puzzle, but she looked so nervous.

'Go to the loft right away,' my mother said.

'OKay, otherwise people will discover me, that I am alive, and my father will get into trouble?' I didn't wait for her to finish her speech because I thought I understood the situation, so that I quickly moved to the loft and hid myself cautiously. I was waiting for those people to leave my home and then I could ask my parents about the whole story of my funeral. My mother seemed to forget me in the loft for a long while and didn't come to tell me to go down.

'Mum, can I go out now? Are they all gone?' I called my mother when I saw her pass by the loft, but she was still very busy and didn't reply.

I slipped out without being noticed because it was so boring to stay in the small loft where no light and sound would be allowed at that moment. When the sunshine dazzled my eyes, I felt a bit weak; that's perhaps because I didn't have any water and food in the loft for the whole night. Anyway, it was so good to see the sun again. In a quite good mood now I greeted everyone I met on the street. Nevertheless, no one replied and it seemed to me that all of them tried to ignore me on purpose. I was not sure if their attitude was related to the mystery of my funeral.

'The weather is so lovely, isn't it?' Finally, an old friend of mine smiled to me and talked. I was so happy and couldn't wait to run to her although my legs were so weak and couldn't really exert any strength. However, my ardour had cold water poured on it in a second when I realized she was talking to the person behind me. I became so depressed with all the things that happened to me in those few days and I really wanted to find out the reasons for those strange situations. I walked back home slowly with my sad heart which was so alone. I stood behind a tree with the feeling of being helpless. I so wanted to go home, but I was not sure if it was a right time for me to appear to my funeral. From my place behind the tree I turned to observe my family. Strangely, I saw my father was in sorrow, and my mother and my sister lowered their heads with tears.

'Why are you so sad? I'm here; I'm here looking at you. Please raise your heads and look at me alive.' It was so vexatious and hopeless when they didn't know me and

I was there to talk to them. It was more worrying because I couldn't make a sound anymore.

When the funeral knell was ringing, I couldn't help but levitate to a river. There was a bridge in front of me, but I didn't dare go over that bridge so that I chose to hold the bridge piers to jump on the water to cross the river. In a twinkling, my brain became blank as though it had experienced a great thunder from the clear sky. The funeral of mine was real; everything was real; the only thing I didn't know was my death. I was dead.

The sun dazzled my eyes again, but this time it was real sunshine that came through my window to wake me up from this death dream. I was so pleased that I was breathing.

♩

'God must love you very much. Your dream led you to experience the exact progress of death which is recorded in some old books.' This was the reply when a friend of mine heard about my dream.

'It's so horrible when no one but yourself knows you exist. I don't want to believe we can't entirely disappear after death. What should we do if our spirits still can feel things in the world? Death becomes my nightmare if our spirits eternally exist.' I think I believed the God loved me quite a lot, but I doubted a bit about the progress of death.

'I know you want to free yourself after death. But, as I know, your dream was just about the same as those records of death in those old books. For example, it is said we normally won't know we are dead till we hear the ringing of the knells; and we will be very weak under the sun and our feet will not really tread on the land when we die; the most relevant thing is, we will be scared to go through the bridge and will choose to find some way to jump on the water to cross the river, which is just the same as you did in your dream.' My friend kept scaring me with his knowledge of death from books. 'And I can tell you about the name of that bridge, I think it is the so-called *Nai Ho Bridge* which means no way to return anymore.'

'No way to return? Where will we go after crossing that *Nai Ho Bridge*?' I was really scared by that strange bridge.

'We will be taken to see *Yama* who is the God to judge whether we are good people or not in our whole lives. After the judgement of *Yama*, we will follow the way which should lead us to our next lives as human beings or as animals. The results will depend on how many wrongdoings there are in our current lives. After a long way through, we will reach a gate where an old lady will stand to give us a soup called *Meng Po Soup*. The surname of this old lady is *Meng* so that the soup was named after her surname. She will tell us to forget everything and to start a new life with a blank mind while we are drinking the soup, and then she will push us down to the place we need to go to.' My friend described the rest of the progress of death, which I didn't dream about.

'It sounds so terrible to be pushed down with all memories gone all of a sudden.' I frowned when I imagined the situation of losing my memories.

'Yes, you may be shocked and scared when you are falling down to the way of transmission of souls; thus you will cry and turn to a new baby again to be born.'

Oh, dear, I spent such a long time to grow up to be an adult, but still must be born and experience the lengthy progress of growing again and again. I don't really like this theory of transmission of souls. But I think I am quite a coward because I worry about the existence of our spirits according to the experience of my dream. It seems to me that I have to believe that we will also be born countless times to the world. Otherwise, where should we go and what should we do if our spirits never vanish?

I don't think I have any other choice but try to be as good as possible in this life to accumulate my luck for my future lives.

Dear Su Yen

I have bought a nice little 100-year-old book which recounts the ancient Greek myths. It has, for example, that story of Proserpine; also Orpheus and Eurydice, Psyche, Pandora and many others. The myths are fantastical of course, but they deal with basic human characteristics such as love, trust, revenge, courage, friendship, jealousy, sadness, loss and so on, so that they have captured our imagination for thousands of years and many of the names are used by modern-day psychologists to express mental conditions. Psyche herself was a brave little human who fell in love with a god and had to go through all sorts of trials before she could be with him. The other gods were so impressed that they made her immortal; hence 'psyche' has come to mean 'soul' and psychology is the study of our non-physical self.

Dear Roy

The Ancient Greek Myths! I will like it very much. When you asked me about my original thoughts about coming here, actually I wanted to come because I had seen so many movies and pictures and read myths about England, Italy and Greece. The architecture, ancient culture, arts and so on mean that for me the life here is like a dream or heaven. However, the problem was, I couldn't enjoy those beautiful things because I learnt them in Chinese, which meant it was very difficult to see the original souls of those things. So, when I was fifteen years old, I decided I wanted to come here for those dreamy expectations. Then, when I grew up, I felt also that studying in only a small island was not enough for a life, and I wanted to explore my life by learning different knowledge and skills from other countries. Now, I want to stay here because my dream is coming true. You know that I always wish to have any opportunity to learn to appreciate poems with old books and with ancient architecture and its beautiful stories. And now I feel more and more peaceful and happier and happier when sharing English culture every week. Usually, after being busy for a whole week, I can get rid of my worry, stress and unhappiness by living my dream for a little while in this way.

Dear Su Yen

I'm glad you liked *Proserpine*. I suggested that it was beautiful in a melancholy way. Melancholy is not quite the same as sadness although the dictionary says it is. The more aware we are of beauty the more we are also aware of its vulnerability so that an experience of beauty always has an element of sadness. Therefore melancholy is a sense of beauty made more poignant by knowing we cannot hold on to it. It is sometimes said to be the proper state of mind for a poet; it is also said to be part of English character. You will find many poems are melancholy in this sense. One role for the poet is perhaps to express sadness, disappointment and loss in ways which are beautiful, sympathetic and universal so that we know that we are not alone.

Another idea of melancholy is that it is awareness of past sadness which in some curious manner we enjoy because it moves our emotions, but it doesn't involve or threaten our real lives. In a similar way we enjoy a sad or tragic play or movie. In 1742 a poet, Sneyd Davies, wrote of this 'pleasurable sadness' he felt on a visit to the ruins of Tintern Abbey:

Here, O my friends, along the mossy dome
In pleasurable sadness let me roam:
Look back upon the world in haven safe,
Weep o'er its ruins. at its follies laugh.

There is a difference between knowledge of past sadness and an awareness of the fragility of our present lives, but they seem to be related. Here are some more lines from *Proserpine*. A 'lure' is a trap: no one can trap time.

We are not sure of sorrow,
  And joy was never sure;
Today will die to-morrow;
  Time stoops to no man's lure ...

Many thinking people in Victorian times, especially after the publication of Charles Darwin's ideas of the Theory of Evolution, found difficulty in accepting the Christian religion although usually they went through the formalities of religious observance because they saw it as important for society. Elsewhere in the poem Swinburne says, 'dead men rise up never,' which is a direct contradiction of Christian belief. Many people at that time found the ideas and stories of the ancient classical world very attractive. Another poem which takes a similar, perhaps rather more cynical, attitude to life and death is *The Rubaiyat of Omar Khayam*, a free translation made in the nineteenth century by Edward Fitzgerald of an ancient Persian poem by Omar Khayam, which you might enjoy. *Rubaiyat* just means written in verses of four lines each, what we call quatrains. But although Fitzgerald's poem says this life is the only one we have he still seems to suggest that we should be respectful of the dead. In a beautiful walled garden in the grounds of Broughton Castle in Oxfordshire there is a sun-dial, a sun clock, with these lovely lines from the Rubaiyat engraved round the edge.

The Rubaiyat of Omar Khayam, by Edward Fitzgerald
(1809–1883)

I sometimes think that never blows so red
The Rose as where some buried Caesar bled;
*   That every Hyacinth the Garden wears*
Dropt in its Lap from some once lovely Head.

And this delightful Herb whose tender Green
Fledges the River's Lip on which we lean—
*   Ah, lean upon it lightly! For who knows*
From what once lovely Lip it springs unseen!

♪

'I can't believe that English people have birth and death ceremonies both in the same place, and where weddings are held too! Although it seems quite natural now for me to see English people eating in a churchyard, it still surprises me when I think about this cultural characteristic in depth. I often see weddings, memorial services or any sorts of either happy or melancholy events; all have been held in the church where I work over the weekends.'

'I don't understand why you're so surprised about this. Is it so different to your culture?'

I was not surprised to hear this question because I thought not many English people would understand what I felt about their different attitudes to death.

'It is rare for us to use the word beautiful to describe a funeral. In the Chinese culture, a funeral is rather a place flooded with weird feelings, controlled by mysterious traditions. Death is still so heavily related to pain and suffering, so that it is an unspoken taboo for us to speak of death at formal occasions like family dinners, particularly in the presence of elderly members.'

I think this answer was not vivid enough to show our English friend the way we treat death in our culture, for his face looked puzzled.

'I remember once we couldn't have any peace from day to night because of a funeral held by our neighbour. If it had been in winter-time, it might have been slightly better because the dead body wouldn't have gone smelly so quickly.' I was telling a story about my experience after a person died next door.

'I don't understand why it was smelly. Don't they put the dead body in a coffin? If so, it shouldn't be smelly.' My friend still seemed very puzzled.

'Traditionally, they have to choose the right day at the right time, based on the lunar calendar, to nail down the coffin, and then to wait for another right day with the right time to bury or cremate it. But, they couldn't find the most suitable time, even after a month, so the terrible smell from the decomposing body was sent to us now and then by the gentle summer breeze.' I explained slowly for my friend to *feel* the situation.

'It sounds so stressful.' He sounded shocked.

'Oh, yes, it was horrible, but it isn't the most stressful thing in a Chinese funeral. The music and crying from day to night going on throughout the whole ceremony till the day of burial or cremation was the hardest experience for me. When I was at my grandmother's funeral, it was all like acting. I know I shouldn't say so, but I really felt like that.'

My friend explained the meaning of an English funeral. 'Your system is quite difficult to understand because, for us, the funeral is the time for people to remember and give thanks for the whole life of the deceased person. Of course, it is sometimes hard to remember good things if the person didn't seem do anything much that was good when he was alive. But the priest still will try hard to say something good for his family to remember about that person.'

'I think we have the same purpose for a funeral, but it's just presented in a different way to remember the dead person. In my grandmother's funeral, we hired a woman leading crier from a professional company. She held a microphone to cry so loudly in the beginning of the line, and demonstrated how to creep on all fours while crying out loud till the leader told us to stop.'

I imitated the professional cry to make him understand it easily with my talented mimic skill.

'*Very professional*!' My friend nodded, but he was laughing very much at my mimicking.

'Sometimes, at midnight, one of my aunts would call all the daughters to come around my grandmother's coffin at a special chosen time to start crying after my aunt counted down from five to one.' I told my friend that not only could the leader do a professional job, so could my aunts.

'How could they start crying immediately if they were not actresses?' My friend seemed very puzzled again.

'I don't know how they managed to do it, but they

really did very well and could stop right away when one of them said, "S*top, time is up*".'

'That's amazing for me to hear. I really can't imagine the situation. In England we are taught not to show our emotions, especially men. Do your men cry too?'

I told him more about this sort of crying business in our country. 'Sometimes some people will choose to hire a group of five young boys from the funeral company to cry by the coffin or the tomb. Those boys are trained very well and can cry following the music beats, and they also can start and stop bursting in to tears anytime by the orders of the leader.'

'What's that for? Is there any meaning to that professional crying?' He finally couldn't help asking this question although he knew it might appear to be critical of my culture.

'Yes, the meaning is simple; those professional criers are trained to lead people to feel very sad and to bring the relatives into the right mood to burst into tears straight away. And I think they find that is a sort of relief for them. I think it was quite useful because all members of my family were crying so sadly and they expected me to do so as well although I wasn't affected by their funny sound. But I just couldn't cry at all and was always falling asleep during the whole process, even though it was difficult to sleep in that situation.' I told the truth honestly, although it might have sounded cold-blooded.

'Yes, I can see that it must have been too noisy and uncomfortable to sleep easily there.' My friend simply thought that noise was the main reason.

'No, the sound was not the main thing that woke me up during the long funeral ceremony. The biggest problem was the Taoist priest hosting the funeral who continually told us to kneel down, to stand up, to turn right and to turn left while he was *pattering* for my grandmother. My mother hit me many times when I was asleep and didn't follow the priest's orders properly.'

My friend laughed out loud when I again described the situation with mimicry.

'Can this traditional funeral still be seen in your country now? If we had that situation next to a house in England someone might call the police to come if it was too noisy and smelly.'

'I think English people might not understand why we didn't call the police, but it was only for the reason of respect because we thought the family was in sorrow for their dead relative, even though it was so annoying indeed. But I think this traditional funeral can be seen only in some remote countryside areas these days because most people now are living in tower blocks which don't have any space for holding a funeral like that. It was a very special experience for me to see our traditional culture for death at my grandmother's funeral. However, I did wonder whether my grandmother was happy with her funeral or whether perhaps she felt it was too noisy for her to sleep peacefully in her coffin.'

In the church where I work in England, the church vault has been converted into a café. On a typical sunny and relaxing summer day, people sit comfortably next to a tomb or even on the grass in the graveyard, sipping their coffee and enjoying their meals with children running and chasing around from tomb to tomb. After I had visited more places and seen more of this *strange* image in this country, I learnt to understand the true meaning of the saying: death is part of life, or as I heard in the beautiful funeral service, 'In the midst of life we are in death'. Certainly everyone will die one day, and I remembered those people who had gone so calmly to their deaths, such as Anne Boleyn and Thomas More, or that English poet-soldier who thought it was glorious to die for England.

My friend explained that was because the Christian religion claims that Christ had conquered death (I heard that in the church too), that the soul will go to a much happier place in heaven, and that the body is not important, so true believers would be happy to die and would be sorry only for their friends left behind. But he thought that often those ideas had been used just to persuade poor people to put up with their unfair lives on earth. He said, however, that although English people are not afraid of the dead, we should treat the tombs with respect and not damage them or do bad things there. Certainly English funerals are very dignified and usually no one cries very much. On the whole I think I prefer the English way, though sometimes I think it is good to cry if you are sad.

Dear Su Yen
Here is the poem that I promised to send you, about one person's grief. The first part is sad in a beautiful way (it always brings tears to my eyes); the second is beautiful in a sad way. Do you see how the pause at the name Heraclitus

in the first line and the repetition of, 'They told me,' is like a sobbing voice?

Heraclitus was a philosopher who lived 2500 years ago in Miletus which was then a Greek city in Caria, but is now in modern Turkey. Although the poem expresses grief, it also celebrates the joy of talking about ideas, and about the pleasure of remembering those conversations. There is nothing about ghosts or about heaven and hell, but only the nobility of life and friendship. See how the poet uses 'you' in the first part when he is talking of the poet's death, but the more traditional, or even religious, 'thou' in the second part when he expresses his conviction that these things can never die.

Heraclitus, by William (Johnson) Cory (1823–1892)

They told me, Heraclitus, they told me you were dead,
They brought me bitter news to hear and bitter tears to shed.
I wept as I remember'd how often you and I
Had tired the sun with talking and sent him down the sky.

And now that thou art lying, my dear old Carian guest,
A handful of grey ashes, long, long ago at rest,
Still are thy pleasant voices, thy nightingales, awake;
For Death, he taketh all away, but them he cannot take.

Dear Roy

The beginning of the poem vividly shows the deep grief of the poet who couldn't believe the truth, although he knew it was true, and he even couldn't say the truth from his sorrowful heart. It's so difficult to accept the situation that someone, who often talked to you happily for so many sunrises and sunsets once, is lying forever with the last sunset. The word 'lying' evokes in me feelings of peaceful, imperceptible unravelling, and melancholy. I can't find the exact words to present those feelings which are just too exquisite to be shown in words. Perhaps that's why English funerals are normally so quiet and peaceful.

For Death, he taketh all away, but them he cannot take.

This line, for me, outpours the incessant grief, together with all the memories which could hardly be taken away by death. All the sadness lapses into silence; I think it's the English way to confront the sadness of parting for ever.

This is such a great poem which naturally led me to ignore the dates and to believe that Heraclitus was a real friend of William Cory. When I realized that the poet was born more than 2000 years later than Heraclitus I felt the magic of space-time interlacing in the poem.

拾叁

13

COUNTRYSIDE
鄉村情懷

Xue and I went for a walk in Port Meadow one day after dinner. It was the first time I had been there although Xue said she jogged there quite often when she was a student and lived nearby. Port Meadow is such an unusual part of Oxford and made us feel so harmonious with nature. I could not help taking pictures with my mobile as the scenes were so like those water-colour landscape paintings we often see in our art books. Xue frowned at the smell of the dung from horses and cattle. On the contrary, I felt somehow that slightly annoying smell was also part of Port Meadow and I hardly took any notice if she did not mention it. As we hopped over the big brown piles on the footpath, I saw horses grazing freely and wandering by the river with weeping willows on the bank. The sun was setting down over the low horizon and a group of geese was flying above the river. This tranquillity was broken only occasionally by the loud cries of a rowing coach on a training boat.

I was amazed by the existence of such a vast untouched wild land in a bustling town like Oxford. I wondered why a land such as Port Meadow could be preserved without having been purchased a long time ago by the university or some rich college for building more houses. Yet it is not a deserted land, and there seems to be a certain care taken with the fences and footpaths. I remembered that when we entered the gate we saw a board showing a short history of Port Meadow: it said Port Meadow is a very large area of common land in Oxford. *Common land*? This sounds a very interesting term to me. When I was studying for my Master's I came to realize that the ownership of the land in this country is a very complicated matter. Sometimes we see signs saying 'Private property: no trespassing'. So, as common land, does Port Meadow belong to nobody or to everybody? That reminded us of the movie *Cromwell*. King Charles I, in order to raise money for his court, allowed nobles to take away land from farmers by simply putting up fences to claim the ownership. We were curious to know how Port Meadow could have survived enclosure.

We were talking about these things when we saw a kindly looking English lady, like the ladies in the church, coming towards us. Xue and I looked at each other. 'You ask,' she said, 'you know more about it than I do.'

'Excuse me,' I said, 'Please can you tell us whether we are allowed to walk here.'

The lady laughed, 'Of course,' she said, 'it's common land isn't it!' She saw we were still looking puzzled. 'Perhaps you don't know what common land means.' We looked at each other and nodded.

'Well,' she continued, 'It means that hundreds of years ago certain people had the rights to keep certain animals on it, "in common" you see; that means they all shared all the land instead of chopping it up in little bits, which is what happened in most places.'

'But why does that mean we can walk here now?'

'Well it doesn't really. You see this common is very old. They say an American once asked to see the oldest monument in Oxford, and they showed him Port Meadow. It was listed in Domesday Book in 1086 which said all the Freemen of Oxford were allowed to keep their horses here then. As you can well see there are still horses here. As to your question, the rights refer to the keeping of animals by certain people; other people don't have any rights to be here at all.'

The lady laughed when she saw she had worried us. 'Don't worry,' she said, 'Though you have no right to be here, it's also true that no one has a right to tell you to leave a common, so you can walk here as much as you like.'

She walked off, chuckling at the paradox. I thought, 'What a strange place England is when you start to ask questions'.

Dear Su Yen

Your adventure on the common reminded me of another famous eighteenth century poem, by Oliver Goldsmith. Hundreds of years ago, in mediaeval times, most farming land was shared 'in common' as the lady said. Gradually and for various reasons the land came into private ownership of a few people only and was enclosed with hedges to make the fields which are so characteristic of English countryside today. This process is known as 'The Enclosures' and it reached a maximum in the eighteenth century. At the same time rich landowners were improving their estates to create a visual ideal of natural landscape, based partly on ideas from China, from the new translations of the Roman poet Virgil, and from ideas seen in contemporary paintings from Italy. Blenheim Park at Woodstock is an example. A few 'common' lands still exist; they are mostly used for recreation now as at Port Meadow in Oxford.

This process left many poor people without any land to grow food for their families and sometimes their houses were destroyed as well to improve the view from the land-owner's house. Goldsmith's long poem describes the destruction of one village which is possibly Sutton Courtenay, just south of Oxford, or perhaps it is a village in Ireland. His poem can be criticised because he follows the pastoral tradition of poetry to idealise and romanticise village life before the destruction, but he does describe with sympathy the reality of the destruction itself. Here is just a small extract in which he tells how the 'sweet smiling village' is replaced by 'desolation' and used only by the bittern which is a solitary bird with a mournful sound which symbolises the loss. Now the 'whole domain' is grasped by 'one master' and:

Trembling, shrinking from the spoiler's hand
Far far away thy children leave the land.

He then imaginatively moves from the particular to the general:

Ill fares the land, to hastening ills a prey,
Where wealth accumulates, and men decay.

The enclosures were in fact a necessary process which led to the improvements in agriculture which enabled Britain to feed the world's first industrial population as the country people moved to the towns for work; many others went to start new lives in America which belonged to Britain at that time. But the enclosures also resulted in much poverty and very bad conditions for life, and sometimes starvation, and they could have been managed better. A similar process is going on in some developing countries today as they industrialise.

I hope you can read the whole poem one day. Note first the metre of the poem which is in 'iambic pentameters'. I think you know now that a pentameter is a line of poetry with a metre or measure of five units (and so five 'beats'). Pent is a prefix meaning five. An iamb is a two-syllable unit with one soft and one stressed syllable. A unit of poetry writing is called a 'foot' (it's rather like a bar in music) and there are other sorts of feet which can be used which have different combinations of syllables. The poem has a typical eighteenth century rhyming pattern where each pair of lines rhymes, and so they are called 'rhyming couplets', each one like the ending of an English sonnet, and you have seen how emphatic that can be.

A 'rood' here is a traditional term for a small area of land. A 'tillage' is an area of ploughed or cultivated land. A 'stint' was the ration of land each person was given under the old common land system. Today it means each person's role in a job to be done, usually in succession: 'I've done my stint' means 'I've done my bit'. A 'lawn' is an area of grass: it can be very formal in shape and setting,

or informal and grazed by animals, which is the meaning
here.

The Deserted Village, by Oliver Goldsmith (1728–1774)

    Sweet smiling village, loveliest of the lawn,
Thy sports are fled, and all thy charms withdrawn;
Amidst thy bowers the tyrant's hand is seen,
And desolation saddens all thy green:
One only master grasps the whole domain,
And half a tillage stints thy smiling plain:
No more thy glassy brook reflects the day,
But chok'd with sedges works its weedy way.
Along thy glades, a solitary guest,
The hollow-sounding bittern guards its nest;
Amidst thy desert walks the lapwing flies,
And tires their echoes with unvaried cries.
Sunk are thy bowers, in shapeless ruin all,
And the long grass o'ertops the mould'ring wall;
And trembling, shrinking from the spoiler's hand,
Far, far away, thy children leave the land.

    Ill fares the land, to hast'ning ills a prey,
Where wealth accumulates, and men decay:
Princes and lords may flourish, or may fade;
A breath can make them, as a breath has made;
But a bold peasantry, their country's pride,
When once destroy'd can never be supplied.

    A time there was, ere England's griefs began,
When every rood of ground maintain'd its man;
For him light labour spread her wholesome store,
Just gave what life requir'd, but gave no more:
His best companions, innocence and health;
And his best riches, ignorance of wealth.

Dear Roy

It seems to me that weak and poor people are always the sacrificial lambs for the development and progress of a country from the past to now, no matter in the Eastern or Western worlds. As you said, many people moved to America to have new lives there when their villages were destroyed for providing better views to the only master of the land. I don't know much about history, but I would imagine that's the original reason, deep in their minds, to strive for being independent from Britain and they didn't want to remember where their root was from.

I so enjoyed walking around those classical parks, such as Blenheim Park, only because of their luxurious designs which powerfully shows off lordliness, before I knew this part of history. After reading this poem, I think when I immerse myself in the park next time I will feel that the whole beauty also includes another cruel power of destruction to accomplish what we can see now. I'm not sure whether this feeling will help me to enjoy the historic park in depth or will extinguish my fervour of imagining the luxurious life in the eighteenth century. Sometimes I'm so fearful to know the truth when I desire to know more history behind those remarkable historical sites because the saying, 'a coin has two sides,' is always a norm for everything in the universe; truth sometimes like a sniper's shot violently impales my wonderland. However, I remember my design tutor once said that a good design work should contain the power of destruction to reflect the power of construction.

Dear Su Yen

You will find extracts of *The Deserted Village* in most general books of poetry. Did you download the whole poem from the internet? My American students are always interested in this next part because, for some of them at least, these displaced people were their ancestors. Goldsmith describes the English people waiting on the shore to go by boat to America, 'round half the convex world;' that is, 'halfway around the globe'. It was a very dangerous and unpleasant journey in those days and the voyagers think about all the dangers they will meet when they reach the new land: gloomy forests, 'tigers' or cougars, rattlesnakes, and fierce indigenous people. The emigrants must have been very brave or very desperate, which, as you say, may explain some aspects of the American character.

Far different there from all that charm'd before,
The various terrors of that horrid shore;
Those blazing suns that dart a downward ray,
And fiercely shed intolerable day;
Those matted woods where birds forget to sing,
But silent bats in drowsy clusters cling;
Those pois'nous fields with rank luxuriance crown'd,
Where the dark scorpion gathers death around;
Where at each step the stranger fears to wake
The rattling terrors of the vengeful snake;
Where crouching tigers wait their hapless prey,
And savage men more murd'rous than they...

Good Heaven! What sorrows gloom'd that parting day,
That call'd them from their native walks away...
And shudd'ring still to face the distant deep,
Return'd and wept, and still return'd to weep.

Dear Su Yen

I meant to send this next poem at Christmas when I sent *The Deserted Village* so that you could compare the two. It is another and different treatment of the Enclosure theme. This is not such a high level of poetry. It is written in a form called a 'ballad'; that is, the words and rhythm appear to be simple and straightforward, though the ideas expressed can sometimes be quite complex and subtle.

You could easily imagine this poem being sung in a tavern or pub; nevertheless, it introduces many significant historical facts.

The peasant could live off a few 'ewes'; that is, female sheep, on the common land. But now, although he has been allocated a small share of land in proportion to his common rights, his share is not sufficient to live on and anyway he cannot afford to fence his land, which legally he is now bound to do. He will have to sell his share cheaply to a rich land-owner. The 'little money' which he receives will soon be used up, again like the situation in some countries today. He is too old to find a fresh life in the local town or to go to America. What can he do?

I realise the language will be strange to you so I have interpreted a few lines here.

What little [share] *of the spacious plain*
Should power to me consign [will the authorities allocate to me],
For want of means, I can't obtain [I do not have enough means (money) to fence it],
Would not long time be mine [I shall have to sell it soon].

261

The stout may combat fortune's frowns [the strong people can overcome bad luck]
Nor dread the rich and great [not be afraid of rich and powerful people]
The young may fly [go] *to market towns,*
But where can I retreat?

I hope you will like this because it may evoke your sympathy, which is a form of imagination. The poem was written in 1783. There are a few more terms you may need to know before reading the poem. In 'threescore years' a score is an old word for twenty, so the man is sixty years old, very old in those days; there was no government support for old people then. A 'cot' is a very simple and rough house or cottage. To wish someone in the churchyard, 'I wish the churchyard were his doom,' means to wish he were dead (and buried in the churchyard).

I am happy to say that I have obtained a good edition of *Tales from Shakespeare* and I hope to bring it next week.

The Cottager's Complaint, on the Intended Bill for enclosing Sutton-Coldfield, by John Freeth (1731–1808)

How sweetly did the moments glide,
  How happy were the days!
When no sad fear my breast annoyed,
  Or e'er disturbed my ease;
Hard fate! That I should be compelled
  My fond abode to lose,
Where threescore years in peace I've dwelled,
  And wish my life to close.

Chorus
Oh the time! The happy, happy time,
  Which in my cot I've spent;
I wish the church-yard was his doom,
  Who murders my content.

My ewes are few, my stock is small,
  Yet from my little store
I find enough for nature's call,
  Nor would I ask for more!
That word, ENCLOSURE! to my heart
  Such evil doth bespeak,
I fear I with my all must part,
  And fresh employment seek.

What little of the spacious plain
  Should power to me consign,
For want of means, I can't obtain,
  Would not long time be mine:
The stout may combat fortune's frowns,
  Nor dread the rich and great;
The young may fly to market-towns,
  But where can I retreat?

What kind of feelings must that man
  Within his mind possess,
Who, from an avaricious plan,
  His neighbours would distress?
Then soon, in pity to my case,
  To Reason's car incline;
For on his heart it stamps disgrace,
  Who formed the base design.

Dear Roy

It is not avoidable, and not only in the eighteenth century, that there are still many stories about unfairness between the rich and the poor; or maybe we can say between the powerful and the powerless. I don't know why, this poem reminds me a lot of my own situation before coming to England. I couldn't compare whether physical punishment is more painful than mental punishment since I'm not living in that situation of the cottager of the poem. But I might be able to say I understand the feeling of hoping for death rather than struggling for hopelessness because I mentally experienced huge disasters in my life which made me feel so like the old man whose poor life was pushed hard to the living hell by the plan of Enclosure. On the other hand, as in the Buddhist's belief in cause and effect, maybe the poor person had done something seriously bad in his previous lives, so that he had to experience such a difficult this-life to dissolve his bad *karma* from past lives. Or if he was innocent, but mistreated in his present life in order to help the good progress of his country, the only thing he could do was to wait for the God to redeem him with good fortune for his next life because the God couldn't do anything more to change his fate then and there.

Dear Su Yen

You say you wonder why so many English poems are about the countryside. This may help to explain. Joseph Addison was a writer and thinker who lived at Magdelen College, Oxford, in the first part of the eighteenth century. There is a footpath from Magdelen Bridge still called Addison's Walk. In his essay *The Pleasures of the Imagination*, published in 1712, Addison introduced the idea that the pleasures of imagination and beauty, and of design, could be understood in a *rational* way similar to the experimental approach to science that was being developed so successfully at that time. In particular he argued that Nature stretched the imagination more than did buildings and gardens since these were anyway only the products of our own minds, whereas Nature was much greater. The extract here explains why he thought Nature was the best subject for poetry.

The beauties of the most stately Garden or Palace lie in a narrow Compass, the Imagination immediately runs them over and requires something else to gratify her; but in the wide Fields of nature, the Sight wanders up and down without Confinement and is fed with an infinite variety of Images, without any Stint or Number. For this reason we always find the Poet in love with a Country-Life, where Nature appears in the greatest perfection, and furnishes out all those Scenes that are most apt to delight the Imagination.

In 1697 another poet and writer, John Dryden, had published a translation in English of a set of poems called the *Georgics*. These poems had been written about 1,500 years earlier by a famous Roman poet, Virgil, and they idealised the countryside and the work of farmers. Before Dryden's translation these poems could only be understood by people who were able to read Latin well, but when everyone could read them in English they stimulated a great interest in the countryside and in nature, which has been a particular feature of English life ever since. Addison wrote an essay about the *Georgics*, which was included in Dryden's translation, and this association with Roman ideas seems to have inspired Addison to develop his ideas about the way nature could please and stimulate our minds. Addison helped to introduce this powerful line of thought into English life and it is still there today.

Addison described Virgil's *Georgics* as:

> *...a collection of the most delightful landskips [scenes] that can be made out of field and woods, herds of cattle and swarms of bees, and as appealing, wholly to the imagination. It is altogether conversant among the fields and woods, and has the most delightful part of Nature for its provinces. It raises in our minds a pleasing variety of scenes and landscapes.*

In fact most of the text of Virgil's poem is about very practical advice on farming activities and not perhaps what we would consider imaginative, but maybe it appealed to Addison in the same way that playing at farming appeals to so many people today in our urbanised world.

Dear Roy

The philosophy of Addison's imagination is so interesting because his idea about nature not only shows the best subject for poems, but also tells us where most original design concepts derive from. I remember you told me that many designers have tried to find the most beautiful line in the world and some, like Ruskin, suggest that the most delightful line should be found in nature, in his case in the Alpine Mountains, rather than in an art studio. This reminded me that the logo of Coca Cola was one good example: the designers kept changing the bottom curve of the logo slightly all the time for many years because they tried to draw the most elegant curve to finish up with, although they thought they could never achieve the aim.

On a short course on art history at Oxford University I'm studying now, I learnt some arguments for design principles which are also around the subject of nature. No matter whether it's the concept of a preference for stylizing nature or for the idea of imitating nature closely, the debate never gets away from nature. I feel I can appreciate the idea that English poetry is mostly about the subject of nature if it's all right for me to think about Addison's imagination from a design aspect. Furthermore, I admire poets much more than designers because it requires greater knowledge and logic to present imagination through words, particularly in poems which have to be consistent with rhythms and rules, than through visual design works. Addison's idea of nature now greatly raises my interest in learning English poems of the countryside.

Dear Su Yen

The month of June is almost here. This is the month of hay-making. Farmers cut the long grass which has been left to grow in selected fields and in a few days the sun and wind dry the grass so that it can be stored and used to feed the farm animals in the winter. Of course the farmer tries to cut the grass when he judges there will be several days' fine weather, not always easy in the English climate. It is perhaps the happiest time on the farm when the weather is warm and the hay is sweet smelling and soft. Traditionally everyone would help – relations, friends and neighbours – so it was a very jolly time, but everyone knew also how important it was for the farmers to be able to feed their animals through the long winter when the grass does not grow.

The tall flower-heads of most grasses, although not colourful, are very delicate and elegant. In traditional agriculture the grass field would include many wild flowers, especially clover, and these would attract large friendly bumble bees, colourful butterflies and many other insects. When all this is at its most luxurious and most vigorous is the time when it must be cut down to be made into hay; the delicate flower heads lie on their sides in rows and slowly die. Various artists and writers have ascribed noble qualities to the grass and to the hay that it becomes: such as sacrifice and endurance. The brief life and death of the grass is used as a metaphor in religion to remind us of the brevity and impermanence of our lives.

Early in the seventeenth century King James I ordered a new translation of the Bible to be made. It is known as the Authorised Version or as the King James Bible. Although the language may seem difficult and old-fashioned now, it is very beautiful and, together with Shakespeare, has enriched our language over four hundred years with many expressive and memorable sayings and has influenced the way people wrote and spoke themselves. Strictly the writing is not poetry, but it is on the border of prose and poetry and has a rhythm which is lacking in some modern poetry. One of the most obvious features is the use of the old verb-ending 'eth' instead of the modern 's'. So 'falls' becomes 'falleth' and 'comes' becomes 'cometh'. This is quite easy when you get used to it and is one of the characteristics which give the language its rhythm and solemnity. The words are especially impressive when read aloud in church, as they were intended to be.

Here is a short extract from the Old Testament Book of the Prophet Isaiah which has many beautiful lines. Cry does not meant to weep, but to cry out, or shout, or to proclaim. The Lord here is not a person: Christians often refer to God as the Lord.

> *'The voice said, Cry. And he said, What shall I cry?*
> *All flesh is grass, and all the goodliness thereof is as the flower of the field:*
> *The grass withereth, the flower fadeth: because the spirit of the Lord bloweth upon it: surely the people is grass.*
> *The grass withereth, the flower fadeth; but the word of our God shall stand forever.'*

And from the New Testament Book of Peter:

> *'All flesh is as grass,*
> *and all the glory of man as the flower of grass.*
> *The grass withereth,*
> *and the flower thereof falleth away'.*

Our Service of Burial has the moving line:

*'Man that is born of woman hath but a short time to live ...
He cometh up and is cut down like a flower'.*

These images and metaphors would have been very familiar when most people lived in or close to the countryside. The words, too, would have been familiar since they were regularly read out in churches across the land. I always feel these words have helped people to accept death as a natural and inevitable part of the cycle of life and therefore, in a strange way perhaps, as beautiful and noble. Among the many men and women who cut and gathered the dead grass, which has now been transformed in to a store of life-sustaining hay, some at least must have meditated on the symbolism of what they were doing. But perhaps the words are not so powerful today and mowing the lawn does not have the same symbolism.

By the way, your comments about approaching an understanding of poetry through design were very perceptive because Addison's main purpose in writing that essay was in fact to try to introduce a new natural style of garden and landscape design based on a poetic view of nature. Conversely, Alexander Pope in his introduction to his translation of the *Iliad* uses garden design to express the difference between Invention and Judgement in poetry.

Dear Roy

I had no idea about this drying of grass for animals because I never saw that sort of agricultural activity in my life. But I can imagine the scene of cutting grass amongst tombs in our Tomb-sweeping Day of the early spring which is the only day we are allowed to cut grass around the tombs of our ancestors. I remember I once went to south Taiwan with my parents for the Tomb-sweeping Day when I was very young. Maybe I was too young to feel death at that time; I was very excited to meet all our relatives by the tomb of my grandmother in such a tranquil countryside which was so different from the environment of my home. The air spread the smell of the spring; the whole scene was full of fresh green and the delicate pink and white flowers joggling with the breeze. Traditionally, it was the time for the whole family to reunite to remember our ancestors.

I think I was about eight to ten years old at that time. It was the only time I joined with the whole of my mother's family because traditionally we are supposed to think much more of the family of the father and not of the family of the mother. But this time we went to the tomb of my grandmother who is the mother of my mother; she died very early when I was under five and my parents didn't allow me to see the funeral because in Chinese life it is not good for very young children to go near death. So the first time I saw a funeral was the one for the mother of my father when I was thirteen years old.

However, when we started to cut the grass, I realized it was not as easy as I thought when thorns pierced my clothes and scratched my skin. The ductile grass was unbelievably so hard to be cut down and I always hurt myself somehow. When I removed and pulled out the grass with my hands, live insects and worms underneath appeared to my eyes, which was quite scary to me. I then shortly dropped out from the work of cutting grass when my relatives warned me to be careful of those bloodsucking worms underneath. I would never have known the environment inside the grass wasn't as quiet as a picture appears to be, but was very busy like a city, if I hadn't joined in the work.

Hence, I did find these words from the Bible interesting because they brought back all those memories, but I also thought about my own feeling of mourning the death of grass which is sacrificed for human activity and is also a metaphor of the live activity of insects and worms underneath who are sacrificed along with the grass; for me it reflects the long death of our ancestors in different layers of time. But the cut grass in our culture was burnt, which I feel is more divine in a sense, than being stored in the barn waiting to be eaten by animals.

I like to think of those people working happily in the fields because I feel better about them than about those poems of complaint of people leaving their land: they are too painful for me to feel at present.

Dear Su Yen

You said once how you rescued a book of Robert Browning's poems, because it spoke to you, and that one day you would read it. Well, here is a start since we are thinking about the English countryside. You remember the story about Elizabeth Barrett, his wife. They went to live in Italy, as many well-off English people used to do, because it was better for Elizabeth's health. He remembers with pleasure all the intense details of the English countryside, which can only be enjoyed by walking or sitting quietly and which we do not see driving along in a car today. I always feel though that his poems are not as well crafted as they might be; they seem to be a little unfinished or untidy, especially when compared to the careful constructions you described for Chinese poetry. The correct emphasis of the words does not always coincide with the correct emphasis of the rhythm of the line. Check it out and see what you think. I was taught that Browning did not try to write in the way words ought to be written, nor even in the way words are spoken, but he wrote as he thought, and thoughts are always unformed at first.

Home Thoughts, From Abroad, by Robert Browning (1812–1889)

> *Oh, to be in England*
> *Now that April's there,*
> *And whoever wakes in England*
> *Sees, some morning, unaware,*
> *That the lowest boughs and the brushwood sheaf*
> *Round the elm-tree bole are in tiny leaf,*
> *While the chaffinch sings on the orchard bough*
> *In England—now!*
>
> *And after April, when May follows,*
> *And the whitethroat builds, and all the swallows!*
> *Hark, where my blossomed pear-tree in the hedge*
> *Leans to the field and scatters on the clover*
> *Blossoms and dewdrops—at the bent spray's edge—*

That's the wise thrush; he sings each song twice over,
Lest you should think he never could recapture
The first fine careless rapture!
And though the fields look rough with hoary dew,
All will be gay when noontide wakes anew
The buttercups, the little children's dower
—Far brighter than this gaudy melon-flower!

Dear Roy

I think English poems are beautiful and romantic, even when they are translated into Chinese language. You told me that 'Romantic' in art does not mean love, but is about one person's struggle seeking something very special or beautiful which probably never existed or could exist, just as Burne-Jones wished for his *Sleep of Arthur*. I like them also because they are like songs with their rhythm which would be beautiful even if I did not understand the words. I read some English poems in Chinese versions before I had the courage to read original ones, and I, and some of my colleagues also, liked sometimes to quote some line of an English poem in our design concepts to show our abstract ideas and just for the mysterious feeling that we had from our limited understandings of the poems. When I learnt more about the backgrounds of those poems from you, I realised that what I had enjoyed before was only about what I imagined from those English poems which seemed so mysterious and out of reach like stars on the sky that they attracted me so much although I did not understand them.

A colleague of mine from university discussed English

poems with me a few months ago. I had a funny feeling in my mind when she told me how clever English poets were in the way they dealt with words and the whole structures for their poems, because I knew she read them in Chinese and didn't know much about the backgrounds of those poems. It was such an interesting experience for me to cross two cultures while reading one poem. A Chinese designer discussed how wonderful those English poems were, using her undisciplined imagination which was thoroughly different to what I learnt from my English tutor. Maybe this imagination is not quite the same as the imagination of Addison's ideas of nature, but it perhaps has some philosophical similarity. When poets formed their poems about nature with elaborately chosen words, they infused their imaginations with nature, and when we read their poems we're picturing the scenery in our minds with our own imaginations of nature following their words. When things are outside of our own experience in the poems, as in Taiwan when I had never seen English countryside, we can only use our imaginations completely to feel the world of the poems. Such as the 'wise thrush': I would picture the character of the bird and feel the word 'wise' was a reaction to the personal emotion of Browning. As you know, in Chinese poetry we often look for opposites. Perhaps Browning is regretful to think that he has not been so wise to live in a foreign country and to miss that 'careless rapture'. The rest continues to show an artistic conception of yearning for the scenery of the English countryside in April as the morning dew melts away and the grass is green and fresh in the bright sun of midday. Although it is a simple picture and seems to be reachable, it is not reachable for him just then or ever, for even if he was there it would not be complete because it would only be part of his life.

I think I can understand the feeling that Browning missed the English countryside although I'm not English, because English countryside is well known as a terrestrial heaven for many people in Taiwan and in other countries. Every corner of the countryside is a picture post-card in our imagination, all country houses are like small cakes standing on the fields surrounded by trees, birds, colourful flowers and often with water around. I don't know how to describe in words, when it is like dreaming for me to live in such a variety of pictures, not just in two-dimensional scenery, but also with sounds and smell and touch which I enjoy so much in real three-dimensional space. I always answer those who envy me in such a picturesque country, that I also envy myself in England.

拾肆
14

REMEMBRANCE
紀念

On our way to work in the church of St Mary's on a sunny Sunday morning in early November, Xue and I heard a very loud sound, like a cannon firing, from the direction of the University Parks. I did not pay much attention and thought it might be some ceremonial or commercial event going on in the park. But Xue was so curious and kept asking: 'Su Yen, what do you think the sound is? Could it be an army parade in Oxford now and a cannon is being fired? Is it for the Remembrance Day?'

'What's the Remembrance Day for?' I was puzzled about everything that morning.

'I heard it's to remember those fallen soldiers in the wars, but I'm not very clear about the story of the day. Let's see this!'

Xue's curiosity does sometimes lead to some interesting discoveries, so we walked quickly up to the University Parks and peeped in through the wrought-iron gates. Indeed, there on the grassy ground, was a cannon! Several soldiers dressed in field uniforms were firing it. We could even feel the shaking of the earth when we were near. On their uniforms the soldiers were wearing the little red flower that so many people here start to wear after the beginning of November. It seemed that for quite a while recently we had often seen people, particularly old gentlemen and ladies, selling that little red flower; we could not really name it, but we thought it must be special.

Xue was excited to see the cannon and soldiers as she has an unusual boy-like interest in the history of wars. She kept talking while we were walking towards the church. She felt that the numbers of the cannon-firing must have some sort of meaning, although we did not count carefully. What we saw just then in the University Parks reminded her of a ceremony she had seen on TV one day in November two years ago when she was staying with an English family. The ceremony had been led by the Queen to remember the soldiers who died in the great wars. All of the attendants, from the boys' choir to the elderly soldiers and the Queen herself, were wearing the same red little flower. I can also remember now that on the way to Buckingham palace there is a pavilion with a wreath woven with the same red little flowers lying on the monumental stone to commemorate soldiers.

For the dead soldiers of the wars: are all their names on the memorial tablets in the churches? I have seen that every church has a tablet and I watched once as Roy read silently through the names of the dead soldiers and he told me they had all died for their country, and he did it out of respect, and I saw tears in his eyes. And why a little red flower for the fallen soldiers? The puzzle makes me feel I'm an outsider of English culture, but it seems this might be a slight opening of a door for me to explore more about England.

Dear Su Yen

You asked me to tell you the story of the flowers. It is not a pretty story. Most of the intensive fighting in the Great War of 1914–18 took place on agricultural land in a large area of Northern France and Belgium. When the earth was disturbed by exploding shells and by soldiers digging shelters, thousands, millions maybe, of poppy seeds which had been dormant in the soil for many years germinated and flowered. Thus many men died in beautiful fields of flowers and so the poppy was taken as a symbol of the war. The colour of the poppy is also the colour of fresh blood.

I promised I would send you some of the work of the War Poets whose subject was that Great War of 1914–1918; it is now usually called The First World War, but at the time people did not know there would be another one.

This poem by Rupert Brooke was written in 1914 and so is from the early idealistic phase when England was still at the height of her power and confidence. The qualities expressed in the poem of patriotism, courage and passionate belief in the idea of England would have been shared by many upper class Englishmen at that time. It is a reflection of the sentiments expressed by the classical Roman poet, Horace: *'Dulce et decorum est pro patria mori'*; translated from the Latin it means, roughly: 'Beautiful and fitting it is to die for one's country'.

By the next year, 1915, Brooke was dead, dying from the not very glorious effects of blood poisoning while on military service. There were no antibiotics then and many soldiers died of infected wounds. The first modern antibiotic, *Penicillin*, was developed in Oxford during

1928-1938, but it was the Americans who recognized its military value and developed it on a large scale. Later it would save my life, so I have reason to be grateful to Oxford, and to the Americans.

Quite apart from its military content the poem is a wonderful evocation of the influence of growing up in England on a privileged young man of the time:

> ... *whom England bore, shaped, made aware,*
> *Gave, once, her flowers to love, her ways to roam.*

These feelings for the country might not have been appreciated by poor working class people living in the large industrial cities; nevertheless, most people were intensely patriotic in those days and many ordinary men volunteered to join the war. Later, the government compelled them to go and fight anyway, and today we do not share exactly those feelings of unreserved patriotism, partly because of that war; nevertheless the poem remains a very beautiful one on its own terms. And in fact many people still love England, and soldiers do still die for their country.

It was a tradition of England, though no longer, to bury its soldiers in the countries where they died. There are British cemeteries in many countries around the world and perhaps we still like to think there are little bits of England everywhere. Maybe that is better than feeling how sad it is that the person is alone in a strange country:

> ... *there's some corner of a foreign field*
> *That is forever England.*

No one at that stage had any idea how long and dreadful the war would become. Other poets came to express the suffering, and the pity and the sorrow, of war. Perhaps Brooke would have done so had he lived longer. Do you notice the poem is in the form of a sonnet, eight plus six lines? See how the poet enlarges his theme in the second part.

The Soldier, by Rupert Brooke (1887–1915)

If I should die, think only this of me:
  That there's some corner of a foreign field
That is for ever England. There shall be
  In that rich earth a richer dust concealed;
A dust whom England bore, shaped, made aware,
  Gave, once, her flowers to love, her ways to roam,
A body of England's, breathing English air,
  Washed by the rivers, blest by suns of home.

And think, this heart, all evil shed away,
  A pulse in the eternal mind, no less
Gives somewhere back the thoughts by England given;
Her sights and sounds; dreams happy as her day;
  And laughter, learnt of friends; and gentleness,
  In hearts at peace, under an English heaven.

Dear Roy

This poem, *The Soldier*, when I first read it (before reading your comments) I thought comprised all the feeling I had when I was here for the first year. I'm not a soldier, but I can understand the feeling they are willing to die for their country. Although this is not my country, I want to dedicate my life to England (if I'm good enough).

I feel very strange when I have this feeling, because I also miss my home town, but I just didn't have any thought like this when I was in Taiwan (why? because we don't have any castles in Taiwan?).

I was very moved by those words:

… there's some corner of a foreign field
That is forever England.

He must have missed England very, very much, and didn't know when he would be able to return to England. In this sentence, it seems he knows that he might not come back at all, and his body will stay in a foreign field; only his spirit always longs for England, under an English heaven.

Dear Su Yen

Here is another poem from a 'war poet', Wilfred Owen. It is not beautiful; it was not meant to be. It is a protest against the waste, squalor and loss of war.

Owen describes the parody of a funeral for young men whose bodies were blown to pieces or left rotting without a name in the mud of the battlefield. In a civilised funeral there would be a dignified 'passing bell' tolling for the passing of life; there would be 'orisons' (prayers); candles; a choir singing; a 'pall' (a cloth, maybe a flag) draped over the coffin; many flowers of remembrance.

But, what bells for these, he asks? Only the continuous sound of the guns. What prayers? Only the deadly stuttering of the machine-guns. But no 'mockeries,' no hypocrisy. No choirs, but the terrifying screaming of the high explosive shells overhead; and the bugles (military trumpets used for commands) which called them from the 'shires,' the counties of England, 'sad,' because they have lost so many men. No choir-boys ('singers') holding candles; only the light fading in their dying eyes. Their only cloth the pallor (unhealthy whiteness) of a young woman's face as she learns of the death of a sweetheart, brother or father. Their flowers the tender thoughts of patient minds who must wait a lifetime without them. It was the custom in England, when someone in a house died, to draw down the window blinds, so each evening when it grows dark and the blinds are drawn it will be a painful memory.

When I describe it like that I think you can see it is a very angry poem, although restrained and succint. I told you twenty thousand British soldiers were killed in one morning, and one million in the whole war. Wilfred Owen was killed when the war was nearly over in 1918. Many of those killed were our best young people. There are about ten thousand villages or parishes in England and only in thirty-two of these did all the soldiers come home. In those days women expected, and were expected, to get married. Now one million women could never find husbands.

Note that Owen says, 'What bells for *these*', not, 'those': these are people near to him. There was a comradeship and understanding between those who were fighting, which at the same time estranged them from the people at home who could not comprehend their sufferings. The poem uses the figure of speech called 'metaphor' where ideas are represented by other images, often quite different.

Regarding our talk today: Anthony Trollope wrote *The*

Way We Live Now. And if you want to see inside another English church or go to a service there just check that it is a public service; usually there is a list near the door: common worship, matins, Eucharist or vespers are all public services, or you could ask someone in the church. Private services are usually funerals, christenings or marriages; quite often some people who are not family or friends may attend, usually local people. But if a strange lady turns up at a man's funeral the family may think she was his secret girlfriend. There will be some good services for Easter in the cathedral. Sit near the back and in the service just stand up, sit or kneel when everyone else does. But if most people go up to the front of the church to receive communion you should not go up. Often there is a collection where someone from the church brings a small bag around and everyone puts some money in it for the church.

Anthem for Doomed Youth, by Wilfred Owen (1893–1918)

> *What passing-bells for these who die as cattle?*
> *Only the monstrous anger of the guns.*
> *Only the stuttering rifles' rapid rattle*
> *Can patter out their hasty orisons.*
> *No mockeries now for them; no prayers nor bells;*
> *Nor any voice of mourning save the choirs, –*
> *The shrill, demented choirs of wailing shells;*
> *And bugles calling for them from sad shires.*
>
> *What candles may be held to speed them all?*
> *Not in the hands of boys but in their eyes*
> *Shall shine the holy glimmers of good-byes.*
> *The pallor of girls' brows shall be their pall;*

Their flowers the tenderness of patient minds,
And each slow dusk a drawing-down of blinds.

Dear Roy

Obviously Owen wrote a quite opposite poem from Brooke's *The Soldier*. Owen's poem is full of anguish, pain and desperation. I remember a Chinese poem that describes a battlefield after fighting: the glory of a general is proclaimed upon millions of bleached bones. The glory of war I thought I admired from *The Soldier* is so over-shadowed by Owen's sadly pale picture of the family and friends left behind to bear an ever-lasting trauma of knowing their beloved vanished into nameless lands without even a proper place to be remembered.

I remember we were chatting once about the Great War, after Xue and I saw the church memorial tablet for soldiers sacrificed in the war. You told us that, when the war broke out, British men volunteered to go to the frontline to fight the Germans, and that people somehow were expecting a glorious war. We were both so amazed to find out Britain did not have large trained armies, all ready to be summoned, but its people could be so brave to volunteer. Unlike the ancient battles fought in England before, as we learnt from you, the Great War did not move from one battlefield to another, but was fought in long trenches and it lasted four years. With the appalling figures in your letter, I understand why many interesting books I have rescued have talked about how deeply the Great War transformed the society and the people. Like a person, a country can also be a metaphor as a phoenix, the bird which renews itself by rising again from the ashes of his own funeral pyre. I believe the innocent lives lost in the war and the pain inflicted on those who survived have not been wasted and have been leading us to a better course if only we can learn from them.

Dear Su Yen

Certainly in the midst of the war people hoped that the world could be made a better place afterwards. It was called, 'The war to end all wars'. Unfortunately it was not.

Here is a third poem from the war poets. The 'fallen' means all those who were killed and so fell down. Of course the wounded fell down too, but the idea is used on memorials especially for those who died: 'For the fallen'; 'To those who fell'. It seems the words 'Dead' or 'Died' were too painful and final.

The fourth verse (or stanza) of Binyon's poem is read out every year at the Remembrance Day ceremonies, nominally on the 11th day of November which is the date the war ended, but in practice usually the nearest Sunday. The poem lies somewhere between Brooke's unquestioning patriotism and Owen's bleak picture. By the end of the war everyone knew it had been a disaster, but on the other hand people could only come to terms with this if they felt there had been something dignified and noble about it too. Binyon's poem seems to achieve that.

The Great War not only caused many deaths, it changed society deeply. There was reaction against all the values which were seen to have led up to the war: patriotism, traditional culture and art, respect for authority, religion. So many men were needed in the army that women did what had been men's jobs. The war stimulated socialism, women's rights, internationalism, and modern art and architecture, though these trends already existed. It also made people question their ideas about the superiority and confidence of Western values.

For the Fallen, by Laurence Binyon (1869–1943)

> *With proud thanksgiving, a mother for her children,*
> *England mourns for her dead across the sea.*
> *Flesh of her flesh they were, spirit of her spirit,*
> *Fallen in the cause of the free.*
>
> *Solemn the drums thrill: Death august and royal*
> *Sings sorrow up into immortal spheres.*
> *There is music in the midst of desolation*
> *And a glory that shines upon our tears.*
>
> *They went with songs to the battle, they were young,*
> *Straight of limb, true of eye, steady and aglow.*
> *They were staunch to the end against odds uncounted,*
> *They fell with their faces to the foe.*
>
> *They shall grow not old, as we that are left grow old:*
> *Age shall not weary them, nor the years condemn.*
> *At the going down of the sun and in the morning*
> *We will remember them.*
>
> *They mingle not with their laughing comrades again;*
> *They sit no more at familiar tables at home;*
> *They have no lot in our labour of the day-time;*
> *They sleep beyond England's foam.*

But where our desires are and our hopes profound,
Felt as a well-spring that is hidden from sight,
To the innermost heart of their own land they are known
As the stars are known to the Night;

As the stars that shall be bright when we are dust,
Moving in marches upon the heavenly plain,
As the stars are starry in the time of our darkness,
To the end, to the end they remain.

Dear Roy

For the Fallen reads like a very beautiful song. I could picture a bereaved and loving father singing softly to his son and never wanting to wake him to face the sufferings of the world. It is a sort of lullaby for the nation.

'As the stars that shall be bright when we are dust.' It is so beautiful to believe that those fallen young men become like stars in the heavens. Now I wonder if the peace I receive from looking up at a starry night sky is from them. You said stars do not move, but the earth moves. So their lofty spirits are always like loyal soldiers who safeguard us through the dark night.

Dear Su Yen

This next poem is about a different sort of war, although people still were killed of course. It was a time when armies were very small and individual courage and skill very important. I think Rupert Brooke may have gained some of his attitudes from those ancient times for, as a classically educated Englishman, he would have been familiar with these stories.

The oldest-known Western poem is the *Iliad*, the story of the Trojan War which took place between the Greeks (strictly, the Achaeans) and the Trojans about 1200 BC. The poem is said to be by a man called Homer, but no one knows if such a person ever existed. It is very long and has many stories which have inspired countless other poems, paintings, sculptures, references, sayings and films ever since. Early in the eighteenth century the poet Alexander Pope translated the *Iliad* from the ancient Greek language. This translation was very popular and earned enough money for Pope to live and to think independently for the rest of his life whereas artists and poets in those days were often dependent on rich patrons. I have extracted and put together some lines from Pope's poem to tell the story of the death of Hector, the Trojan's greatest warrior. The previous day Hector had killed Patroclus, the friend of the greatest warrior on the other side, Achilles. It was partly Achilles' fault, because he had refused to fight that day after the king had annoyed him. As always we blame people most when the fault is really our own, and Achilles was determined to kill Hector.

The Greeks have chased the Trojans into the city of Troy. Although Hector's father, King Priam, pleads with him to come in also, Hector bravely decides to remain outside the city and fight alone; but he is suddenly and strangely afraid when he sees Achilles' shining spear and plumed helmet. Hector runs away and is pursued by Achilles. Hector tries to run close to the gate-towers of the city so his friends can shoot arrows at Achilles, but Achilles cleverly turns him the other way. Three times they run around the walls of the small city.

The scene becomes unreal, as in a bad dream: 'As men in slumbers ...' they run; their 'sinking limbs' (tired legs) will not go where they want. Hector cannot get away, but Achilles cannot catch him. The whole world seems concentrated on that small space, the plain, between Troy and the sea; the 'gazing gods lean forward from the sky' as though they were watching a play. The gods, who want Achilles to win, decide they must do something. Minerva agrees to descend from the sky and make herself appear as Hector's warrior brother, Deiphobus.

Minerva's trick works. Thinking he now has support, Hector turns to fight Achilles; but first he wants Achilles to agree that whoever wins will treat the other's body with respect and return it to his family for proper burial. Achilles angrily refuses and throws his spear at Hector who skilfully avoids it and believes he now has the advantage. But Minerva secretly returns the spear to Achilles and when Hector throws his javelin accurately at Achilles Minerva's 'heavenly shield' deflects it. Hector calls for help from Deiphobus, but of course 'no Deiphobus was there'. Hector now knows the gods are against him and that he will die and resolves to die bravely so that he will always be remembered.

It is believed that the story of the *Iliad* was remembered and told for many centuries before it was written down. It is interesting to think that two and a half thousand years ago people would have been listening to this story of Hector and Achilles.

The words 'fly' and 'flies' may be confusing. They do

not mean fly as a bird, but to flee or run away.

Selection from *The Iliad of Homer: Book XXII*, translated
by Alexander Pope (1688–1744)

'Ah! stay not, stay not! guardless and alone;
Hector! My loved, my dearest bravest son!
Methinks already I behold thee slain,
And stretched beneath that fury of the plain.'

But fixed remains the purpose of his soul;
Resolved he stands, and, with a fiery glance,
Expects the hero's terrible advance.

Thus pondering, like a god the Greek drew nigh.
His dreadful plumage nodded from on high.
The Pelian javelin, in his better hand,
Shot trembling rays that glittered o'er the land.

As Hector sees, unusual terrors rise.
Struck by some god, he fears, recedes, and flies.
He leaves the gates, he leaves the wall behind.
Achilles follows like the wingéd wind.

No less fore-right the rapid chase they held,
One urged by fury, one by fear impelled;
Now circling round the walls their course maintain,
Where the high watch-tower overlooks the plain

By these they passed, one chasing, one in flight:
The mighty fled, pursued by stronger might.
Swift was the course: no vulgar prize they play,
No vulgar victim must reward the day,
Such as in races crown the speedy strife:
The prize contended was great Hector's life.

Thus three times round the Trojan wall they fly.
The gazing gods lean forward from the sky...
Unworthy sight! The man beloved of heaven,
Behold, inglorious round yon city driven!

My heart partakes the generous Hector's pain:
Hector, whose zeal whole hecatombs has slain...
Now see him flying; to his fears resigned,
And fate, and fierce Achilles, close behind.

Oft as to reach the Dardan gates he bends,
And hopes the assistance of his pitying friends
Whose showering arrows, as he coursed below,
From the high turrets might oppress the foe,
So oft Achilles turns him to the plain:

He eyes the city, but he eyes in vain.
As men in slumbers seem with speedy pace
One to pursue, and one to lead the chase,
Their sinking limbs the fancied course forsake,
Nor this can fly, nor that can overtake.

The watching gods, who favour the Greeks, decide they must make Hector stand and fight: not to help him, but hoping he will be killed by Achilles. Minerva treacherously offers to appear as Hector's warrior brother, Deiphobus. In this disguise she speaks to Hector:

'Too long O Hector, have I borne the sight
Of this distress, and sorrowed in thy flight:
It fits us now a noble stand to make,
And here, as brothers, equal fates partake.'

Minerva's trick works; Hector turns and challenges Achilles:

'Enough, O son of Peleus! Troy has viewed
Her walls thrice circled, and her chief pursued;
But now some god within me bids me try
Thine, or my fate: I kill thee or I die.

Yet on the verge of battle let us stay,
And for a moment's space suspend the day;
Let Heaven's high powers be called to arbitrate
The just conditions of this stern debate.

...I swear; if, victor in the strife,
Jove by these hands shall shed thy noble life,
No vile dishonour shall thy corpse pursue:
Stripped of its arms (the conqueror's due)
The rest to Greece uninjured I'll restore:
Now plight thy mutual oath, I'll ask no more.'

'Talk not of oaths,' the dreadful chief replies,
While anger flashed from his disdainful eyes,
'Detested as thou art, and ought to be,
Nor oath nor pact Achilles plights with thee...
To such I call the gods! One constant state
Of lasting rancour and eternal hate;
No thought but rage, and never-ceasing strife,
Till death extinguish rage, and thought, and life.'

He spoke, and launched his javelin at the foe;
But Hector shunned the meditated blow:
He stooped, while o'er his head the flying spear
Sang innocent, and spent its force on air.

Minerva watched it falling on the land,
Then drew, and gave to great Achilles hand,
Unseen of Hector, who, elate with joy,
Now shakes his lance, and braves the dread of Troy.

'Boasting is but an art, our fears to blind,
And with false terrors sink another's mind.
But know, whatever fate I am to try,
By no dishonest wound shall Hector die.

But first, try thou my arm; and may this dart
End all my country's woes, deep buried in thy heart!'
The weapon flew, its course unerring held;
Unerring, but the heavenly shield repelled
The mortal dart ...

Hector beheld his javelin fall in vain.
No other lance nor other hope remain.
He calls Deiphobus, demands a spear;
In vain, for no Deiphobus was there.

All comfortless he stands: then, with a sigh:
'Tis so—Heaven wills it, and my hour is nigh!
'Tis true, I perish, yet I perish great;
Yet in a mighty deed I shall expire.
Let future ages hear it and admire!'

Prone on the field the bleeding warrior lies,
While, thus triumphing, stern Achilles cries:
'At last is Hector stretched upon the plain,
Who feared no vengeance for Patroclus slain.
Then, prince, you should have feared what now you feel:
Achilles absent was Achilles still'.

Dear Roy

It's so unfair that a warrior is slaughtered by another mightier warrior because of the gods' decision. Even when we were at school far, far away in the East, we knew of this legendary invincible Achilles who was feared both by gods and by men. There might be many poems, or odes perhaps, to exalt Achilles as people usually bow to strength and power. In this sense, the poet wrote a rather unusual and difficult poem to capture, with such an effort and detailed strokes, the last moment of a brave but doomed hero who is facing desperately Achilles' glittering helmet.

Sometime ago, I found a very old book called the stories of the *Iliad* and the *Aeneid*. I think the first one must be based on the long poem you mentioned which is supposed to have been written by Homer. After a few pages, I became quite saddened with the stories as it seems to me that all the battles are first settled between gods and goddesses from both sides and the warriors simply fulfil the divine decisions no matter how hard they pray to their divine protectors before going onto the battlefield. Nearly all battles are fought in the same pattern except that the names of the warriors are different and the gods and goddesses who interfered are different. I put that book away thinking that, if I only could know ancient Greek, one day Homer's poem could be more enjoyable and exciting with word choice, structure and metre as you explained about English poetry. But when I read your version aloud in my room the poem began to come alive. Hector was cheated by Minerva; maybe he knew that would happen, which is why he ran away at first; he clearly was a brave man as we see at the end, and he seems to have been a better man than Achilles was. Poor Hector, he must feel very helpless when he realised he was so alone and was not supported by the gods after all. I wonder if the gods had fair reasons to decide who should win the war. In Chinese culture, we believe that if the gods want us to suffer, there must be reasons. All our sufferings will release us from sin which relates to the Buddhist theory of cause and effect.

Perhaps real life is sometimes unfair for all of us and we just want to run away from it, but we have to face it in the end. Even so great a warrior and hero suffers from fear and desperation to meet his fate; I cannot imagine what an ordinary soldier who does not even want to be a warrior would go through in long horrible wars like the World Wars with almost everything of his life left behind in his home country. It is so heavy a topic and the poem makes it beautifully and unbearably heavier. If those people who led them to the great wars could have read more of the poems like this and had the same empathy for soldiers great or small, would the chances of world-wide wars have been reduced? Sadly, I know this is only a good hearted dream as wars are still breaking out in many places in our own times even when such great progress of civilization and humanity has been achieved.

拾伍

15

SYMPATHY

同理心

Dear Su Yen

In those grand houses that you saw, the large chimneys used to be swept by making small boys as young as four years (they had to be small) climb up and sweep the soot down. This poem illustrates the point that by the eighteenth century educated people were not writing only about religion and love, but were becoming aware of and concerned about the conditions of the poor. Often these boys were orphans and the orphanage was glad to find a way to get rid of them by finding them any job. It was hard, dangerous, unhealthy and cruel work. Sometimes the master would light a little fire underneath the boy to make him climb faster. The wounds, and the chemicals in the soot, led to sores and cancers. This way of sweeping chimneys was made illegal only as recently as about 1865. This is another side of English culture which, like the religious persecutions, was unpleasant.

The Chimney-Sweeper's Complaint, by Mary Alcock (1742–1798)

> *A CHIMNEY-SWEEPER'S boy am I;*
> *Pity my wretched fate!*
> *Ah, turn your eyes; 'twould draw a tear,*
> *Knew you my helpless state.*

Far from my home, no parents I
Am ever doomed to see;
My master, should I sue to him,
He'd flog the skin from me.

Ah, dearest madam, dearest sir,
Have pity on my youth;
Though black, and covered o'er with rags,
I tell you nought but truth.

My feeble limbs, benumbed with cold.
Totter beneath the sack,
Which ere the morning dawn appears
Is loaded on my back.

My legs you see are burnt and bruised,
My feet are galled by stones,
My flesh for lack of food is gone,
I'm little else but bones.

Yet still my master makes me work,
Nor spares me day or night;
His 'prentice boy he says I am,
And he will have his right.

'Up to the highest top,' he cries,
'There call out chimney sweep!'
With panting heart and weeping eyes,
Trembling I upwards creep.

But stop! no more—I see him come;
Kind sir, remember me!
Oh, could I hide me under ground,
How thankful should I be!

The main interest of the poem lies in its awareness and concern for the human condition at a particular period. However, as a poem it is not very good. You know by now the distinction between versification and poetry. The poem has an easy rhythm and simple rhymes. But not only does the poet fail to relate the particular subject imaginatively to a universal perception of human compassion and justice, she doesn't even make the boy seem very real to us or appeal effectively to our natural sympathies despite her graphic description. We would not expect beautiful ideas to be present because of the subject of the poem, but there are no striking or memorable lines or phrases at all, nor lines which express a complex idea in a few words, which is one of the qualities of poetry. Of course this must be so because the poet has chosen to write the whole poem as though the little uneducated boy was speaking and it would be incongruous if he used fine words. Perhaps that was not a good plan.

We saw this distinction between poetry and versification in the two poems on the same subject of enclosure, *The Deserted Village* and *The Cottager's Lament,* but the *Lament* is a better ballad than this one. William Blake wrote a couple of poems about chimney sweeps. Here, in this short extract, he expresses in only a few lines the betrayal and hypocrisy surrounding their condition.

A little black thing among the snow,
Crying 'weep! weep!' in notes of woe!
'Where are thy father & mother, say?'
'They are both gone up to the church to pray'

I said once that to appreciate a poem you must read it aloud many times or, if silently, then slowly in the mind, as though it were aloud. Tennyson, says in *The Idylls of the King*:

As when we dwell upon a word we know,
Repeating, till the word we know so well
Becomes a wonder, and we know not why.

Dwell here means to think about something for a long time, not to live as in a house. So a good poem will become a wonder as we repeat it. But I'm not sure that Mary Alcock's poem is worth repeating in that way: what do you think?

Dear Roy

Before thinking about the poem itself I felt so sad about the situation in the eighteenth century described in your introduction which is more interesting and sensitive than the poem itself. Hence, I could imagine why the poet chose those words to make the poem in this way.

I think it would have been better though to construct a piece of prose or a short story with more emotional expression rather than a poem like this. I feel she put too many adjective words into the complaint of that boy. I wonder, in that poor condition, how those very young boys could have such mature thoughts as to sue their masters when there was too much hard work to their little life. So, maybe it would be better if she could use a third person's description to show this pity.

I think versification is *just* writing verse with a regular metre and rhyming words, but poetry is more than that: it stimulates imagination and sympathy, or shared feelings, deeply. I feel this is not a bad poem, though perhaps it is not a good one. But this poem does not evoke my sympathy deeply because, although his life sounds very hard, the boy seems more like a character in a musical.

Dear Su Yen

You are right to see that a very young, uneducated boy would not speak like that. We could express your idea by saying that the poem lacks *authenticity* in this respect and maybe that is why it does not arouse our sympathy. However, 'sue' is not just a legal term: it can mean to plead or ask. I think the poet's description of the details of the boy's hard life probably is authentic.

Here is another poem from the eighteenth century. This one is more thoughtful. You have seen this period portrayed in movies and in real buildings as being very elegant in its architecture, music and costumes. Many luxurious houses were built in that time and filled with elegant furniture and fittings, and with elegant people, and these surroundings still give much pleasure to many visitors today as you have seen at Chatsworth House or Blenheim Palace or at Uppark. The period is also known as the *Age of Reason* because by then it had become accepted that problems should be examined by rational discussion and practical experiments. Even human character and feelings were analysed in rational ways rather than in religious or emotional ways, and this is often shown in the poetry.

An attractive aspect of many of the poems written in the eighteenth century is their display of great human sympathy with the conditions of ordinary people; side by side with the elegant and intellectual life there was a great deal of poverty and hardship and both public and private life could be vicious and cruel; topics such as these may be used as subjects for poetry.

This poem is called *Elegy Written in a Country Churchyard*, and it was written by a man called Thomas Gray. First he sets the scene; but before you read it I see there are several unfamiliar words for you. A 'curfew' is a time when all people have to be in their homes for the night, usually marked by the ringing of a bell; to 'toll' is, of a bell, to ring or be rung; 'knell' you know is the ringing of a bell for a death, in this case for the dying of the day; 'lowing' is the sound that cattle make; 'lea' or ley is a grass field; 'tinklings' are the sounds of the little bells which sheep used to be made to wear round their necks; a 'fold' is the temporary enclosure where the sheep would be gathered for the night; 'yon' means 'yonder, 'or 'over there'; 'elm,' as you know, is a type of tree which was once characteristic of the English landscape until these trees were all destroyed by a disease in the 1960s; and 'rude' does not mean bad mannered, but simply uneducated or simple. You have discovered that in England the light of daytime fades very slowly into night in a period we call 'twilight,' unlike in Taiwan where, you told me, the darkness comes more quickly.

Elegy Written in a Country Churchyard, by Thomas Gray
(1716–1771)

> *The curfew tolls the knell of parting day,*
> *The lowing herd winds slowly o'er the lea,*
> *The ploughman homeward plods his weary way,*
> *And leaves the world to darkness and to me.*
>
> *Now fades the glimmering landscape on the sight,*
> *And all the air a solemn stillness holds,*
> *Save where the beetle wheels his droning flight,*
> *And drowsy tinklings lull the distant folds.*
>
> *Save that from yon ivy mantled tower,*
> *The moping owl does to the moon complain,*
> *Or such as, wandering near her secret bower,*
> *Molest her ancient solitary reign.*
>
> *Beneath those rugged elms, that yew-tree's shade,*
> *Where heaves the turf in many a mouldering heap,*
> *Each in his narrow cell for ever laid,*
> *The rude forefathers of the hamlet sleep.*

Gray paints a word-picture containing all the elements of a late summer evening in the English countryside and which could be found in a thousand villages. Farming, both pastoral and arable, is over for the day; the twilight is thickening so the everyday world becomes difficult to see; the late-flying chafer beetle tells us it is summer; everything becomes quiet except for distant sounds.

There are five beats to a line in this poem and the combined rhythm and words seem to lead naturally to the voice falling off as though going to sleep. The feeling is dignified and solemn.

But Gray does not go to sleep. The mounds in the turf, or grass, tell us he is in a burial ground as night approaches. As a man of reason, however, he is not at all troubled by thoughts of ghosts. He wonders instead about the lives of all those people who have lived in the village over hundreds of years. Educated and powerful persons might have despised poor and uneducated labourers, and treated them badly, as we shall see in another poem, but Gray sees a nobility and honour in their limited lives and that, if they had been given the opportunity, some of them might have achieved great things.

> *Perhaps in this neglected spot is laid*
> *Some heart once pregnant with celestial fire;*
> *Hands that the rod of empire might have swayed,*
> *Or waked to ecstasy the living lyre.*

Someone whose heart was 'pregnant,' or fruitful, with 'celestial fire' might have been a great writer or preacher; another might have been a great statesman and ruled an empire; another might have been a great musician. Gray sympathetically recognises how lack of educational opportunity and 'penury,' or poverty, had limited their lives and perhaps made them bitter.

> *But Knowledge to their eyes her ample page*
> *Rich with the spoils of time did ne'er unroll;*
> *Chill Penury repressed their noble rage,*
> *And froze the genial current of the soul.*

You know now how poets often change the order of words to create rhythm and other effects so I expect you can work out what the first two lines of that verse mean. However, although Gray is sympathetic to the lack of opportunity for these villagers, he still expresses in other verses the attitudes of the pastoral tradition in art of seeing the rural labourers' lives as healthy and fulfilling, as did Goldsmith, unlike another other poet, George Crabbe, as we shall see.

There are many more verses to this poem, too many for me to type them all here. You can find it in your anthology. It is one of the best known of English poems; I should just add that it has some memorable and often-quoted lines as well as that first verse; for example:

Full many a flower is born to blush unseen,
And waste its sweetness on the desert air.

And:

Far from the madding crowd's ignoble strife
Their sober wishes never learned to stray ...

Far from the Madding Crowd is the title of a well-known novel by Thomas Hardy.

By the way, you know that different types of poems and subjects have their own names. This poem is called an 'elegy' because it represents deep thinking about a serious idea.

Dear Roy

I can imagine people staying in a churchyard at night in England, but can't believe that anyone, except grave-robbers perhaps, dares stay around graves at night in Taiwan. English churchyards are peaceful and melancholy which might be the reason that Gray was in the mood to write this poem which started beautifully from *The curfew tolls the knell of parting day, And leaves the world to darkness and to me*; and continued to be an elegy showing the dark side of the village life rather than a happy and carefree countryside.

As I learnt from my mother, countryside provides fresh air, wide sight and pleasant sounds by nature, which are not so satisfactorily offered in a big city. Apart from the fact that people have plenty of opportunities to be educated and to develop their lives in towns, city life also has many disadvantages, such as too much competition, so that people lack exercise and easily develop short-sighted eyes or tension. Perhaps one day an uneducated life style will be suggested to be the most suitable for human beings although we all think people desire to learn knowledge and to be able to choose their preferences of life styles; and then many people will prefer to drop back to the simplest life style without much civilization. However, the most serious problem then will be the big shortage of natural environment which has not all ready been over-developed.

I somehow believe this idea may happen one day, although most people from under-developed countryside still try to seize a chance to go to big cities where there are supposed to be most opportunities for people to change their life quality. I remember my father once told me that it's the best choice for children to grow up in a city rather than in a pretty village even though we all think countryside is healthier than a city, because the reality of the city does not allow people to be too naïve to survive in the world. Maybe Gray had the same conflict of both sides of country life in his mind as he described the beauty of the countryside in the village so much in his poem while he cared about the lack of opportunity and education for the poor villagers.

> *Full many a flower is born to blush unseen,*
> *And waste its sweetness on the desert air.*

These two lines could imply a genius was born but wasn't educated enough and just wasted his talent in a rough village; but it also could be a warning that a healthy person may be born with rubicund face as *a blushing flower* and yet waste his health trying to survive in the poor air of a place without much nature.

Dear Su Yen

You have seen that many poems about the countryside show it as being a happy carefree place where work is enjoyable, or perhaps where not much work seems to be done at all. This is a poet's view of countryside: poets usually, though not always, being people who did not have to do physical work for their living and who were free to appreciate the beauty of the countryside and sometimes fantasise about the lives of the poor people who lived and worked there. This idealisation of country life in art and poetry is known as the Pastoral Tradition in art and can be traced back through the Roman poet Virgil to the Greek Theocritus. It is quite possible that pastoral farming (that is, looking after grazing animals) in the warm Mediterranean climate was quite a pleasant life, but arable farming, cultivating the soil, in the colder wetter weather of Northern Europe was not. Some English poets in the seventeenth and eighteenth centuries would make a link with the Ancient World by giving classical names to their imaginary characters; for example here are just a few lines from one of our greatest poets, John Milton.

L'Allegro, by John Milton (1608–1674)

> *Hard by, a Cottage chimney smokes,*
> *From betwixt two agèd Okes,*
> *Where Corydon and Thyrsis met,*
> *Are at there savoury dinner set*
> *Of Hearbs and other Country Messes,*
> *Which the neat-handed Phillis dresses;*
> *And then in haste her Bowre she leaves,*
> *With Thestylis to bind the sheaves; ...*

Milton is best known for his great poem *Paradise Lost* which describes how an over ambitious angel in heaven was expelled and became God's opponent, the Devil. Interestingly, Milton suggests that God needs the Devil as you said the lamb needs the tiger. Some of Milton's early poems, however, are considered as not being very good.

L'Allegro has good qualities, but the point here is what a rather elegant picture of country life the poem suggests with its classical characters, Phillis, Corydon, Thyrsis and Thestylis, and words such as, 'savoury,' 'neat-handed' and 'bowre,' or bower. Nearly a hundred years later a country parson, or priest, George Crabbe described, as he says, 'What forms the real picture of the poor,' in a very different way. He starts by mocking the idealised image of country life presented by many other poets who imagined rural labourers writing poems and playing flutes while they watched their sheep.

The Village, by George Crabbe (1754–1832)

> *Fled are those times, if e're such times were seen,*
> *When rustic poets praised their native green;*
> *No shepherds now, in smooth alternate verse,*
> *Their country's beauties or their nymphs' rehearse; ...*
> *Yes, thus the Muses sing of happy swains,*
> *Because the Muses never knew their pains:*
> *They boast their peasants' pipes; but peasants now*
> *Resign their pipes and plod behind the plough;*
> *And few, amid the rural tribe, have time*
> *To number syllables, and to play with rhyme, ...*

Crabbe acknowledges that farms and fields are charming for the owners and maybe for people who have nothing better to do than look at them.

> *I grant indeed that fields and flocks have charms*
> *For him that gazes or for him that farms;*
> *But when amid such pleasing scenes I trace*
> *The poor laborious natives of the place, ...*

Then shall I dare these real ills to hide
In tinsel trappings of poetic pride?

As a village priest Crabbe has seen the real living
conditions of the labourers; he does not see their poor
cottages as poetically picturesque.

By such examples taught, I paint the cot,
As truth will paint it, and as bards will not: ...
Can poets soothe you, when you pine for bread,
By winding myrtles round your ruin'd shed? ...

Ye gentle souls, who dream of rural ease,
Whom the smooth stream and smoother sonnet please;
Go! If the peaceful cot your praises share,
Go, look within, and see if peace be there;
If peace be his—that drooping weary sire,
Or theirs, that offspring round their feeble fire;
Or hers, that matron pale, whose trembling hand
Turns on the wretched hearth th'expiring brand!

Crabbe expresses particular sympathy for those who
are not strong or healthy enough to carry out the hard
work.

Amid this tribe too oft a manly pride
Strives in strong toil the fainting heart to hide;
There may you see the youth of slender frame
Contend with weakness, weariness, and shame:
Yet urged along, and proudly loth to yield,
He strives to join his fellows of the field;
Till long-contending nature droops at last,
Declining health rejects his poor repast,
His cheerless spouse the coming danger sees,
And mutual murmurs urge the slow disease.

Dear Roy

I was unfortunately one of the ignorant people who imagined the life in the countryside was just like that scene of *rural labourers writing poems and playing flutes while they watched their sheep.* We do have these sorts of traditional ballads and paintings presenting that image in Taiwan and we all learnt to sing those ballads which were supposed to be being sung by those little boy shepherds in the farms.

However, what I learnt about real country life in the past was not so picturesque when our tutors at high school showed us the works of Van Gogh who famously painted many poor lives around his countryside. In my short experience of seeing the world, I haven't seen any sort of hard country life yet, so I can't really say that I can possibly understand the difficulties just by reading Crabbe's poem. Nevertheless, I am touched when I read through the long poem, particularly the two lines:

I grant indeed that flocks and fields have charms
For him that gazes or for him that farms ...

The idea here clearly shows the sheer contrast of charms between people who look at the scenery and those who work in the farms. Perhaps life is always like that, some are in a great happiness when some are in a deep sorrow, though all of us stand on the same Earth with faithful sunshine.

Dear Su Yen

Yes, Crabbe makes the point specifically that this hard life was mainly for the benefit of other people when he describes the work of the shepherd, so different from the supposed happy scenes of pastoral poetry.

Oft may you see him, when he tends the sheep,
His winter-charge, beneath the hillock weep;
Oft hear him murmur to the winds that blow
O'er his white locks and bury them in snow,
When, roused by rage and muttering in the morn,
He mends the broken hedge with icy thorn: ...

These fruitful fields, these numerous flocks I see,
Are others' gain, but killing cares to me; ...

I wonder, do you find this poem beautiful? I feel its deep understanding and genuine compassion, and the authenticity—for Crabbe really knew these people's lives, are perhaps more beautiful than those poems of Browning or Shelley. What do you think?

Dear Roy

Maybe people all know the world that has two sides, and most of them prefer to look at happy scenes rather than to face to cruel reality because lives are bitter at all different levels for everyone. When people don't even have enough courage to overcome their own pain, including physical and mental pain, how could they truly appreciate any beauty in the hard lives from other people's stories?

Naturally I also enjoy reading happy pastoral poems

because they are so beautiful. But I now gradually am not fearing to learn how to comprehend the other side of so-called stories of poor lives, because their beauty arises from authenticity, which helps me to think about whether I could be that wise to see the beauty of my own happiness among the misfortune in my life in the same way as I try to understand the beauty of those poems. There is a well- known, but not normally well-understood, saying: 'perfection contains deformity'. Perhaps the most beautiful poem should embrace both bright and dark sides of a scene.

Dear Su Yen,

As we are thinking about sympathy in poetry perhaps you would like to learn a little more about the poet Alexander Pope. His body was seriously deformed and his health was poor, yet none of this is evident from his poetry which is elegant, lively, succinct and witty, which does not mean that it was funny, but that it was clever and learned. Pope can be seen as a classical poet in the modern sense. He worked at the end of what is termed the Augustan age, roughly the time of Queen Anne and early Georgian in the first half of the eighteenth century, when after the Civil War of the previous century the British began to see themselves as the new Romans, referring to the first Roman emperor Augustus who also brought order, stability and culture after a civil war. Seeing themselves in this way not only influenced British architecture and poetry, but powerful men often had their portraits painted or statues made showing them wearing clothes in the style of ancient Rome. I tell you this because otherwise you might be puzzled when you see such portraits in great houses or museums, but those people didn't dress like that normally.

A modern French scholar and writer, André Maurois, in his book, *Voltaire*, a biography of that great French philosopher, describes the classical style (the translation is by Hamish Miles):

> *...the classic spirit is a perfection of form imposed on strength of feelings. A great classic is not an insensitive creature; he has the same passions as a great romantic. But ' he is shaped by the habit of speaking, writing, and thinking in the midst of a drawing room assemblage.' The choice of words has lightness of texture. The writer avoids technicalities, pedantries or crudities, which are painful or tiresome in agreeable company. He strives for clarity and swiftness, and expresses his personal sufferings in the form of general maxims rather than lyrical outpourings, because violence is in bad taste. But there are outcrops of passion showing through the transparency of the maxims, and awareness of the existence of that underlying passion gives the great classics their own beauty.[1]*

Pope had the skill of using a few well-chosen words to great effect, an ability which came perhaps from studying classical Latin. His style is light and easy to read and he does not use words which might be offensive or generally obscure although he does assume the reader has a knowledge of classical civilisation; for example, the

---

1 Originally published in France as *Voltaire* by André Maurois © Editions Grasset & Fasquelle, 1935. English language translation *Voltaire* by André Maurois, p. 8-9. © Hamish Miles, 1952.

Sceptics and the Stoics referred to in the poem below are ancient schools of philosophy; maybe that is clear from the poem anyway. Pope was enthusiastic about the new natural style of garden design, as promoted by Addison, and wrote poems which express the new design principles very effectively and memorably.

Here is a short extract from a long poem by Pope concerning human nature and life. The term 'Man' traditionally is used generically to mean human beings and thus includes women, although no doubt at that time Pope would be thinking mostly of men's lives.

An Essay on Man, by Alexander Pope (1688–1744)

> *Know then thyself, presume not God to scan,*
> *The proper study of mankind is Man.*
> *Placed on this isthmus of a middle state,*
> *A being darkly wise and rudely great:*
> *With too much knowledge for the Sceptic side,*
> *With too much weakness for the Stoic's pride,*
> *He hangs between; in doubt to act or rest,*
> *In doubt to deem himself a God or Beast,*
> *In doubt his mind or body to prefer;*
> *Born but to die, and reas'ning but to err;*
> *Alike in ignorance, his reason such*
> *Whether he thinks too little or too much:*
> *Chaos of thought and passion, all confused;*
> *Still by himself abused or disabused;*
> *Created half to rise, and half to fall;*
> *Great lord of all things, yet a prey to all;*
> *Sole judge of truth, in endless error hurled:*
> *The glory, jest, and riddle of the world!*

'Presume not God to scan,' he says: don't think you can understand God, so don't waste time trying to. The proper subject for human beings to study is themselves. This attitude reflects a disillusion with religious dogmatism after nearly 200 years of religious and political strife, and the subsequent development of a secular society in the Age of Reason which followed an Age of Belief. You might be interested to know that for some people in England at that time China, as they understood it, which was not very well, seemed to be a model of a secular and rational society where wars of religion were unknown and where civil harmony was valued more highly than personal expression.

The words 'Know thyself,' or 'Know yourself,' were written over the door of the most important temple of the Ancient Greeks. These words do not mean to understand yourself in the self-centred indulgent way people sometimes aim to do today, but to understand your nature as a human being, in the context of other human beings, that is as part of society, and the nature of that society also. This is a classical attitude, and possibly a Chinese Confucian one as well. There was a great awareness in Pope's time of a need to rebuild a shattered and fearful society after two centuries of religious and political wars. Pope is suggesting that we human beings are too imperfect to have any right to be arrogant or dogmatic.

Pope identifies the contradictions and dilemmas that are characteristic of human personality. He doesn't talk about his personal problems directly or even distastefully, as a Romantic or modern writer might do, but now you know his physical condition you might like to read the rest of the poem and see whether you think he is perhaps talking about himself indirectly in the classical manner. With a brilliant mind trapped in a deformed body (he needed to wear a sort of corset everyday just to stand up) his daily dilemma is perhaps reflected in these lines, although Pope expresses this as a universal condition:

In doubt to deem himself a God or Beast,
In doubt his mind or body to prefer;

Pope was not an aristocrat, but he had made a large amount of money early in his life with his translation of Homer and his social life was aristocratic. It is unlikely that he knew much about the conditions of the poor or cared in the ways that Crabbe and Blake would care. His sympathy was of a different kind: for the difficulties of coming to terms with life as a human being, whatever one's condition.

Dear Roy

This poem truly reflects the progress of human beliefs, which started moving from surrendering all hope to the God to the predominance of human nature in eighteenth century England. I would imagine that is because religious and political powers, too strongly twisted together, had caused many wars and killings in Europe in the past. I remember those movies *Richard III*, *A Man for All Seasons* and *Cromwell*. Many people, like Pope, might want to remind people not to destroy each other for their different beliefs in a God who was beyond human understanding.

However, the idea I read from his poem is that we live in a society surrounded by other human beings, which is the most practical and interesting philosophy for us to learn to deal with each other to make our world better and better. So, the first and most complicated thing is to understand and to face the truth that human nature comprises both sides of greatness and fault in all their aspects.

I was most impressed by the line, 'Great lord of all things, yet a prey to all'. I think it's the core idea that shows why people can't stop contending for power and profit for all time, although the subtlety of human nature has been expressed from thousands of years ago by many well-known philosophers throughout the world. Now I think I can understand why the English can reach the highest level of dealing with the spiritual and normal worlds with a great peaceful open-minded attitude, because they've learnt to make good progress by meditating and carrying out their lives at the same time, each in moderation.

鳳凰戲牡丹

Phoenix & Tudor Rose

319

拾陸

16

MERRY CHRISTMAS

聖誕快樂

From my childhood it has always been a great desire of mine to have a real English Christmas like those I saw in movies and paintings, because they look so full of magic and hope, though I never had any Christmas like those in my life in Taiwan. I have now spent four Christmases in England and each one has been a stage in my reviving. Maybe it's because I want to believe, or maybe because I'm lucky, but when Christmases come in England my wishes often magically come true even more than my own expectations. From those I called the *Beginner's Christmases* to the *Real English Christmas*, I opened my heart to embrace all my life with a true smile as I've been walking into English culture gradually and naturally. The learning of English culture has made a good path for me to improve myself to deal with my mind.

I can't remember now how I had that courage to come to England with only a visa, a little money and a small case containing a coat and a few clothes which were even not enough for me to pass a winter; especially for me, such a spoiled girl who even never carried a heavy bag to walk home from a supermarket or never went to a traditional market to buy meat or any raw food to cook for myself in my life before. I thought I was so brave to learn to live alone with my strong will, relying on the tiny hope of studying here for my future, and I admired myself a great deal that I was flexible to adapt myself from a luxurious life to such a constrained life so quickly. It was such a big confusion and problem during the first year of my stay in England; I couldn't really believe that I would be able to see my Russian friend with whom I studied in New Zealand for three months and with whom I shared a long-time wish that we should overcome our problems to study for our Master's in Europe, and then we must meet to celebrate our success of studying abroad.

The first magic of my Christmas here saw my wish come true just as though it was in a movie. We met at Oxford Station, had coffee in a cosy English pub facing my dreaming Oxford High Street, and we went to a supermarket for our Christmas shopping which was my first time of seeing the many products and foodstuffs prepared for a 'real' Christmas. While she was cooking her Russian Christmas dinner for me my friend told me how they celebrated their Christmases in Russia. After dinner we decided to have something which we had never tried before, because it was only for English Christmases. It was called Christmas Pudding. We were not sure if we had cooked it in the right way that time, but it was for us a taste of our '*Beginners' Christmas*' in England. We wouldn't say it was tasty, but it was so new and exciting for us to explore more about how English people share Christmas Pudding on such an important day with their families.

Now my mind was not alone anymore. At least I knew some other people would be also brave like me, or even more brave, to struggle for their wishes as I and my

Russian friend did; it was just that just I hadn't met them.

I was often stuck in our traditional rules which maybe it could be argued do not fit the contemporary age, but it was not easy for me not to be suffocated under those rules when I had grown up in such a typical traditional family. My wandering life across the whole of Taiwan from the North to the South never really set me free at all, but bound me more tightly according to my increasing age. But now I'm educated by England, my soul is truthfully freed by English culture and English tradition which I think are mostly open-minded and are full of respect for different cultures. This perhaps is the main reason why English people see deeply the importance of protecting their own culture while they've learnt to accept other cultures in their kingdom.

When I eventually entered a university to study for my Master's degree I knew I never need worry about my life for a whole year and could concentrate on my study with all my heart. I stayed in our library very often to learn my profession and to enjoy looking at so many old books with my own imagination. When I found many old poetry books were on sale in our library, I so desired to have them and to read them only to fulfil my dreamy image of English culture. However, the magic of my second Christmas here didn't show in a normal Christmas way. I know I shouldn't say it was lucky, but it was really a rare opportunity when I heard Roy had fallen off a ladder on his boat and couldn't go anywhere, but just sat to read poetry by the fire and email poems to me during his Christmas holiday. I grasped the chance eagerly and decided to stay in my room to study those poems as much as possible. I was not sure whether it was only because Roy really couldn't move at all that he could 'enjoy' reading my replies about these poems, or whether he was somehow truly interested in my innocent understandings of English poetry. He encouraged me a great deal to think about them with my own thoughts while learning English culture. It was so hard when I had to work out the meanings of words and tried to have my own ideas between my culture and English culture, but it was so much fun because I thought I would become more clever and open-minded by doing this brain exercise during the whole winter vacation. Amazingly it did work very well and my study improved so much from the second semester of my first Master's to my second Master's the year after. I think the improvement of my study was not only because my English improved quickly (although I know it's not perfect still), but also because my mind was becoming peaceful and calm while reading poetry.

If I could say what I've learnt most from those poems, I would think it is to see a new meaning of what I call *Trinity* in my life. It came to my dream that Xue gave me a little green glass vase in the shape of a Cotswold cottage. She knows how much I would love to have a little English house where I could surround myself with books and music. Strangely, on the base of the vase was moulded the word *Trinity*. I asked Xue what that meant. She said that in China they were taught there was no God, but that in Singapore she had been told that Christians believe the God has three forms, a Trinity of Father, Son and Holy Spirit. But in the dream different ideas came into mind, which sub-consciously helped me to understand my life, and when I woke up I remembered them and told Xue. A long time ago people were born with the original character of the deity within their innocent and pure souls. However, the deity went away, as the Holy Grail went away in the Arthur legends, when the enlargement of humanity brought avarice, jealousy and infatuation, and then a new subject of humanity dominated a new study for human beings to deal with each other and to think of themselves. Eventually, in a third stage, pure self became sublimated with humanity in a way of real understanding of human beings. This circle could not only be run in a lifetime, or in the many lives of a person as we think in Buddhism; but also could be seen as the progress of society for many generations in the changing world. Nevertheless, in the stages of my life I think I'm only repeating the progress of seeing the meaning of Trinity which many predecessors already understood well, from hundreds or even thousands of years ago, and kindly shared their wisdom with us by handing down many poems or other literary works so that we might enjoy the crossing over of space-time friendships like the one shown in my most favourite poem, *Heraclitus*, by William Cory.

I locked many old memories in my inner heart when they seemed to hurt me too much. But the pain was revealed slowly and gently and was healed bit by bit as I read more and more poems and thought about them more and more freely with my own life experience, which gradually has been constructed to be the whole story of my life, for the past and the future. I did feel pain sometimes, but I don't want to refuse to recall all the memories in my mind when they've been part of my life and part of me. I would like to call my second English Christmas the '*Healing Christmas*' both for Roy's hurt back and for my hurt mind, though they were not comparable.

After the *Healing Christmas*, I came to appreciate English culture much more in depth and avariciously wanted to know more, more and more. Perhaps it's an ideal that I never need to wake up from the dream of immersing myself in this ancient air. But the reality usually is not that kind to people to let them have their dreams in the daytime. It was such an inexpressible difficulty for a foreigner like me to study amongst a group of English professionals. However, before I became too frustrated by my poor knowledge of English culture, the '*Civilizing Christmas*' came to save me in time. The book *Civilization*, one of my Christmas gifts, recalled all my childhood dreams of mediaeval European scenes in a moment, and my hope was lit again to explore more about this mystical country. However, my English was still not good enough to understand that book, so my enthusiasm could only be a great motivation for me to check every new word in a dictionary and use it as an English-learning book for a start. I didn't know if it was useful or not when I spent all my winter vacation to read that book, but was never clear about what I was reading for two months; but Roy told me that he could see a big improvement from reading my assignments for my course tutors. I would like to believe he was right, especially when I saw my marks were regularly increasing all the time to the end of my Master's.

Following closely the *Civilizing Christmas*, a chance to work in the ancient University Church of St Mary's in Oxford High Street brought me nearer to the English culture. The job helped me to enter a church freely without feeling myself to be an intruder. I would think it is also the God's gift because I once made a wish for working in a church so that I would feel free to pass in and out of the Christian space naturally, although Roy told me that I could enter a church anytime if I wished. From the first week of my work in the church shop I was so excited that I was the one who held the key to open and close the mediaeval church and the tower. More importantly, I wasn't a tourist anymore. It's such a super feeling when Xue and I can say, 'The bell is ringing from our church'. 'Our church.' How marvellous for us to feel that we are part of the mediaeval church.

I was working one December afternoon with Ann, who is a friendly English lady in our church shop, when she kindly invited Xue and me to join her family Christmas dinner; significantly, her invitation brought us into a '*Real English Christmas*'.

After quite some homework and consultation with my other English friends, I finally decided my gift package: a bottle of wine, a box of biscuits, one scent bottle decorated with traditional Chinese paintings, and one silk lipstick case embroidered with Chinese roses. This combination of Western and Eastern cultures made me a bit anxious about the day when I would present the gifts. My nervousness disappeared right away when I saw Ann's friendly smile outside our flat under the sunshine.

It was so lovely when I saw the pretty house in front of us with a small Christmas Tree twinkling at the door. 'Make yourself at home.' Ann encouraged us to feel at home, 'You just relax, relax and relax today.' I felt so warm and cosy the moment I stepped into the house and followed her into the living room where she introduced her husband John to us. As usual in a movie where English people always have dogs or cats in their houses, a pretty, gentle, white cat quietly appeared at John's feet and looked at us tenderly. The picture of a movie then came to reality: an English gentleman, with his beautiful cat at his feet, was reading a profound philosophical book in the afternoon sunlight in an English house. Again we found what we are normally experiencing everywhere in England: two foreigners, amazingly, went in to this English movie and started a very lively conversation there.

The dinner started when Ann's son and daughter-in-law arrived. I couldn't feel I was in reality all the whole night there. We talked about everything, including Oxford, cats, English lives and religious beliefs. Somehow they started making jokes on the topic of death. Xue then burst into laughter and told me that she was so surprised about the way English people can talk about death during Christmas, because it's the most serious taboo in Chinese culture to mention anything about death or unpleasant things during New Year.

It was really a happy time for me to enjoy English

culture so closely by joining Ann and her family in the festive dinner. Magically, for that night I left all my troubles behind and enjoyed myself so much on the *Real English Christmas* family day.

According to the miracles of my four Christmases here, I daringly pray to the God that I so want to have a real cosy English house, as Ann and John have, to welcome all the Christmases to come with the magic of me bringing pleasure to light hopes for other people's dreams, as I have received these years, bit by bit for years and years, till one day people's hearts are all full of magic and hopes all over the world.

THE AUTHORS
作者簡介

Su Yen was born in 1978 and grew up in the close family of a senior government official in Taiwan. After obtaining her Diploma in Advertisement Design at Shilin High School of Commerce in Taipei City in 1997, Su Yen spent a year working for a high-class woman's fashion house. In 1998 Su Yen went to university in Kaoshiung and gained her first degree in Interior Design. Su Yen's first impressions of the buildings of Oxford transformed her interest from being a modern designer to the study of the development and conservation of historic buildings. Following her first Master's Degree in Spatial Planning at Oxford Brookes University in 2007, she obtained a second Master's Degree in Historic Conservation at Oxford Brookes University in association with the University of Oxford.

Roy trained first as a scientist and then as a landscape designer with a particular interest in the history of ideas in design. His doctorate was on the subject of landscape beauty and its conservation. For over twenty years Roy gave regular courses at Rewley House (later Kellog College) in the University of Oxford on Historic Houses and Gardens with special emphasis on the contexts of ideas at different periods. These courses were provided for visiting alumni and academics from a number of American universities including Chicago, Austin-Texas, North- western, Michigan State and Virginia, and for the American Bar Association. For the last twelve years Roy has been a tutor in English language for international post-graduate students in the School of the Built Environment at Oxford Brookes University. Roy has published two academic books (*Designs on the Landscape*, Belhaven, 1991; and *Starting Research*, Pinter, 1994) and various papers and articles.